The Conservation of Decorated Surfaces on Earthen Architecture

Proceedings from the International Colloquium
Organized by the Getty Conservation Institute and
the National Park Service

Mesa Verde National Park, Colorado, USA
September 22–25, 2004

Edited by Leslie Rainer and Angelyn Bass Rivera

THE GETTY CONSERVATION INSTITUTE

LOS ANGELES

Front cover: View of a traditional dwelling, northern Ghana (photo: Thierry Joffroy, CRATerre-EAG, 1997). Back cover (clockwise from top left): Detail of *Babban Gwani,* Bauchi, Nigeria (photo: Ishanlosen Odiaua, 2004); painted earthen plaster on the interior of Room 121, Cliff Palace, Mesa Verde National Park (photo: Angelyn Bass Rivera, 1999); detail of a screen wall, Adarko Jachi shrine, Ghana (photo: Thierry Joffroy, CRATerre-EAG); and detail of *Banqueting Scene with Dancers* (EA37984), wall painting fragment from the Tomb of Nebamun, British Museum (photo: Corinna Kenyon).

© 2006 J. Paul Getty Trust

Getty Publications
1200 Getty Center Drive, Suite 500
Los Angeles, California 90049-1682

Christopher Hudson, *Publisher*
Mark Greenberg, *Editor in Chief*

Patrick Pardo, *Project Editor*
Leslie Tilley, *Manuscript Editor*
Pamela Heath, *Production Coordinator*
Hespenheide Design, *Designer*

Printed in Singapore by Imago

Every effort has been made to contact the copyright holders of the photographs and illustrations in this book to obtain permission to publish. Any omissions will be corrected in future editions if the publisher is contacted in writing.

Library of Congress Cataloging-in-Publication Data

The conservation of decorated surfaces on earthen architecture / edited by Leslie Rainer, Angelyn Bass Rivera.
      p. cm.
   Includes bibliographical references.
   ISBN-13: 978-0-89236-850-1 (pbk.)
   ISBN-10: 0-89236-850-0 (pbk.)
1. Mural painting and decoration, Ancient—Conservation and restoration. 2. Decoration and ornament, Architectural—Conservation and restoration. 3. Earth construction. 4. Architecture, Ancient. I. Rainer, Leslie H., 1960– II. Rivera, Angelyn Bass.
   ND2560.C66 2006
   751.7'30288—dc22
                      2005030987

Contents

PART THREE

Historic Buildings

PART FOUR

Living Traditions

Foreword

We are delighted to present this most recent volume in the Proceedings series of the Getty Conservation Institute. These proceedings are the result of a four-day colloquium held September 22–25, 2004, that focused on the conservation of decorated surfaces on earthen architecture. The colloquium was co-organized by the Getty Conservation Institute (GCI) and the National Park Service (NPS) and hosted by Mesa Verde National Park, with support from the US/ICOMOS Specialized Committee on Earthen Architecture and the Colorado Historical Society. It brings us particular pleasure to introduce this publication on the occasion of Mesa Verde's centennial as a national park.

The idea for a colloquium was proposed at the US/ICOMOS Earthen Architecture Specialized Committee meeting in Philadelphia in 2001. The choice of Mesa Verde National Park as the colloquium venue was ideal given the extensive research and conservation that has been accomplished there on the twelfth- to fourteenth-century Ancestral Puebloan alcove sites. It followed similar collaborative colloquia organized by the GCI and the NPS on site reburial, held in 2003, and shelters for archaeological sites, held in 2001.

The GCI and the NPS share a commitment to the conservation of cultural heritage and the dissemination of information to the public. The GCI has a long-standing commitment to the conservation of earthen architecture, from its work on the Terra Project in collaboration with CRATerre-EAG and ICCROM to its field projects in Egypt, West Africa, and China, which exhibit wall paintings and decorated surfaces on earthen plasters. Likewise, the NPS has carried out extensive research and conservation of wall paintings and architectural finishes on archaeological and historic sites throughout the United States.

The partnerships established and cultivated through these colloquia and other scholarly meetings are invaluable, especially when working in multidisciplinary fields such as the conservation of decorated surfaces on earthen architecture, where architectural and wall paintings conservation, archaeology, site management, science, and anthropology converge. Through collaboration among professionals and dissemination of information, we can work together to develop successful conservation strategies and plan for the future of our diverse cultural heritage.

This volume comprises a selection of the papers presented at the colloquium, which brought together fifty-five professionals from eleven countries to discuss the conservation of wall paintings, decorated plasters, and surface finishes made of earth or on earthen architecture. The program was divided into themes focusing on the conservation of earthen architectural finishes at Mesa Verde and other archaeological sites, in museums and historic buildings, and as living traditions. Presentations and discussion were followed by site visits in Mesa Verde National Park. The program also included a public lecture at the Anasazi Heritage Center and a four-day postcolloquium tour to sites in the region with decorated earthen architecture.

We are grateful to volume editors Leslie Rainer (GCI) and Angelyn Bass Rivera (NPS) for the time and energy they spent preparing these proceedings for publication and for their work organizing the colloquium. Through these proceedings, we hope not only to disseminate the information shared at the colloquium but also to promote further discussion and research on the conservation of these fragile and diverse architectural finishes worldwide.

Timothy P. Whalen
DIRECTOR
The Getty Conservation Institute

Larry T. Wiese
SUPERINTENDENT
Mesa Verde National Park

Preface

Leslie Rainer

For millennia, people in all cultures have decorated the surfaces of domestic, religious, and public buildings. Among the most significant modes of surface decoration are wall paintings, sculpted bas-reliefs, and ornamental plasterwork. Decorated architectural surfaces convey immense meaning and provide insight into civilizations through the forms, materials, and techniques used in their creation. They also display the symbols, stories, signs, and patterns of the cultures that produce them. Decorated surfaces are significant as expressions of the culture and the craftsmanship of a people at a given moment in time.

Earthen architecture in particular has been a canvas for a rich array of surface decoration over the ages. The diversity of forms this has taken is seen across West Africa, where earth is applied as textured patterns, relief decoration, and as vibrant paintings. In China and Europe, wall paintings on earthen plaster grace tombs, religious structures, and homes. Earthen architecture across the Middle East shows elaborate decorative patterns in paint and relief. Further variations include wall paintings on lime plaster on colonial adobe structures, and archaeological sites with polychrome relief and painted surfaces in the Americas.

Globally, as traditional techniques have been influenced by the use of modern materials, an even greater variety of plasters and paints is being employed. The diversity of materials and techniques is virtually endless, but the common denominator is the use of earth in the structure, substrate, or surface. The problems posed by the conservation of these decorated surfaces can be complex due to the heterogeneous characteristics of the earthen materials and their vulnerability as surface layers.

Awareness of the global diversity of traditions and techniques has led to efforts worldwide to conserve both the materials of decorated surfaces on earth and the traditions that produced them. Because such surfaces are integral to the larger architectural context, their conservation is complicated by the need to take into consideration the entire construction system. Specialization in this area of conservation has evolved over the past century as specific methodologies have been developed that recognize the physical and chemical characteristics of earthen building systems, as well as the wide range of materials used for their decoration.

Successful conservation in this area clearly demands an understanding of the deterioration mechanisms of the earthen building materials and the plasters and paints used in the surface decoration. The complexity of this endeavor points to the necessity of a multidisciplinary, integrated approach to conservation. Thus, training that combines a fundamental understanding of the conservation of earthen architecture with conservation of wall paintings and architectural finishes is critical to the development of appropriate conservation strategies for the long-term preservation of this heritage.

The aim of the colloquium "Conservation of Decorated Surfaces on Earthen Architecture" was to bring together a broad group of international professionals, including conservators, cultural resource managers, materials scientists, engineers, architects, archaeologists, anthropologists, and artists who specialize in the conservation and care of decorated surfaces on earth in different contexts, and to provide them with a forum for both presentation of their recent work and in-depth discussion of key issues, challenges, and future directions in this area. In organizing the colloquium, four different contexts for decorated surfaces were identified: archaeological sites, museum practice, historic buildings, and living traditions. Each of these contexts affects the ways in which decisions are made about conservation, including treatment, maintenance, and resource management.

Archaeological Sites

On archaeological sites, the excavation and exposure of surfaces, once maintained, then abandoned and often buried, frequently results in drastic changes in environmental conditions, which can be detrimental to their preservation. While minimal intervention is advocated to preserve as much original information as possible for future study, this must be balanced with more extensive conservation measures to ensure preservation and presentation of the exposed decorated surfaces for the long term.

Museum Practice

Wall painting fragments in museum settings present unique conservation challenges, since they have been removed from their original physical and cultural context. The practice of detaching wall paintings may seem inappropriate to us today, but there are many examples of detached wall paintings on exhibit or in storage in museums around the world. These fragments were largely collected in the nineteenth and early twentieth centuries, as artifacts or works of art whose value was foremost to educate, in the belief that they would best be safeguarded in a museum setting. Museums must address the complex issues of storage, access, display, and interpretation of decontextualized fragments. At the same time, conservators must address issues of retreatment of wall painting fragments where deterioration may be directly or indirectly related to the museum environment.

Historic Buildings

Conservation of wall paintings and decorative schemes in historic buildings often requires not only treatment of the surface and support but comprehensive conservation and maintenance of the structure as well. The selection and use of compatible repair materials is often one of the main concerns in the conservation of surface decoration and wall paintings. Additionally, the continued or adapted use of historic structures often threatens preservation of the decorated surfaces due to overpainting or building modifications.

Living Traditions

Decorated architectural surfaces in vernacular settings, where the art and traditions are still being practiced, present complex issues regarding continuity and significance of cultural practices, the evolution of traditions, and the authenticity of original fabric. In these circumstances, issues of material conservation are closely linked with the sociocultural issues of the creative process and the transference of knowledge and traditional techniques. These include the use of appropriate materials, maintenance, and preventive conservation measures to retain the cultural value of the surfaces being preserved. Whether reviving a tradition or working with the living artists who create decorated surfaces, the continuity of the tradition allows conservation of both the material fabric and the cultural practices that produce them.

The collected papers in this volume illustrate a wide range of issues related to the conservation of decorated surfaces on earthen architecture in these different contexts. They explore a number of questions: What do we conserve? How do we conserve it—and for whom? Are we conserving the material as a museum object, as fragmentary evidence of the past on an archaeological site, or as an integral element of the architecture in situ? Are we preserving the artifact itself, or the tradition that created the decorated surface?

As reflected in the papers, in different cases all of these approaches have been taken. Historically, certain approaches have prevailed at different times, but aspects of each continue to be practiced today, depending on the context, specific goals for treatments, choices of conservation materials, and changing philosophies. And, while there is certainly more work to be done in all areas, a century of conservation of decorated earthen architectural surfaces has resulted in significant developments in both the philosophy and techniques for their conservation.

The work of architectural and wall painting conservators, scientists, archaeologists, anthropologists, and artisans has provided us with knowledge and insight into the sensitive nature and the complex conservation issues of decorated architectural surfaces on earth. Through their research and experience, specialists working in this area have contributed to the field by developing appropriate conservation strategies for these surfaces. Their work has laid a foundation for further study and research specific to these wall paintings and plaster finishes.

The state of the conservation of decorated surfaces on earthen architecture today is a convergence of material conservation and preservation of the traditional craftsmanship that created the structures and decorated the surfaces. The current trend to conserve decorated surfaces as an integral part of the architectural ensemble, in a cultural context, while maintaining the traditions of constructing and decorating earthen architecture, represents a positive step toward a holistic approach to their preservation.

The dissemination of information is vital to the advancement of this specialized area of conservation. Through the publication of current research, including papers presented at the colloquium and a bibliography of selected references regarding decorated surfaces on earth, these proceedings aim to contribute to the study and conservation of this unique and universal aspect of the cultural heritage.

Acknowledgments

The colloquium "Conservation of Decorated Surfaces on Earthen Architecture" and this volume of proceedings resulted from the efforts, enthusiasm, and energy of many individuals and institutions, whom we would like to acknowledge here. Foremost, we thank our fellow members of the organizing committee, Mary Hardy, Claudia Cancino, Kecia Fong, and Rebecca Carr, for their creativity, good humor, and dedication in helping plan and lead the colloquium. We greatly appreciate the support and direction we received from Jeanne Marie Teutonico, associate director, Programs, the Getty Conservation Institute (GCI); and Linda Towle, chief, Research and Resource Management, at Mesa Verde National Park.

We are deeply grateful to the institutions and individuals that provided generous financial and in-kind support, including the GCI, Terra Project, Getty Publications, the National Park Service's Challenge Cost Share Program, Bandelier National Monument, Mesa Verde National Park, the Colorado State Historical Fund, and US/ICOMOS individual members and specialized committees.

Special thanks go to the speakers and participants, who brought their diverse knowledge and expertise to Mesa Verde National Park for four days and who openly shared their experiences and viewpoints throughout the colloquium. We would like to recognize the moderators of the sessions, George Abungu, Giacomo Chiari, Anthony Crosby, and Susan Thomas, who guided the sessions and discussions following the presentations and added their insights to each theme. To the authors of the papers included here, we thank each of you for your contribution. Without the efforts, expertise, and cooperation of the participants, moderators, and organizing committee, the colloquium and this volume would not have been possible.

We thank the GCI staff who helped plan, coordinate, and implement the colloquium, including Annette Snelling, Michele Astorian, Virginia Horton, and Nick Swarts. We are indebted to Valerie Greathouse of the GCI Information Center, who was assisted by Amel Chabbi and Claudia Cancino, for their hard work and perseverance in the research and compilation of the bibliography published in this volume. From Mesa Verde National Park, we thank Sue Johnson-Erner, Larry Nordby, Preston Fisher, Flint Boardman, Paul Blomgren, and all the staff who facilitated logistics, provided the audiovisual and computer support, and led site visits, as well as ARAmark Mesa Verde Company for the excellent service at their lodge and restaurant and on the postcolloquium tour.

We would also like to acknowledge Kathy Fiero, formerly with the National Park Service at Mesa Verde, who spearheaded conservation efforts throughout her twenty-year tenure there and who generously shared her knowledge of the site with participants. Mary Slater of the National Park Service at Bandelier National Monument was an essential liaison for the media session and the postcolloquium tour. Also from the National Park Service, we acknowledge Barbara Romero and Mary Padilla for administering the National Park Service's Challenge Cost Share grant.

Many thanks to Susan Thomas and the staff of the Anasazi Heritage Center, who shared their museum and laboratories with the colloquium participants during the museum session and public lecture held there. We also acknowledge J. J. Brody, professor emeritus at the University of New Mexico, for presenting the stimulating public lecture sponsored in part by the Colorado Historical Society/State Historical Fund.

Finally, we are extremely grateful to all of those who worked on the publication of this volume, particularly Patrick Pardo, assistant editor, Getty Publications, who oversaw the publication process; Leslie Tilley, who provided thoughtful copy-editing of the manuscript; Gary Hespenheide, who attended to the design; Pamela Heath, who handled production; Cynthia Godlewski and Chris Seki, who did a tremendous job of coordinating the authors and editors; Kristin Kelly, assistant director, Dissemination and Research Resources at the GCI; and all of our colleagues at Getty Publications.

Opening Dedication

Delbridge Honanie/Coochsiwukioma
Cliff Palace

Yes, I am happy that all of us are gathered here this morning

Getting to know each other.

I am happy to see your many faces from the four directions.

The workers here at the park, and the fine food that has been

Prepared for us, I am thankful for.

With you, faces of the four directions, what we will experience

And see, I am happy about.

Now we have descended to this ancient sacred community,

Home of my ancestors, who welcome and are happy about your visit.

From their ancestral spirit let us experience their traditional knowledge

And wisdom, as we stand here in meditation and pray with them.

With open minds, let us ask questions and seek answers, then take these

Teachings back home with us, and share with our children and people.

With happiness and strength let us journey in our gathering.

Kwakhai.

Thank you.

Archaeological Sites

Introduction

Giacomo Chiari

The archaeological section in this volume comprises four papers that are very different from one another in content, geographical distribution, and issues discussed. Each of them provoked interesting discussion among the participants during the colloquium on the subjects listed below in the form of questions. While acknowledging that they are far from being resolved, I present them here with the hope that they may be the object of further reflection and debate.

A change of scale in archaeological investigation can make the use of nondestructive techniques, including satellite imagery, possible and very useful. Could it be that excavation will no longer be necessary?

Abbasid earth architecture at Samarra, Iraq, was investigated by Alastair Northedge by studying historic photographic documentation and satellite images. The map of the town made using satellite imagery shows a level of detail comparable to maps of archaeological excavations. However, while the urban plan can be obtained in this way, the full richness of the historic and artistic finds is missing. Yet, in times of extreme change such as uncontrolled urbanization, it may well be that this type of information is the only kind that can and should be retrieved, in order to stop the voluntary and planned destruction of archaeological sites.

Detachment of decorated surfaces, once a common treatment, is no longer acceptable. Are there any exceptions to that general rule? Under what circumstances, if any, can removal and relocation be acceptable?

The paper by Eric Miller, Pamela Rose, and David Singleton presents the Taharqo wall painting rescue at Qasr Ibrim, in Egypt, now a small island in Lake Nasser, which was created by the Aswan High Dam. The painting is the last remaining of the Twenty-Fifth Dynasty and therefore unique. The chances of imminent and total destruction were high. Is this reason enough for detachment, which involves a complete loss of the contextual value of the painting?

The paper is limited to the first phase of the operation, and the final conditions of the mural remain uncertain. Those who argue against any form of painting detachment and transfer point out that in the protected museum setting there are numerous detached mural fragments that are decaying and deeply in jeopardy. Given the enormous number of mural paintings in danger, it may be wiser to concentrate efforts on saving the ones that can be maintained in situ, with most of their values preserved. Others argue that if one can do something to save a mural that faces imminent destruction, it should perhaps be detached, although this solution should be adopted only in extreme cases and after having proven that there is no other alternative for its preservation.

How can architectural plasters on large, exposed, complex sites be preserved and interpreted successfully in situ? How can the iconographical study be used toward the interpretation of the site, and how does it relate to the conservation of the architectural finishes?

The two-part paper on Mesa Verde in this volume by Rebecca Carr and Larry Nordby presents both the management tools being used to survey and document the plaster finishes and to prioritize conservation needs and the significance of the finishes. At Mesa Verde, where there are at least eighty-four alcove sites with surface finishes, a comprehensive plan for survey, documentation, and stabilization is being developed. This was shown in the example of the Archeological Site Conservation Program's ArkDoc database, which has been designed to help address conservation and management issues. Such tools can be used to strengthen the link between site significance and treatment planning and implementation, as well as interpretation. Regarding conservation, even with limited resources, it is necessary to focus not only on remedial treatment of the plasters but also on determining and mitigating the causes of deterioration.

In conclusion, it was shown that significant advances have been made toward conservation of decorated architectural finishes in situ on archaeological sites. However, serious preliminary study of the conditions and conservation issues of the decorated surfaces and the related architecture must be done first. This entails a thorough condition survey of the surface finishes and the related architectural context, analysis of the survey data, and identification of the conservation issues. The technical tools for in situ preservation are available, and are continuously being enhanced and improved.

A method for long-term evaluation of the results of conservation treatments is yet to be determined, but the participants held in common an understanding that monitoring and maintenance are essential to the preservation of decorated architectural surfaces on earth.

Abbasid Earth Architecture and Decoration at Samarra, Iraq

Alastair Northedge

Samarra is located 125 kilometers north of Baghdad on the Tigris river (Fig. 1).[1] The present-day city of 200,000 inhabitants is sited on the east bank of the river, surrounding a shrine commemorating the tombs of the tenth and eleventh imams of the Twelver Shi'a sect of Islam and the site where the twelfth imam disappeared in AD 874. In this area, the river plain of the Tigris is two to three kilometers wide, and fertile; however, the steppe to the west is arid and dry, and to the east, green but without trees. The rainfall, 100–150 millimeters per year, is inadequate to support agriculture without irrigation.

In ancient times, the region was little settled, but in the sixth century AD the Iranian Sasanian dynasty dug a major irrigation canal, called in Arabic al-Qatul al-Kisrawi, with its inlets north and south of Samarra (Fig. 2). This enterprise led to the construction of palaces and hunting reserves, which culminated three centuries later, in 836, in the Abbasid caliph al-Mu'tasim choosing the site for a city to house the court and the main military base of the army.

The Abbasids were the second hereditary dynasty of caliphs in Islam,[2] and came to power as a result of the Abbasid Revolution, in 750. Opposed to the Umayyad caliphs of Damascus, they settled in Iraq, and the second Abbasid caliph, al-Mansur, founded Baghdad in 762–66. Al-Mu'tasim (833–842), eighth caliph of the dynasty, had a problem of conflicts between his elite guard of Turks from Central Asia and the population of Baghdad, and so preferred to found a new military base to the north at Samarra, which was renamed Surra Man Ra'a ("He who sees it is delighted"). As it happened, the seven succeeding caliphs decided to stay there, until the last, al-Mu'tamid, died in 892, when his successor settled again in Baghdad.

In this time, the city expanded enormously, mainly as a result of the architectural enthusiasm of the caliph al-Mutawakkil (847–861), until it reached a solidly built-up area of 58 square kilometers, with related construction spreading over about 164 square kilometers. However, the city's unfertile surroundings provided insufficient local resources for it to maintain that size, and, after the departure of the caliphs at the end of the ninth century, soon collapsed into the area of the modern city—35 hectares at the beginning of the twentieth century (now larger). The ruin field of the city, mainly composed of earth mounds, survived well into the twentieth century and only began to be built over and cultivated in the 1960s (Fig. 3). Today, according to a satellite image dated to about 2000—before the present troubles—about 7.5 square kilometers of the main built-up area visible in 1924 has been totally lost to archaeology,[3] although the remains are also much more worn down than before. The lost area is mainly under the modern town, and thus is also the heart of the Abbasid city. Detailed reports on the consequences of the recent battles, from November 2003 onwards, remain thin, but the fighting has been principally within the modern town. By contrast with the pillage of archaeological sites in southern Iraq that occurred both during the 1990s and since the war of 2003, no reports have emerged of clandestine excavations at Samarra.

Archaeological interest began at the beginning of the twentieth century, with competing teams of German and French archaeologists. In 1907 and 1909, the French architect Henri Viollet conducted two campaigns (Viollet 1909, 1911). The German Ernst Herzfeld made a first visit to Samarra in 1903, and then excavated in two grand campaigns in 1911 and 1913. Two preliminary reports were published shortly after the fieldwork.[4] After the First World War, a monumental series of

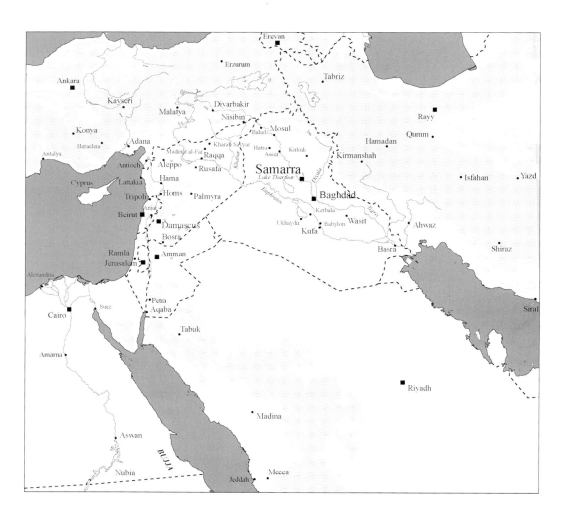

FIGURE 1 Map showing the site of Samarra.

six volumes of the *Ausgrabungen von Samarra* were published between 1923 and 1948. The two volumes that particularly concern this article were *Der Wandschmuck der Bauten von Samarra und seine Ornamentik* (The Wall Decoration and Ornamental Motifs of the Buildings of Samarra), which appeared in 1923, and *Die Malereien von Samarra* (The Paintings of Samarra), which appeared in 1927. No publication of the architecture excavated was made. A recent project has targeted this lack, and the first of two volumes treating the architecture of the first campaign in 1911 was published in 2003, T. Leisten's *Excavation of Samarra,* vol. 1, *Architecture, Final Report of the First Campaign 1910–1912*.

The Iraq Directorate-General of Antiquities restarted excavations between 1936 and 1940, and published as *Hafriyyat Samarra' 1936–1939,* in 1940. Excavations of the Directorate-General continued in the 1960s and 1970s. From 1980 onwards, a massive and heavily financed project of excavation and restoration was launched, which continued on a lesser scale until 1990.[5]

In 1983, the author undertook a project to record all the surviving remains of the city, surface and excavated, with the intention of preserving what was known of one of the world's largest ancient cities. In the end, three campaigns were conducted in the field, in 1983, 1986–87, and 1989. The plan was made largely by photogrammetry, based on air photographs taken in 1928 and 1953. The first volume, *The Historical Topography of Samarra,* is in the course of publication, and the second volume, the *Archaeological Atlas of Samarra,* will be finished shortly.

The Site

Essentially, the complex was composed of a caliphal city, called Surra Man Ra'a, which extended south from the Caliphal Palace (Dar al-Khilafa)[6] along both sides of a monumental avenue over a distance of 7 kilometers.[7] The markets and mosque were located along this avenue. To this central element were agglomerated a number of separate cantonment

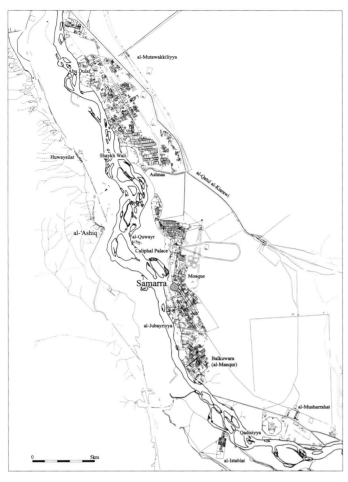

FIGURE 2 Overall plan of the archaeological site of Samarra.

FIGURE 3 Aerial view of the central city (1953).

units: hunting reserves, racecourses, and housing for major military units and other royal servants, including the palace staff. The cantonment units most often follow the palace-avenue plan of the caliphal city, but on a lesser scale. None were fortified. Under al-Mutawakkil, more units were added, doubling the city size. Most notably these included the palaces of Balkuwara and Istablat, and the new caliphal city of al-Mutawakkiliyya, which covered 1,165 hectares. The latter was built in 859 and abandoned only two years later, at the end of 861.

Of all this construction, the following have been excavated:

- The Congregational Mosque of al-Mutawakkil, with its spiral minaret (Creswell 1940: 254–65; Leisten 2003: 35–57)

- The Abu Dulaf Mosque (Creswell 1940: 278–82; Leisten 2003: 58–68)
- About 39,000 square meters out of 125 hectares of the Caliphal Palace (Creswell 1940: 232–45; Hammudi 1982; Northedge 1993)
- Parts of the Balkuwara Palace (Creswell 1940: 265–70; Leisten 2003: 69–71, 81–104)
- The Qasr al-'Ashiq (Creswell 1940: 361–64; Leisten 2003: 105–11; Hamid 1974)
- Some 50 houses[8]

Construction Techniques

Ancient Mesopotamia had a long tradition of construction in unfired mud brick, little else being available in the alluvial plain of southern Iraq. From the third millennium BC onwards, the proportion of fired brick increases in monumental architecture, and in the sixth century BC Babylon of Nebuchadnezzar, much monumental architecture was in fired brick (Oates 1979). Samarra is the last urban archaeological site in Iraq where much fine architecture can be found in unfired materials. (In fact, the ancient tradition of using unfired earth materials was still common there in village architecture at the end of the 1990s.)

At Samarra, the large area of construction necessitated the extensive use of unfired construction, with a minor proportion of fired brick. Four types of construction can be distinguished.

- **Coursed earth construction.** In this technique, wooden shuttering may have been used to shape the form of the wall, including half-round buttresses.[9] Then earth was tamped down in courses of approximately 50 cm and left to dry before the next course was added. The coursing is frequently visible. This technique was used for major enclosure walls and the walls of houses.
- **Mud-brick construction.** At Samarra, the mud bricks are 27 × 27 × 5 cm, and are mortared with a gypsum mortar, which is more resistant than the bricks themselves. This technique appears to have been considered superior to coursed earth construction, and is used in the public rooms of some major houses.[10] An associated technique of using large mud bricks, 46 × 46 × 11 cm, with mud mortar, is used for the walls of the slightly earlier Octagon of Qadisiyya, dated before 796, at the south end of the ruin field. The towers use reed mats between courses of bricks. A second related technique of bricks with a high admixture of gypsum, or pure gypsum, is used in the palace of al-'Ashiq.
- **Fired-brick construction.** Fired bricks measure 27 × 27 × 5 cm, with gypsum mortar between the courses. Fired brick was used for major fine construction. In the vast majority of the fired construction, the bricks have been removed for reuse elsewhere, leaving the trenches where the wall had been. Only six buildings in Abbasid Samarra have retained their fired brick.[11]
- **Rubble stone construction.** In the Upper Palace at Huwaysilat, the surviving lower parts are built of rubble stones in gypsum mortar, a technique typical of western Iraq and Iran, where poor-quality stone is plentiful (DGA 1940: figs. 3–4).

On the interiors, there is evidence of gypsum plastering. Floors were most commonly of fired-brick tiles, approximately 50 cm square, where flooring is recorded. The little evidence that has been preserved of roofing suggests mainly flat roofs of wooden beams. In unusual cases, there is evidence of brick domes and barrel vaults, which use the pitched-brick construction of Mesopotamia and Iran.[12]

It should be noted that construction techniques at Abbasid Samarra, being an imperial capital that was built rapidly, were not necessarily typical of the local region. The army was mainly composed of Central-Asian Turks, eastern Iranians, and Egyptian Bedouin who are called al-Maghariba (westerners) in the sources (Northedge 2005). It would be reasonable to suppose that many of the builders were of these origins, although others were drawn from all around the region.[13] However, they were constrained by the materials available.

Architecture at Samarra, as far as is known, is nearly universally single-story (Fig. 4).[14] Outer walls are often reinforced with half-round buttresses. Reception rooms are most commonly in the form of a T-*iwan* (a rectangular open-fronted hall with a transverse pillared portico in front, accompanied by two side rooms and facing onto a courtyard), but closed halls with a portico at each end are also widely known. Dome chambers with four basilical halls are also known in the palaces. In the larger houses and palaces, family apartments composed of a courtyard with seven or more surrounding rooms can be identified. It should be emphasized that, as on the order of 20,000 houses are known in Abbasid Samarra, many different combinations of a similar theme can be identified, from small houses to the greatest palaces.[15]

Decorative Techniques

In the larger houses (i.e., those excavated) the most common decorative technique of the reception rooms is a carved stucco dado about 1 meter high (Fig. 5). In five of the excavated large houses and two of the palaces, fragments of wall paintings placed above the dadoes have been recovered.[16] In the Caliphal Palace (Dar al-Khilafa), there are cases where the stucco dadoes are replaced by carved marble, either a border of a pearl motif, or elongated hexagonal tiles. In the debris of the Caliphal Palace, the German expedition of 1913 recovered fragments of luster-glazed tiles, one of the first two examples of this famous technique in the Islamic world. There are also tesserae of glass wall-mosaics, but no panel has been recovered to show the motifs. Glass panels were recovered from the Mosque of al-Mutawakkil.

Stucco Panels
The stucco used in decoration is composed of a fairly pure gypsum with an admixture of earth. Gypsum is a widely avail-

FIGURE 4 Plan and photo of House no. 5 (1983).

FIGURE 5 Vine-leaf-style stucco, from the Circular Basin in the Caliphal Palace.

able material, found as nodules in the soil on the steppe land east of Samarra (Herzfeld 1912: 14–15). One hundred forty-one abandoned kiln sites have been identified, probably dating to the first half of the twentieth century, and production was certainly continuing in the 1980s.

Stucco panels are normally placed in the reception rooms; side rooms are normally not decorated.[17] The panels are most commonly dadoes, 1 meter high on the lower walls (Figs. 5 and 6), but borders to doorways are also known, as are borders to decorative niches (Fig. 7).There are two cases in houses of a carved stucco *mihrab* niche, one with a relief inscription (Herzfeld 1923: 226–27; DGA 1940: fig. 57).[18]

The first volume of the German publication *Der Wandschmuck* brought out a typology of Samarran decorations that continues to be used today. It was divided into three main styles: the first, called the bevelled style (or *Schrägschnittstil*); the second, characterized by cross-hatched lobes; and the third, defined by vine leaves with four holes. The sequence was based on the relative frequency of the styles. At a later date, K. A. C. Creswell reversed the sequence (which he labeled styles A, B, and C), arguing correctly that the vine-leaf style was chronologically earlier (Creswell 1940: 286–88). As German speakers tend to use Herzfeld's numbering and English speakers tend to use Creswell's denominations, it seems better to avoid confusion and simply use the names: bevelled style, cross-hatch style, and vine-leaf style. On the whole, Herzfeld's division into three styles has survived the test of time well, but, as we shall see, there is a certain degree of overlapping.

The Vine-Leaf Style

The vine-leaf style is defined by a dense mass of vine leaves, each of which is characterized by four holes (Fig. 5; Herzfeld 1923: 183–225). Only rarely are bunches of grapes found. In the style found at Samarra, the vine leaves are placed in and around frames, which have pearl borders. The geometric forms of the frames are various: circles, rectangles, hexagons, octagons, crosses, ovals, and polylobed medallions. Elsewhere, the use of frames is not so frequent, notably at Raqqa in Syria, where the earliest dated examples of the vine-leaf style are found in the settlement of the caliph Harun al-Rashid in the period 796–808 (Meinecke 1991, 1999). Meinecke thought that the origins of this style evidently lay in classical decoration, but the fact is that this style is very different from stucco decoration before 750, and it is mostly found in Iraq and further east. At any rate, at Samarra it is found in the earliest buildings, the palaces at Huwaysilat (DGA 1940: pls. 4–32), and the circular basin in the Caliphal Palace (al-Hayani 1996), but also in a late building—the Qasr al-ʿAshiq, which may have been begun in 877 (Herzfeld 1923: ornaments 262–63, 265).

The Cross-Hatch Style

The cross-hatch style retains the medallions of the vine-leaf style, but replaces the vine leaves with teardrop and other abstract motifs, which are decorated with relief cross-hatching (Herzfeld 1923: 117–82). In some panels, the cross-hatching degrades into simple dots (Fig. 6). The style is often associated with the vine-leaf style; motifs from the two are combined together in the Bab al-ʿAmma of the Caliphal Palace (Herzfeld 1923: 257–59). By contrast, it is not known before Samarra. Whereas vine leaves can be described as originating in classical or Middle Eastern art, the cross-hatch style has no known origin in the region. The only idea so far put forward is Dimand's, who proposed sources in Indian temple art, which can only be described as quite distant (Dimand 1952). More work is required on this subject.

The Bevelled Style

The bevelled style is the most famous of the Samarra decoration techniques, a highly abstract mass of trefoils, half-palmettes, and palmettes, all defined by a sloping or rounded cut (Fig. 7; Herzfeld 1923: 10–116). Late versions can be identified by patterns of four holes (al-Jannabi 1981, 1982). Borders of rounded pearls for niches are known.

It is clear that this style is a secondary development at Samarra, but was certainly in use by the time of the early palace construction of al-Mutawakkil, for example, Sur ʿIsa,

FIGURE 6 Stucco panel of the cross-hatch style in the Samarra Museum.

FIGURE 7 Bevelled-style façade as excavated in the Balkuwara Palace. Courtesy of Staatliche Museen zu Berlin – Museum für Islamische Kunst, Photo no. Sam 249. Photo: Ernst Herzfeld, 1911/12.

probably built at the same time as the Congregational Mosque in 849–52 (Northedge 2001), or House no. 4 (Hanin 1985–86). During the reign of al-Mutawakkil (847–61), its use became general, and the majority of buildings employ the style. It is also found on wood panels (e.g., Herzfeld 1923: taf. xiv, xvi, xxv), and marble (e.g., Herzfeld 1923: taf. xix). Ettinghausen (1952) saw a long subsequent history to the bevelled style in Iran, but in its original format it was limited to Samarra, Raqqa, and Tulunid Egypt in the ninth century. As in the case of the cross-hatch style, it has no known antecedents in the Mediterranean or Near East. In this case, there is widespread agreement that it has its origins in Central Asia in Steppe art (Bernus-Taylor 1988). The one figural panel found in the Caliphal Palace is a painted relief frieze of two-hump camels (Herzfeld 1927: taf. lxxvi). Nevertheless, little is known about Steppe art of this period, and doubts remain.

Wall Paintings

Wall painting is relatively rare at Samarra, being found only in parts of the Caliphal Palace, notably the so-called Harim, and in five houses (Herzfeld 1927; DGA 1940: figs. 46–53). The paintings have all been found as fragments in the rubble, through collapse of walls and, often, later robbing of the bricks. Only one panel was partially preserved in situ, in House no. XIII of 1911 (Herzfeld 1927: taf. lix). There is one case of nonfigural painting, in House no. 4 of 1936 (DGA 1940:

figs. lxxiv–lxxvi), which is mostly composed of diamond and quatrefoil patterns; the majority of the remainder, as far as can be deduced from the fragments, were basically figural with patterned borders and frames. Animals are common, mainly a wide variety of different birds, commonly partridges and ducks, but also including parrotlike creatures (Herzfeld 1927: taf. xxv, xlviii–xlvix). The human figures are depicted with black hair and pale skin. Herzfeld interpreted many beardless figures as women, but this seems unlikely in the context of the society of the time, where women were hardly ever mentioned. A good example is the most famous scene from the "Harim" of the Caliphal Palace, where two figures are depicted pouring wine into bowls (Fig. 8). Herzfeld thought they were female dancers, but the consensus now seems to be that they are young men, wearing versions of the long Arab shirt. However, a fundamental reanalysis of these paintings is overdue, and without that, secondary commentaries are not worth much.

Ceramic Tiles

As noted, glazed ceramic tiles were found in the debris of the Caliphal Palace, one of the first two examples of this famous technique in the Islamic world, the other being the mosque of Kairouan in Tunisia (e.g., Creswell 1940: 308–20). They are polychrome luster tiles in hexagonal and square formats. The hexagonal tiles are sprinkled with the different red and yellow-

FIGURE 8 Watercolor reconstruction
of the painting of two wine-pourers
from the "Harim" of the Caliphal
Palace. (Source: E. Herzfeld, 1927,
Die Ausgrabungen von Samarra 3,
Die Malereien von Samarra [taf. ii]
Berlin.)

FIGURE 8 Watercolor reconstruction of the painting of two wine-pourers from the "Harim" of the Caliphal Palace. (Source: E. Herzfeld, 1927, *Die Ausgrabungen von Samarra* 3, *Die Malereien von Samarra* [taf. ii] Berlin.)

green tints, to imitate marble, but the square tiles carry a circular garland which in one case bears the figure of a cock. Other tiles are monochrome luster, with a circular motif on a white ground (al-Jannabi 1981, 1982). It remains uncertain whether they were in a storeroom, as supposed by the excavators, or in an upper story of a tower pavilion that had collapsed (Sarre 1925: 50–54).

Summary of the Decoration

The decoration of Samarra was largely composed of stucco and painting, with a small input from other techniques. The massive domination of stucco, much in excess of what has been found elsewhere, was largely due to the ample supply of raw gypsum. The ninth century was a period of relatively strong iconoclasm in Islam: compare, for example, the powerful figural art of the Umayyad period and the miniature paintings of the post-Mongol period. It is not surprising that the stucco decoration, the most widespread, is almost entirely nonfigural. The contrast with the figural wall paintings is all the stronger. Those paintings are found in the Caliphal Palace and in the zone of houses around the palace

where the Turkish military leaders, who had a relaxed view of Islam, lived.

Conservation and Politics

Conservation of the decoration in the field remains a serious problem, and has scarcely been addressed. As noted above, much of the decoration has survived in fragments, poorly or not at all attached to walls of differing degrees of stability.

During the more than twenty years of the regime of Saddam Hussein, Iraq was largely a closed country, cut off from the outside world. A desire for conservation of the cultural remains at Samarra certainly existed, along with a political desire to restore the glories of the Abbasid Caliphate, on the model of the regime's restoration of Babylon. At Samarra, the overall scheme cannot be said to have been successful, although approximately thirteen million dinars (about twenty-five million dollars at the exchange of the time) were spent in the early 1980s. Access to outside technical assistance was not possible, and only technically primitive methods used. Walls in unfired materials were replaced with commercial fired brick containing high quantities of salts and not expected to last more than ten years. Stucco panels were restored to complete status and extended with new stucco apparently of local origin. There are no paintings conserved on-site.

With the Iraq War of 2003, cultural management work on the site appears to have come to a halt, and at the time of writing the local situation is insufficiently stable to permit field activity. Nevertheless, a new management plan is being prepared for the Directorate of Antiquities, and it is hoped this will be put into effect when the political problems are resolved.

Notes

1 On the history and geography of Samarra, see Herzfeld 1948; Northedge 1995, 2005.

2 *Caliph* is the equivalent of the Arabic *khalifa*, meaning a deputy or successor of the Prophet Muhammad, who died in AD 632.

3 "Totally lost to archaeology" means the site is built over and it would be impossible to excavate more than a small fragment.

4 The first, a monograph entitled *Erster vorläufiger Bericht über die Ausgrabungen von Samarra*, was published after the first season's work (Herzfeld 1912). The second, an article that appeared in *Der Islam* in 1914, covered the work of the second season (Herzfeld 1914).

5 Some of this work has been published in the journal *Sumer*, but some remains unpublished.

6 In earlier literature, the palace was known as al-Jawsaq al-Khaqani. This was an error by Ernst Herzfeld, who substituted the name of one of the subpalaces for the whole. For the arguments, see Northedge 1993.

7 For the plan of Abbasid Samarra, see this author's *Historical Topography of Samarra*, currently in press.

8 The houses from the excavations of Herzfeld in 1911 are published in Leisten 2003: 118–46. The houses are numbered I to XVII. Those excavated between 1936 and 1940 are published in DGA 1940. Ten house sites were excavated, but only nos. 1 to 4, and 9 to 10 were published. Of the work from the early 1980s, the reports published in the journal *Sumer* are al-Jannabi 1981, 1982; 'Abd al-Fattah 1984; Hanin 1985–86; Nadir and Qaduri, 1985–86.

9 No actual evidence has been recovered of the use of wooden shuttering, and it may be that a technique of avoiding the use of so much wood existed.

10 The use of mud brick with gypsum mortar is notably found in House no. 1 of 1981 ('Abd al-Fattah 1984), and Houses no. 5 and 11 excavated in 1940, all situated in al-Mutawakkiliyya.

11 All six were discussed by Creswell (1940). They are the Congregational Mosque of al-Mutawakkil, the Abu Dulaf Mosque, the Bab al-'Amma of the Caliphal Palace, the Balkuwara Palace, the 'Ashiq Palace, and the Qubbat al-Sulaybiyya.

12 Evidence of barrel vaults is preserved in the Bab al-'Amma of the Caliphal Palace, and the undercrofts of the Qasr al-'Ashiq.

13 Evidence of a wide variety of construction is to be seen in the Umayyad desert castles of the first half of the eighth century (Creswell 1969). At Samarra, it is more difficult to distinguish different national traditions, and so far no analysis has been made.

14 The exceptions are a number of tower pavilions in the palaces (Northedge 2001, 2005).

15 The exact figure for the number of houses is difficult to state, for it is impossible to know without excavation whether any individual house was composed of one or more courtyards. The number of complex houses at present is 1,640, and the number of blocks of small houses, which could include five to twenty houses, is 1,969. The number of palaces is forty-one (Northedge 2001).

16 House no. 1 (DGA 1940: figs. 46–53); House no. 4 (DGA 1940: figs. 74–76); sounding C (DGA 1940: fig. 104).

17 An exception is the side rooms of the palace of Sur 'Isa, where carved stucco borders are placed around the doors (unpublished).

18 A *mihrab* is the niche of a mosque oriented toward Mecca.

References

'Abd al-Fattah, Nahda. 1984. Mashru' Ihya' madinatay Samarra' wal-Mutawakkiliyya al-athariyyatayn: Dar raqm (1) wal-shari' al-a'zam fi Samarra'. *Sumer* 43:30–49 (Arabic section).

Bernus-Taylor, M. 1988. *L'Art en terres d'islam.* 1: *Les Premiers siècles.* Paris: Desclée de Brouwer.

Creswell, K. A. C. 1940. *Early Muslim Architecture*, 1st ed., vol. 2. Oxford: Oxford University Press.

———. 1969. *Early Muslim Architecture*, 2nd ed., vol. 1, pts. 1 and 2. Oxford: Oxford University Press.

Dimand, M. S. 1952. Studies in Islamic ornament 2. The origin of the second style of Samarra decoration. In *Archaeologia Orientalia in memoriam Ernst Herzfeld*, ed. George C. Miles, 62–68. Locust Valley, NY: J. J. Augustin.

Directorate-General of Antiquities (DGA). 1940. *Hafriyyat Samarra' 1936–1939*, 2 vols. Baghdad: Government Press.

Ettinghausen, R. 1952. The "beveled style" in the post-Samarra period. In *Archaeologia Orientalia in memoriam Ernst Herzfeld*, ed. George C. Miles, 72–83. Locust Valley, NY: J. J. Augustin.

Hamid, 'Abd al-'Aziz. 1974. New lights on the 'Ashiq Palace of Samarra. *Sumer* 30:183–94.

Hammudi, K. K. 1982. Qasr al-khalifa al-Mu'tasim fi Samarra'. *Sumer* 38:168–205 (Arabic section).

Hanin, Q. R. 1985–86. al-tanqib wal-siyana al-athariyya fi dar raqm 4 fi Madaqq al-Tabl. *Sumer* 44:158–81 (Arabic section).

Hayani, H. H. al-. 1996. al-birka al-da'iriyya dakhil qasr al-khalifa—Samarra'—tanqib wa-siyana. *Sumer* 48:89–103 (Arabic section).

Herzfeld, E. 1912. *Erster vorläufiger Bericht über die Ausgrabungen von Samarra.* Berlin: D. Reimer.

———. 1914. Mitteilung über die Arbeiten der zweiten Kampagne von Samarra. *Der Islam* 5:196–204.

———. 1923. *Die Ausgrabungen von Samarra 1, Der Wandschmuck der Bauten von Samarra und seine Ornamentik.* Berlin: D. Reimer.

———. 1927. *Die Ausgrabungen von Samarra 3, Die Malereien von Samarra.* Berlin: D. Reimer.

———. 1948. *Ausgrabungen von Samarra 6, Geschichte der Stadt Samarra.* Hamburg: Eckardt und Messtorff.

Jannabi, K. al-. 1970. *Masjid Abi Dulaf.* Baghdad: Directorate-General of Antiquities.

Jannabi, T. A. al-. 1981. al-tanqib wal-siyana fi Samarra' 1978–81. *Sumer* 37:188–211 (Arabic section).

———. 1982. Islamic archaeology in Iraq, recent excavations at Samarra. *World Archaeology* 14:305–27.

Kennet, D. 2001. The form of the military cantonments at Samarra: The organisation of the Abbasid army. In *A Medieval Islamic City Reconsidered,* Oxford Studies in Islamic Art 14, ed. C. Robinson, 157–82. Oxford: Oxford University Press.

Leisten, T. 2003. *Excavation of Samarra,* vol. 1, *Architecture, Final Report of the First Campaign 1910–1912, Baghdader Forschungen* bd. 20. Mainz: von Zabern.

Meinecke, M. 1991. Early Abbasid stucco decorations in the Bilad al-Sham. In *Bilad al-Sham during the Abbasid Period* (Proceedings of the Fifth International Conference on the History of Bilad al-Sham), ed. M. A. Bakhit and R. Schick, 226–67. Amman: University of Jordan.

———. 1999. Abbasidische Stuckdekorationen aus ar-Raqqa. In *Rezeption in der islamischen Kunst* (Bamberger Symposium), ed. B. Finster, C. Fragner, and H. Hafenrichter, 247–65. Stuttgart: F. Steiner.

Nadir, M. A., and Qaduri, A. 'A. 1985–86. al-tanqib wal-siyana al-athariyya fi dar raqm 5 fi Madaqq al-Tabl. *Sumer* 44:182–98 (Arabic section).

Northedge, A. 1993. An interpretation of the Palace of the Caliph at Samarra (Dar al-Khilafa or Jawsaq al-Khaqani). *Ars Orientalis* 23:143–71.

———. 1995. Samarra. In *Encyclopaedia of Islam*, 2nd ed. (1954–). Leiden: Brill.

———. 2001. The palaces of the "Abbasids at Samarra." In *A Medieval Islamic City Reconsidered*, Oxford Studies in Islamic Art 14, ed. C. Robinson, 29–67. Oxford: Oxford University Press.

———. 2005. *The Historical Topography of Samarra*, Samarra Studies 1. Oxford: British School of Archaeology in Iraq.

Northedge, A., and D. Kennet. Forthcoming. *Archaeological Atlas of Samarra*, Samarra Studies 2. Oxford: British School of Archaeology in Iraq.

Oates, J. 1979. *Babylon.* London: Thames and Hudson.

Qadi, Sabah Mahmud al-. 1995. Mashru' tatwir madinatay Samarra' wal-Mutawakkiliyya "Masjid Sur Isa." *Sumer* 47:57–60 (Arabic section).

Qaysi, Rabi al-. 1967. al-siyana al-athariyya fi Qasr al-'Ashiq fi Samarra'. *Sumer* 23:183–90 (Arabic section).

———. 1969. Jami' al-malwiya fi Samarra'—takhtit wa-siyana. *Sumer* 25:143–62 (Arabic section).

———. 1970. al-Malwiya manarat al-masjid al-jami' fi Samarra'. *Sumer,* 26:277–84.

Rice, D. S. 1958. Deacon or drink. *Arabica* 5:15–33.

Robinson, C., ed. 2001. *A Medieval Islamic City Reconsidered.* Oxford Studies in Islamic Art 14. Oxford: Oxford University Press.

Rogers, J. M. 1970. Samarra, a study in medieval town-planning. In *The Islamic City*, ed. A. H. Hourani and S. M. Stern, 119–55. Oxford: B. Cassirer.

Sarre, F. 1925. *Ausgrabungen von Samarra 2: Die Keramik von Samarra.* Berlin: D. Reimer, E. Vohsen.

Susa, A. 1948–49. *Rayy Samarra' fi 'Ahd al-Khilafa al-'Abbasiyya*, 2 vols. Baghdad: Matba'at al-Ma'arif.

Viollet, H. 1909. *Description du Palais de Al-Moutasim fils d'Haroun-Al-Raschid à Samara et quelques monuments arabes peu connus de la Mésopotamie*, Mémoires présentés à l'Académie des Inscriptions et des Belles-Lettres, 12, 567–94. Paris.

———. 1911. *Fouilles à Samara en Mésopotamie. Un palais musulman du IXe siècle*, Mémoires présentés à l'Académie des Inscriptions et des Belles-Lettres, 12, 685–717. Paris.

The Taharqo Wall Painting Rescue at Qasr Ibrim, Egypt

David Singleton, Eric Miller, and Pamela Rose

The removal of architectural elements from sites in Egypt is, these days, rarely done, as conservation in situ is preferred whenever possible. An exception to this rule is the subject of this paper: the removal and conservation of a unique wall painting (a full-length royal portrait) from an earthen structure at Qasr Ibrim. Because the painting was in danger of imminent destruction, the decision was made to remove it from the wall and house it in a museum. This paper describes the circumstances leading up to the decision and details the process of removing and transporting the wall painting.

The Site

Qasr Ibrim is situated on what was a high promontory on the east bank of the Nile. Its commanding and isolated position made it a natural fortress, and it had a long history of habitation, from around 1000 BC to the early nineteenth century.

Following commencement of the Aswan High Dam project and in response to an appeal by UNESCO, the Egypt Exploration Society began archaeological excavation there in 1963. With the rising water level, the promontory became an island in 1975.

The Wall Paintings of the Taharqo Temple

Two wall paintings were discovered in the 1970s on the northeast and northwest walls of the sanctuary of a small mud-brick temple built by the Kushite pharaoh Taharqo (690–664 BC) (Plumley and Adams 1974: 229; Plumley 1975: 20). Each depicted a full-length figure of the pharaoh standing in front of a god. At the time of their initial discovery, the paintings were partly documented through photographs and drawings, and a brief report on their content and condition was prepared by a member of the archaeological team. The room containing the paintings was then backfilled with sieved soil and left.

The section of wall painting from the northwest wall (Fig. 1) was the subject of the rescue mission. In addition to the figure of the pharaoh, the remains of a cartouche, containing his name, can be seen above his head. The figure facing Taharqo is probably the god Amun. The dismantling of a later apse, inserted when the temple was converted to a Christian church, led to the discovery of the continuation of the northwest painting scheme; it includes at least one more figure standing with its back to Taharqo.

The underlying stratigraphy of the wall painting (Fig. 2) consists of a coarse mud-and-straw plaster that was applied to the mud-brick wall in a layer approximately 2 cm thick. This is coated with one or two layers of a finer, light brown plaster containing clay, sand, and a variety of chopped vegetable matter. On top of this is a white ground, approximately 1–2 mm thick, on which the painting is executed. The white ground contains an aggregate of fine sand.

The Significance of the Wall Paintings

Wall paintings of this date are extremely rare and are of considerable art-historical importance. The only other surviving example on mud-brick known to the authors is from Building A1 at Kawa in Sudan, and it preserves the figures only up to knee level (Welsby 2002; Haywood 2002). The presence of the upper bodies of the figures at Qasr Ibrim, and especially the remarkable rendition of the head of Taharqo in an elaborate crown, is unique.

FIGURE 1 The Taharqo temple during excavation work in 2000. Note the waterline and mud deposit on the lower portion of the painting. The remains of the east wall are on the right of the photo, and the apse of the church is still in situ in front of Taharqo's legs. Courtesy of the Egypt Exploration Society.

FIGURE 2 The upper portion of the image of Taharqo (2000). The stratigraphy of the preparation can be seen in the damaged portions of the painting. Part of the eighth-century cathedral is visible over the top of the wall, at the top-right corner of the photo. Courtesy of the Egypt Exploration Society.

The Effect of the Rising Water Level

The level of Lake Nasser rose dramatically in autumn 1998 to its highest level ever recorded (181.3 meters above sea level), reducing the area of the site by half from its fullest extent. The archaeological deposits readily carried water farther up into the ground, well above the actual water line. Since the expedition at that time worked on-site every other year (due to financial and logistical constraints), the expedition returned to the site in January 2000. By this time the water level had fallen by about 1.5 meters from its highest level, but had in the meantime destroyed the southeast and southwest areas of the temple, including most of the painting on the northeast wall of the sanctuary. A few fragments survived of the collapsed northeast painting, but the majority of it had disappeared without a trace. The loss of the southeast wall had caused the soil covering the northwest painting to shift, exposing the top 10–15 cm.

The dampness of the soil as a result of the earlier high level had encouraged vegetation, especially acacia bushes, to become established on the site, particularly in the area around the Taharqo temple. There the thick layer of mud from the dissolution of the walls has proved an exceptionally fertile base. These plants' root systems continue to draw up moisture into the soil.

As a result of the recent damage, it was decided to re-expose the northwest painting in order to assess its current condition, and particularly to look for evidence of water saturation affecting it. Once it was exposed, a line showing the level of water percolation was clearly visible on the surface, some 50 cm above the floor, discoloring the lower part (Fig. 1). The painting was then copied at full size by a professional illustrator and extensively photographed and documented. Since neither the materials nor the expertise was available in that season to do anything further, the painting was covered over again with dry soil and kept in place by a new retaining wall.

After returning from Egypt that season, Pamela Rose, director of the excavations at Qasr Ibrim, sought advice from the British Museum as to the best policy regarding the painting's survival. The main point influencing the discussion was the unpredictability of the level of Lake Nasser. The water level is mainly the result of the quantity of rainfall feeding into the Nile further south, which cannot be predicted. However, the lake level has for the last ten years also been influenced by the requirements of a massive irrigation and development undertaking called the Toshka project, which will carry water from the lake along a newly built canal out toward the western oases. In order for the canal to be filled, the level of the lake has to remain high. Discussions with British engineers constructing the Mubarak Pumping Station at the lake suggested that the water level would be kept as high as possible for the foreseeable future. Under these circumstances it was impossible to predict whether the painting was safe or in imminent danger of destruction from a renewed high water level.

A brief visit to the site by British Museum conservator Eric Miller in February 2001 led to the drawing up of detailed plans for the removal of the wall painting, should it prove necessary. At the time of the visit, the water level was approximately 179.8 meters above sea level, but in the following autumn it rose again to roughly 181 meters. Thus, the water level at the end of 2001 was again approaching the maximum level recorded, and it was decided to proceed with the removal of the painting. The necessary equipment and chemicals were purchased and shipped to Egypt.

Practicalities of Working at Qasr Ibrim

In order to understand the planning and decision-making processes involved in removing and conserving the painting, it is important to understand the practicalities of working at a site like Qasr Ibrim. As part of the Egyptian Supreme Council for Antiquities' requirements for foreign archaeological expeditions, the application to work and papers detailing all expedition personnel have to be submitted at least three months beforehand. Because Qasr Ibrim is on the edge of a security zone, additional permissions must also be obtained from military authorities, and such requests are not always approved. In addition to these administrative considerations, obtaining the specialized materials and equipment necessary to carry out the project also has to be undertaken well in advance, and has, in our experience, taken far longer to complete than the paperwork. Since many of the materials needed are not available in Egypt, they have to be shipped. Extracting them from Customs on their arrival has proved challenging, time-consuming, and unpredictably costly. This is detrimental to the overall project budget, which, as for any major project, must be costed and accepted by the organization financing the expedition well before the work can take place.

In light of all these factors, it is clear that there can be no such thing as a spontaneous response to a crisis at the site, such as a sudden rise in the lake level. Administrative and financial considerations demand that plans be finalized months before the project is scheduled to start. Thus, due to the condition of the painting as seen in 2001, we applied to the Egyptian authorities to remove it in 2002. However, military

permission was not forthcoming for that year, and plans had to be abandoned. The relevant permissions were granted in 2003, shortly before the field expedition was scheduled to begin. Having held the team and last-minute supplies on standby for several months, we were able to undertake the project in February 2003.

The Cyclododecane Method of Removal

All methods of wall painting detachment involve the application of a facing, traditionally an adhesive and scrim applied to the paint surface, followed by a rigid support. At the end of the removal and rebacking process, a residue of the adhesive is left on the painted surface which can be potentially damaging.

The detachment of the Taharqo wall painting depended on the successful securing of the painting by its front surface, so that the section of wall behind it could be dismantled from the back, through to the plaster layers. A temporary backing would then be applied, in order to sandwich and protect the painting and the plaster on its journey back to the Nubian Museum in Aswan. As part of the following year's project it was planned to remove the temporary backing and secure the wall painting onto a permanent backing, which would allow the painting to be studied, stabilized, cleaned, and then displayed. Cyclododecane $C_{12}H_{24}$, an alicyclic hydrocarbon compound, was introduced as a solution in place of a traditional adhesive. After application, cyclododecane (CDD) sublimes at ambient temperatures, leaving no residue, so that the paint layer is consolidated and protected during the removal and rebacking processes. Having decided that a CDD-based technique offered the best chance of removing the painting in a single piece, Eric Miller, conservator, consulted Hans Hangleiter, who had developed this technique with Elisabeth and Erhard Jäers (Hangleiter 2000).

Using data collected at the site and results from field tests (it is illegal to remove samples from Egypt), scientific investigation at the British Museum estimated rates of CDD sublimation under the hot and windy conditions likely to be found on-site. Several significant findings were made: that the sublimation rate of the consolidant and coating applications would not be significant to the process, provided the programmed time frames were not exceeded; that a layer of polyurethane foam bonded to the CDD would not inhibit sublimation; and that the materials in the wall painting were unlikely to be affected by CDD (Hallett and Parker 2002).

As stated, the separation of the support frame from the face of the wall painting is achieved by the loss of the CDD through a (natural or accelerated) sublimation process. At room temperature CDD is a white crystalline solid, and it melts at 59–61°C. The main solvents for CDD are hydrocarbons. Thus, petroleum spirit with a specific boiling range of 100–120°C, was selected as appropriate for the work on the Taharqo wall painting.

The facing system comprised four stages: (1) a consolidant (CDD), (2) a separation layer (CDD), (3) a facing layer of polyurethane foam, and (4) a timber frame. For the first two functions the CDD was mixed with petroleum spirit at different ratios. For the consolidant function, hardening needed to be delayed until the mixture had been applied and penetrated the plaster. This was achieved by mixing equal quantities of CDD and petroleum spirit (w/w) and heating them to 80°C.

To form the separation layer, the CDD needed to harden rapidly on the surface to produce a glassy film. A "melt" coat composed of CDD and petroleum spirit at a ratio of 9:1 (w/w) was selected as most appropriate. It was necessary to allow time for the petroleum spirit to evaporate after each stage. Tests found that twelve hours were required after the consolidation process, and six hours after the separation layer was applied.

The remainder of the process is described in the Expedition Diary, below.

Work Schedule

Because the site at Qasr Ibrim is so remote, it was necessary to produce a very detailed work schedule. Taking dimensions from a photograph of the wall painting when it was last fully uncovered and with the assistance of technical advice from Hans Hangleiter, Eric Miller produced a schedule that broke down the work into defined tasks. Drawings with measurements were added to help visualize each phase. This process was intended to reduce errors and omissions by forcing all decisions at the design stage. Standard risk assessments, health and safety concerns and regulations, and other standards required when working in the UK were all included in this process and adopted as the minimum standards throughout the project. The equipment and materials were then itemized and quantified by task. The resulting list was separated into items to be purchased in the UK and shipped out and those to be purchased in Cairo and Aswan.

Where possible, materials were prepared prior to shipping. For example, the blocks of CDD were pulverized and packed into airtight containers of appropriate size. Direct delivery of solvents to Aswan was arranged through a Cairo agent. The most time-consuming element of the Aswan shopping was purchasing and preparing the timber for the support frame. All the standard equipment for excavation and recording on the site was already on hand at the Egypt Exploration Society's facility in Aswan. Tents and catering arrangements were provided by Pan Arab Tours.

Expedition Diary

The description of the detachment process related below details the logistical and technical aspects of the project day by day. The aim of the rescue was to remove the wall painting from the original wall support, apply a temporary backing to sandwich the painting and underlying plaster, and transport it to the Nubian Museum in Aswan for further study, treatment, and display.

The expedition party comprised site director Dr. Pamela Rose, archaeobotanist Dr. Alan Clapham, conservators Eric Miller and David Singleton, two inspectors appointed by the Supreme Council of Antiquities, two laborers, and two Pan Arab personnel. Pamela Rose and Alan Clapham worked full time with the two conservators on the Taharqo project. The laborers were involved only in the clearance and excavation processes. All daylight hours were worked, with a break for lunch. Midday temperatures of 24°C in the shade and 34°C in direct sun were recorded.

Day 1

Our convoy of three vehicles made the four-hour journey down the west side of Lake Nasser, through the desert from Aswan to the Mubarak Pumping Station. There we were received by a team from Skanska Cementation International, who were working on the pumping station project. The Skanska team loaded us and our equipment onto their boat, the *Layla,* and ferried us to Qasr Ibrim—a 45-minute trip. We immediately established that the wall painting was still standing and set up our camp on an area of the site selected as best able to withstand such intrusion. This was the first and probably the only time that camping on the site will occur. The decision to do so was based on lack of available water transport and the comparatively short period of time we would be there. Disruption to and contamination of the site was minimized as much as possible.

Day 2

The immediate drying out of the wall painting was our priority, so no attention was paid to setting up a work station at this stage. The backfill of soil was cleared away with a *turiya* (a local tool similar to a mattock), shovels, trowels, and brushes. The remains of the stone apse were recorded and dismantled with great care, as many scorpions had made their homes in the soft soil and between the stones.

The lower portion of the wall painting was damp and stained brown from humic material in the mud. Despite the drop in the lake's level, the water percolation line on the painting was about 15 cm higher than it had been in 2000, when the painting had last been exposed. Boundary lines for the detachment were determined (governed by the size of the truck bed) and marked.[1] The overall dimensions of the section were 208 cm high by 272 cm wide.

Day 3

With the backfill removed, a combination of the breeze and the strong sun evaporated the moisture from the wall painting—a necessary step given that any water would prevent the CDD and petroleum spirit from penetrating into the plaster. Then, using a polyethylene sheet as an overlay, an accurate drawing of the painting was made to record its condition.

We set up a work area close to the temple (Fig. 3). A windbreak formed an enclosure in which the gas burners and scales were set up. It also served as a store for all the tools and chemicals. In this area, the CDD and petroleum spirit were weighed out and heated in a double boiler, ready for application. The flat area of the temple floor was used to store the timber and construct the frame. The generator was located nearby.

The first batch of CDD consolidant was weighed into the pan with an equal weight of PET and the mixture heated to 80°C. Application by brush was hampered by the outward lean of the wall: the solution, which we had hoped would flow over the surface and soak in, instead dripped to the floor or ran down the wall like hot wax down the side of a candle. As a result, much of the consolidant cooled before it could be absorbed sufficiently into the plaster. To overcome this, batches were sometimes reheated mid-application, and a towel was wrapped around the pan to slow the solution's cooling. We also erected a double windbreak, which produced still air at the painting surface for the remainder of the applications. Uniform consolidation was then achieved, with the surface of the wall painting appearing saturated, the colors enhanced, and no white or opaque layer on the surface.

The intention was to impregnate only the paint layers and the thin layers of mud plaster beneath. Two liters of the mix (320 g CDD and 320 g petroleum spirit) were allowed per square meter. In the event, a total of 14 L of consolidant were used (2.47 L per square meter).

Day 4

By the time we were ready to begin applying the melt coats, a full twelve hours had passed, ensuring that all the petroleum spirit had evaporated. The surface was hard and resonated when tapped with a knuckle. The windbreak was adjusted to allow for the change in wind strength that had occurred.

Two melt coats were applied in 2 L batches (Fig. 4). Gauze bandage was incorporated into the second coat, especially over voids and undercuts, to ensure that the polyurethane foam layer, when cast against it, would not interlock into any part of the painting or plaster layers.

The support frame was made 4 cm larger (in width and height) than the section being taken to accommodate the

FIGURE 3 The site of the Taharqo temple is located between the two windbreaks (February 2003). Note the vegetation encroaching where water covered the site in 1998. Courtesy of the Egypt Exploration Society.

FIGURE 4 The section of wall painting to be removed has been consolidated and received its first coat of cyclododecane (February 2003). Gauze bandage was incorporated into the second, facing layer of CDD to fill in or cover the missing areas. Courtesy of the Egypt Exploration Society.

mold that would enclose the polyurethane foam layers. It was constructed out of 10 × 5 cm timber (equivalent to a two-by-four). A simple rectangle, with two cross members and temporary diagonals at the corners, the frame's function was to support a mold or "shuttering" comprising a series of battens positioned a minimum of 3 cm from the painting surface (Fig. 5). The space between the CDD and the shuttering was filled with polyurethane foam, which bonded the two together. All faces of the frame were coated with parcel tape and a release agent to keep the foam from permanently bonding the frame to the battens, which would hamper its eventual removal.

The shuttering was made by alternating 3 cm wide timber battens with 10 cm wide polyurethane foam battens (cut from commercially available aluminum-foil-faced sheets). The flexibility of the foam battens allowed them to yield to the pressure exerted by the expanding polyurethane foam, should uneven foaming and polymerization occur. The pressure might otherwise have deformed the wall-painting surface. The timber battens were screwed to the frame and gripped the alternating foam battens. Finally, a 6 × 2 cm batten screwed to the bottom edge of the frame was intended to tuck beneath the section being removed and serve as part of the mold for the backing.

Day 5

The frame was held up to the wall and its edge traced to mark the section that would be removed. Then the plaster was cut down the side and across the bottom with a sharp knife, and the material beneath was cut away to allow the frame to be positioned and bottom batten inserted. The frame was braced against the ground with an A-frame at each end, and the whole structure was anchored with tent pegs pushed into the ground. The joint between the batten and the plaster was sealed with CDD and gauze bandage to create a leakproof floor for the mold. Gaps at the ends and across the top were filled with lengths of a soft, mattress-type foam, which were wrapped in plastic wrap and then gently inserted to conform to the varying widths. The first sets of timber and polyurethane foam battens were then secured to the frame with screws.

The next step was to measure out and mix the polyurethane foam. Polyurethane foam is formed by combining two components: part A, which contains polyetherols and a foaming agent, and part B, which contains di-isocyanate. When parts A and B are mixed together in equal quantities, the reaction causes the original volume to increase by approximately twenty times before the resulting material hardens. This foaming and curing process takes about 10 minutes, at

FIGURE 5 The rectangular timber frame in place, supported by an A-frame at each end (February 2003). The process of building up the shuttering and pouring in the polyurethane foam is two-thirds complete. Courtesy of the Egypt Exploration Society.

which point the foam can be immediately cast against. Half-liter plastic cups were used for mixing the PUF, and three of these were mixed and poured simultaneously.

In calculating the quantities of polyurethane foam required, we had assumed that the wall was flat. It was not. A significant dishing of the surface meant that, although the frame had the desired 3 cm gap along the top and bottom, a distance of 11 cm now existed at the center. Filling this depression pushed our contingency allowances on polyurethane foam to the limit and added weight. The total weight of polyurethane foam cast in the facing was 12 kg.

Day 6

Now that access was no longer required through the frame, two diagonal cross braces were added to the frame as well as two lengths of timber to act as feet. The feet protected the face of the shuttering from projecting objects when the frame was placed on uneven ground and allowed finger space when lifting and putting down the box.

Recording and dismantling the mud-brick structure directly behind the framed section of wall painting now commenced (Fig. 6). The bricks were laid in alternating layers of headers and stretchers, with layers of woven *halfa* grass "matting" between every four courses. The matting consisted of

FIGURE 6 Dr. Rose supervises the partial dismantling of the north wall, which supported the wall painting (February 2003). A corner of the support frame can be seen behind the wall. Note the thick mud-brick walls and multiple phases of building. Courtesy of the Egypt Exploration Society.

halfa grass culm bases that were connected by a single line of palm fiber string woven around them.

This matting may have been indirectly responsible for some of the damage to the wall painting, as it gave rats a route by which to penetrate the brick work. Rat runs within the wall account for both voids within the wall fabric and many small round holes on the painting surface. These holes, and larger ones which had occurred during a period of abandonment, were filled in in Meroitic times (ca. first to fourth century AD), when the temple was refurbished and brought back into use. The smaller holes were filled with mud plaster and the larger ones with lumps of stone, which were then plastered over.[2]

Once we had removed the mud bricks, which were easily separated from the coarse plaster, the plaster layers could then be examined from the back. All, where not burrowed through by rats, were in good condition and well bonded to one another; thus, the thick mud-and-straw layer could not be removed as we had planned. This additional 2–3 cm layer (over the approximately 5.5 square meters of the painting) added considerable unplanned-for weight.

Once the section of wall painting had been completely freed on all sides, the A-frames were unbolted, and the frame was lowered facedown (Fig. 7). An aluminum foil separation layer for the temporary backing was fitted against the mud plaster, and a mold (or casting wall) was built up around the edge of the frame. The temporary backing had been planned as a 6 cm layer of polyurethane foam, but because of the convex curve of the plaster, this backing had to be increased to 14 cm. This used up our full contingency of timber.

Day 7

Because the overall weight of the wall painting and frame was now nearing the carrying limit of the available manpower, it was moved to a site close to the *Layla*'s mooring site before the temporary backing was cast. Carrying the frame that distance (less than 150 meters) over rough terrain took nine of us 45 minutes.

Once in position and leveled, the mold was adjusted to the actual (nonrectangular) shape of the painting, and then sealed. To perform the casting, we used polyurethane foam in 1.5 L batches (Fig. 8). A polyethylene sheet separator and plywood lid were screwed into position as each batch of resin foamed and cured. The offcuts from the polyurethane foam battens were included in the void to ensure there was sufficient foam to complete the backing. On completion of

FIGURE 7 The frame and wall painting having been lowered facedown onto the ground (February 2003). Courtesy of the Egypt Exploration Society.

FIGURE 8 The frame and wall painting with its temporary backing, designed to sandwich the wall painting while in transit (February 2003). The timber mold constructed around the edges of the plaster can be seen. A foil barrier was created on the plaster, and several pours of polyurethane foam cast into the back. The plywood lid, which had been used to contain the foam during casting, was then screwed on to complete the packing process. Courtesy of the Egypt Exploration Society.

this phase, the polyethylene sheet and lid were again screwed down, to offer extra protection during transportation.

Day 8

The crated wall painting was lifted onboard the *Layla* together with all our equipment and rubbish,[3] and taken to the pumping station, where we met our ground transportation. By the end of the day we had the painting safely stored in the basement of the Nubian Museum in Aswan.

Future Work

Over the coming years, the temporary backing will be removed and the wall painting secured to a permanent backing. Once that is in place, a program for a detailed examination of the painting and its cleaning and treatment will be established. A suitable display environment will also be created for the wall painting at the Nubian Museum, which will make it accessible to local and international visitors and scholars.

Conclusion

The water level in Lake Nasser has not, up to now, risen to the same height it reached before 2000, although that threat can by no means be discounted. Although "rescue missions" like the one described in this paper are highly unusual in the present day, the uniqueness of the Taharqo wall painting and the

circumstances threatening it necessitated such measures. All interested parties gave their full support to the effort, and the result has been widely welcomed by those interested in Nubian and Egyptian studies. The painting's display in a museum setting will help to preserve it for the study and enrichment of visitors and scholars in the future.

Notes

1 The painted scheme appeared to continue behind the apse, albeit in a very fragmented and damaged state. Since its removal had not been provided for in our planning, we decided to leave as much support and protection as possible for this section. This would give us the option of investigating it (and possibly removing it) in the future.

2 Several finds were recovered during the removal of the original temple wall and from the areas repaired later. Those from the repair holes, presumably deliberately deposited therein, included two gold-and-glass beads, part of a mold for a *wadjet* eye amulet, several corroded iron and copper-alloy fragments, and part of an iron finger ring with a stone bezel on which was a Hellenistic bearded head in intaglio. From on top of the *halfa* matting layer in a section of the original brickwork came a fine, and apparently unused, reed pen.

3   Disposal of containers posed an additional problem. It was essential to ensure that they were neutral (nontoxic) or flattened before disposal, since useful-looking waste can easily find its way into domestic use.

References

Hallett, K., and J. Parker. 2002. Report no. 2002/1: Evaluation of the use of cyclododecane in the temporary conservation of a painted wall plaster from Qasr Ibrim, Egypt. Unpublished report. British Museum, Conservation Research Group.

Hangleiter, H. M. 2000. Temporary protection of sensitive surfaces: About the usage of volatile binding agents. Deutsche Restauratoren Vereinigung Conference, Berlin, November 2000.

Haywood, C. 2002. The Kushite town and cemetery at Kawa, the 2001–2002 season: Stabilisation and investigation of the wall paintings. *Sudan and Nubia Bulletin* 6:38–41.

Plumley, J. M. 1975. Qasr Ibrim, 1974. *Journal of Egyptian Archaeology* 61:5–27.

Plumley, J. M., and W. Y. Adams. 1974. Qasr Ibrim, 1972. *Journal of Egyptian Archaeology* 60:212–38.

Welsby, D. A. 2002. The Kushite town and cemetery at Kawa. *Sudan and Nubia Bulletin* 6:32–37.

Archaeological Site Conservation at Mesa Verde National Park

Part I   Surface Finish Preservation: A Summary of Current Work for the Archeological Site Conservation Program of Mesa Verde National Park

Rebecca J. Carr

The National Park Service Cultural Resource Management Guidelines define cultural resources as "finite" and "nonrenewable" resources. These resources are so important that "if they are degraded or lost, so is the park's reason for being" (NPS 1998: 1). The guidelines identify key components for cultural resource management, such as research, planning, and stewardship. Research is the basis for management decisions. Thus, inventories, condition assessment, materials identification, and detailed documentation provide the baseline data needed to make preservation, visitor-impact, and visitor-enjoyment decisions.

The term *surface finishes* is used to describe the applied earthen decoration observed on Ancestral Puebloan architecture within Mesa Verde National Park. This includes all pictographs; plastered, painted, or whitewashed walls; and any other architectural surface that has been embellished with applied color. These surface finishes provide an interpretive link that joins the past to the present. Iconography and painted decoration are interpretive tools that represent intellectual thought processes. Just as we embellish the walls of our architecture by painting and plastering them, Ancestral Puebloans painted their architecture hundreds of years ago.

Many of the Ancestral Puebloan surface finish embellishments are symbolic and culturally significant. They are a manifestation of cultural perceptions and iconographic symbolism. As such, surface finishes are an important tool for interpreting the heritage of Mesa Verde National Park to the public. This paper illustrates many of the research methods used to identify the management and preservation needs of this resource.

The research approach adopted by Mesa Verde National Park is based on a hierarchical model that uses physical evidence retained in the features, associations, methods, and sequences of architectural construction (Nordby 2001; Nordby et al. 2002). This hierarchical model is implemented by the Archeological Site Conservation Program (ASCP) to compile information relating to the preservation and interpretation of architectural resources within Mesa Verde National Park. Archaeologists, masons, architects, and architectural conservators work under the umbrella of ASCP to coordinate the documentation, research, and treatment needed to preserve and interpret this resource. The surface finish module within ASCP has two guiding principles: (1) to contribute to the preservation of this cultural resource, and (2) to contribute to the understanding of Ancestral Puebloan architecture. For this purpose, the surface finishes module is an essential part of the larger ASCP program.

The current documentation, analysis, and preservation methods employed by the program are the synthesis of over 20 years of work on this subject. The park contains more than 600 alcove sites, most of which have some level of documentation. The level of previous surface finish documentation varies greatly from site to site. For example, Cliff Palace and Spruce Tree House have detailed site maps and annotated digital profiles that record the deteriorating conditions that affect surface finish preservation. In other cases, site documentation is limited to a plan map, field notes, and/or photographs.

Since 2000, the surface finish preservation module within ASCP has concentrated its efforts on the preservation of the well-known and highly visited sites. This work includes documentation, assessment, and some treatments at Cliff Palace, Spruce Tree House, Balcony House, Long House, and Step House. Work has also been conducted at sites that have exceptional surface finishes, such as Nordenskiold Ruin 12, Square Tower House, and Painted Kiva House. Surface finish documentation, analysis, and treatment have also been conducted using the ASCP method at sites in Utah, New Mexico, and Arizona.

Our approach at each of these sites has centered on the preservation of original construction materials within their architectural context. Therefore, architectural surface finishes at Mesa Verde do not have the benefit of strictly controlled environmental conditions like those used to preserve artifacts in museums. Although a few kiva murals have been physically removed from a site to be conserved and curated in a museum setting, most of the surface finishes in Mesa Verde National Park are maintained within the archaeological site where they were originally constructed. Maintaining these finishes within their architectural context exposes them to fluctuating environmental conditions. Since the roofs and walls of many structures have fallen, the outdoor environment is now imposed upon fragile interior finishes (Fig. 1). Yet the cultural value of these sites to Native Americans, and even to tourists, prohibits the relocation of painted finishes.

Preserving original surface finishes in situ helps to retain their historic integrity and ensures their future research potential. Environmental exposure makes materials compatibility and cyclic maintenance an essential consideration when recommending conservation treatments. Field and laboratory research form the basis for maintenance and monitoring schedules, which ensure the preservation of surface finishes at Mesa Verde National Park. Computer-aided compilation and quantification of this data provides site managers with a useful tool for making site-management decisions. Surface finishes are the most fragile component of this architectural resource; they are most susceptible to fluctuations in environment and to visitor impacts. Deterioration conditions that affect the entire site are first evidenced in the plasters. The cause of such effects may be tracked and mitigated before their detrimental effects are seen elsewhere.

FIGURE 1 The advanced deterioration of a kiva pilaster in Kodak House is attributed to its exposure to an outside environment. The surface finishes on this interior architectural feature were exposed to weathering after the roof of this kiva collapsed. Courtesy of ASCP Digital Archives, Mesa Verde National Park. Photo: Laurel Casjens.

Work during the last several years has provided the park with a solid foundation for quantifying damage through the use of surface finish assessments. The high level of detail that we use to document surface finish deterioration helps architectural conservators identify damage and quantify its rate of change. In most cases, monitoring on a five- or ten-year schedule is sufficient to identify the preservation needs of this resource.

Of the 600 alcove sites within Mesa Verde National Park, eighty-four have extant surface finishes (Silver 1985: 12–28). From 1998 to 2001, Mesa Verde National Park received over one million dollars from the Save America's Treasures Program. This money helped to fund surface finish documentation at Cliff Palace and to conduct a condition survey of backcountry resources. While the existence of surface finishes was not specifically recorded during the condition survey, that survey identified many sites containing surface finishes that are still in need of detailed documentation and conservation treatments.

To date, the surface finishes for only twenty-one sites within Mesa Verde National Park have been documented, and the level of this documentation varies from site to site. Only eight sites have been documented in accordance with the current ASCP standards. One goal of this program is to compile data from earlier surveys into the current ASCP database. Digital comparisons of archival information to modern field data are of great value to the study of surface finish preservation at Mesa Verde National Park and elsewhere. Previous surveys formed their own methodology but often used similar terminology. Thus, the data from prior surveys may be incorporated into the current Microsoft Access database. Compilation of this data will aid park staff in mapping factors that influence the rate of surface finish deterioration. Compilation of surface finish survey data will also establish color, symbolic, and schematic consistencies among recently surveyed sites, enhancing our understanding of the architectural and cultural context for Ancestral Puebloan surface finishes. This will provide a broader picture of the park's surface finish resources.

This paper will elaborate upon the research approach currently employed by the surface finish preservation module within ASCP. The application of surface finish conservation treatments is one step in a larger plan to preserve the integrity, cultural significance, and research value of this irreplaceable resource. The treatment process begins with thorough documentation, assessment of condition, selection of compatible treatment methods, and selection of appropriate treatment materials. Site surveys and materials research are the basis of modern conservation treatment recommendations. These recommendations are implemented in the field, their results are monitored, and follow-up treatments are made as necessary. For the sake of brevity, this paper will omit technical evaluations of conservation treatment materials and construction methods. Instead, case studies will be provided to illustrate recent research applications for the ASCP approach.

The Process: Summary of ASCP Hierarchy of Site Management Actions (Version 2004)

ASCP Level 3 Inventory

The goal of conducting a limited investigation such as an ASCP level 3 survey is to identify new sites and determine the level of data collection needed to make responsible management decisions. Data collected at this level concentrates on sitewide applications. This level of inventory identifies the location of extant surface finishes within each site and provides a brief description of their general condition. The level 3 surface finish inventory form was designed as a quick method for archaeology crews working in the backcountry to identify whether surface finishes are deteriorated and to list where they are located within the site. This form allows multiple crews of archaeologists with varying levels of conservation experience to obtain preliminary surface finish data. It was developed as a means to standardize and correlate the minimum level of surface finish survey data.

ASCP Level 2 Assessment

The goal of an ASCP level 2 assessment is to evaluate architectural conditions and recommend preservation actions. Recommendations are made for monitoring and treatment of each wall within the site. This assessment includes structural investigation, site mapping, numbering walls and features, surveying wall condition, and surveying the surface finishes. Surface finish condition assessment at this level is qualitative, based on visual estimates of surface area affected by each threat and each condition. Archival reports that were identified during the level 1 inventory are compared to level 2 survey data. This establishes a relative rate of deterioration for surface finishes. All of this information is entered into the ASCP database for comparison with other architectural research (Fig. 2).

During the development of this process, previous materials research, accelerated weathering experiments, archaeological reports, and conservation surveys were reviewed to identify the more common indicators of deterioration, architectural

FIGURE 2 The introductory data entry screen for the ASCP database. A link to the surface finish preservation module is highlighted. Courtesy of ASCP Digital Archives, Mesa Verde National Park. Database designed by Cynthia Williams and Rebecca Carr. Graphics by Rebecca Carr.

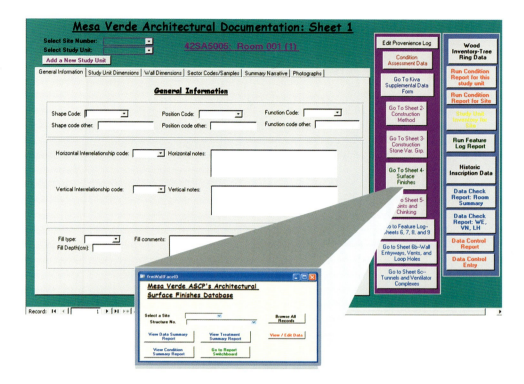

integrity, and cultural significance. Each of these park-specific indicators is assessed in the field and rated according to the amount of surface area affected. Any additional indicators of architectural integrity, cultural significance, research value, or rate of surface finish deterioration are described in the comments section of the level 2 forms.

Once the assessment is complete, level 2 survey data is compiled into the ASCP database. The database assigns a numeric score to each wall based upon the condition, public access, indicators of cultural significance, and architectural integrity. Architectural conservators use this score to prioritize surface finish conservation treatments within Mesa Verde National Park. Only high-priority elevations are given further consideration at the level 1 documentation, analysis, and maintenance stages.

ASCP Level 1 Documentation

The goal of level 1 documentation is to document architectural resources for the dual purposes of cultural interpretation and future research. This level of documentation includes detailed data collection regarding the size, shape, and configuration of architectural elements. This information is entered into a customized database format, which enables researchers to compile and compare various forms of architectural data.

Standard report formats within the ASCP database include prioritization of architectural spaces for treatment. Other report formats list the graffiti, schematic interpretations, color combinations, iconographic images, number of finish layers, and specific surface finish application types according to location within a site and subsequently within all surveyed sites in the park. Each layer of surface finish is assigned a number according to its position in the architectural construction sequence, beginning with the most recent application of surface finish and extending inward until the wall substrate has been reached (Fig. 3). This level of documentation aids archaeologists in forming conclusions regarding the cultural implications of color, design, and iconography and their architectural associations.

Scaled drawings are produced for each priority wall within the site. Scaled photomontages are produced as a complement to the hand-drawn elevations. Each photographic montage is used as a template to record architectural deterioration in the field (Fig. 4). This type of documentation can be conducted using printed media or by entering the condition data directly onto a tablet PC laptop computer. Use of a tablet PC enables architectural conservators to digitize surface finish conditions while observing them on-site. It also provides the conservator with unlimited opportunities to magnify the photographic montage

FIGURE 3 (a) Numbering sequence for the stratigraphy of surface finishes. Each layer of surface finish is numbered and recorded according to its placement on the wall. (b) Data relating to the application method, color, and schematic design are recorded in the field and entered into the surface finish preservation module of the ASCP database. Courtesy of ASCP Digital Archives, Mesa Verde National Park. Database designed by Cynthia Williams and Rebecca Carr. Graphics by Rebecca Carr.

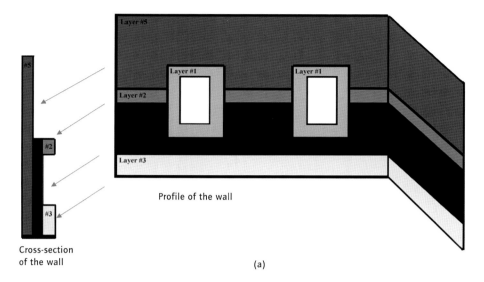

while collecting this data. This increases the accuracy and efficiency of the condition mapping.

Once digitized, these scaled drawings and photographic montages are used to quantify the amount of surface area affected by specific conditions. Each polygon of their surface area provides a quantifiable means for monitoring and assessing the deterioration of extant surface finishes. In this manner, field data may be collected and queried digitally so that changes in the data can be quantified over time. This system has been implemented at Cliff Palace, Moon House, and Spruce Tree House.

Data collection at this level is compiled in the ASCP database and is quantified graphically in AutoCAD and a geographic information system (GIS) program. This enables researchers and conservators to assess the spatial relationships between specific conditions, threats, features, and construction episodes. Graphic documentation establishes a timeline for the construction, habitation, and maintenance of this

FIGURE 4 Documentation for a stabilization treatment conducted at Spruce Tree House in 2002. Before treatments are administered, architectural conservators conduct a graphic assessment of architectural condition. This example of a photographic montage is overlaid with condition and conservation treatment documentation. Courtesy of ASCP Digital Archives, Mesa Verde National Park. Documentation and graphics by Rebecca Carr.

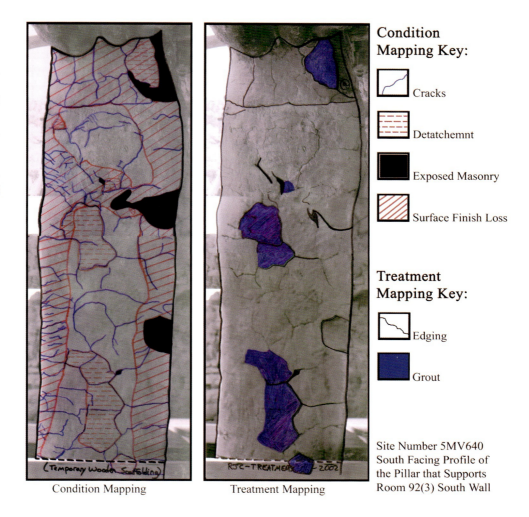

Condition Mapping   Treatment Mapping

Condition Mapping Key:

Cracks

Detatchemnt

Exposed Masonry

Surface Finish Loss

Treatment Mapping Key:

Edging

Grout

Site Number 5MV640
South Facing Profile of
the Pillar that Supports
Room 92(3) South Wall

architecture. It also becomes a monitoring tool to quantify the factors that lead to surface finish deterioration. As a graphic supplement to the more traditional forms of photographic documentation, this method also enables researchers to document painted iconography at a higher level of detail (Fig. 5).

ASCP Analysis Level

NPS-28 states that "the primary purpose of physical documentation and material analysis is to confirm and enlarge upon earlier findings regarding the integrity and historical associations of structures, landscapes, sites, and museum objects. This type of research also improves understanding of conditions aiding the development of treatment recommendations. It is also used to record the significant attributes of a cultural resource before its modification or demolition" (NPS 1998). The University of Pennsylvania Architectural Conservation Laboratory brought many techniques for microscopic, gravimetric, and chemical analyses to Mesa Verde National Park. The goal of this analysis

within the ASCP surface finishes module is to compile data collected through prior surveys and to supplement this data with materials testing. Analysis of original building materials contributes to the assessment, documentation, and treatment recommendations for this resource. Examples of materials analysis include scanning electron microscopy (SEM), petrographic analysis, X-ray diffraction (XRD), X-ray fluorescence (XRF), particle size distribution, pH, soluble salt content, electrical conductivity, water vapor transmission rate, porosity, permeability, and accelerated weathering of facsimile surface finishes (Fig. 6; Carr 2002).

Condition mapping of key architectural spaces at Cliff Palace, Mug House, Long House, and Spruce Tree House has established the detailed baseline data needed to quantify changes in condition over time. When combined with knowledge of the mechanisms that typically induce this damage, mathematical and graphic models are being developed to answer modern research questions. Among these issues are:

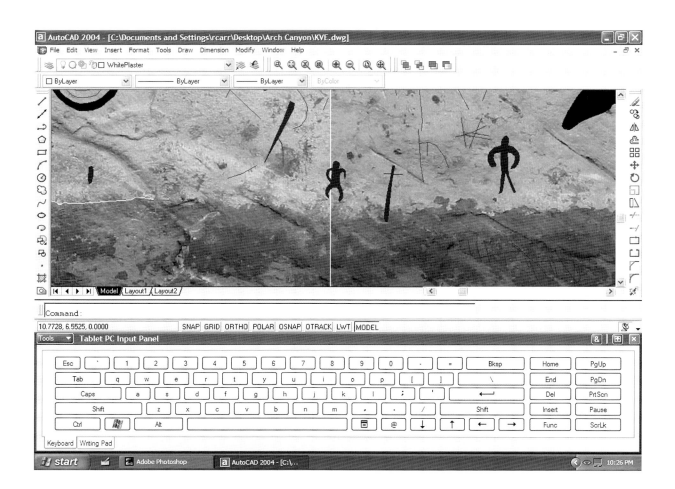

FIGURE 5 Graphics tablet PC screen from the laptop computer used to digitize documentation of surface finishes while working in the field. Graffiti and historic iconography are outlined using AutoCAD 2004. Courtesy of ASCP Digital Archives, Mesa Verde National Park. Documentation and graphics by Rebecca Carr.

FIGURE 6 Materials testing such as this accelerated weathering experiment can aid architectural conservators in their understanding of surface-finish-deterioration phenomena and potential treatment methods. Courtesy of University of Pennsylvania Department of Historic Preservation. Documentation from the master's thesis of Rebecca Carr.

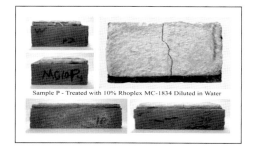

(1) the impacts of natural disasters such as wildland fires and water drainage on the rate of surface finish deterioration, (2) the long-term effectiveness of different conservation treatment materials within different environmental conditions, (3) the carrying capacity for public visitation at specific archaeological sites, (4) the distribution of sites with specific characteristics such as color use, iconography, schematic design, common material sources, etc., and (5) quantified monitoring of changes in surface finishes that are in a state of deterioration.

The ASCP database was designed to enable conservation professionals to track treatments and subsequent actions. Survey information is sorted into the following categories for ease of use: Layer Data, Iconographic Embellishments, Scheme Interpretations, Condition Data, Treatment Data/Recommendations, Monitoring Data, Analysis Results, and Previous Documentation. The percentage of surface area that is evidenced by each surface finish condition is digitally calculated and then tracked within the database. GIS is being explored as a graphic interface between the mathematical models used to quantify and prioritize treatment needs in the ASCP database. GIS spatially overlays environmental data, visitor traffic routes, and the physical properties of earthen construction materials. Digital analysis conducted with AutoCAD and GIS computer programs enable architectural conservators to evaluate the relationship of one condition to another. Digitized survey data is also used to calculate changes in the rate of surface finish deterioration over time. Additional analyses can be conducted with three-dimensional modeling and laser scanning of original surface finishes.

ASCP Treatment and Maintenance Level

Thorough assessment, documentation, and analysis are the basis for making conservation treatment decisions. Once the baseline data is collected and analysis has been completed, cultural resource managers have a realistic data set upon which to base subsequent management decisions.

Conservation treatments are a necessary and immediate means for arresting the rate of surface finish deterioration. Yet, barring removal and relocation of extant surface finishes, this cultural resource remains exposed to destructive environmental elements. Since removal would reduce the cultural value and architectural integrity of this resource, conservation treatments are only one step in a larger preservation process. Examples of surface finish preservation treatments include the redirection of water drainage patterns, injection grouting, edging, masonry stabilization, and maintenance of treated areas. Maintenance, conservation treatment, and monitoring schedules are based on the research conducted in accordance with ASCP standards and guidelines.

Case Study 1: Five Sites Condition Assessment Survey

Mesa Verde National Park's current method of data collection was used to survey five sites during the 2003 and 2004 field seasons[1] (Fig. 7). The sites within this survey were Balcony House, Square Tower House, Long House, Step House, and Nordenskiold Ruin 12. The level of previous site documentation varied from as little as a sketched map and verbal description to detailed archaeological documentation. It had been at least five years since any information relating to surface finish condition

FIGURE 7 Crew members of the Five Sites Condition Assessment Survey study wall surfaces in Nordenskiold Ruin 12 in 2003. Present (from left to right) are David Bleckley, Peggy Alison, Rebecca Carr, Zonna Barnes, and Elizabeth DeGaetanno. Courtesy of ASCP Digital Archives, Mesa Verde National Park. Photo: Rebecca Carr and Elizabeth DeGaetanno.

had been recorded for any of these sites. None of these sites had been brought into the ASCP standardized format.

This survey was organized as an ASCP level 2 condition assessment. The first step in this process was to identify any previous survey reports, excavation records, historical photographs, stabilization records, and site maps. The best map was selected and scanned into AutoCAD. All walls and space designations were updated into the current provenance system, labeled on this map, and entered into the ASCP database. When needed, new architectural spaces identified through this survey were designated on the digital map. All archival records were reviewed, and references to surface finishes, petroglyphs, or pictographs within the archival data were indexed according to the ASCP standardized site provenance system and entered into the database.

Once a map was produced for each site, a condition assessment survey and limited documentation was conducted to identify the preservation needs for this resource. In order to collect this information in a standardized format, the surface finishes form package and associated interrelational ASCP database were used.

The condition of every wall surface within each site was assessed according to the amount of surface area affected by a standardized set of surface finish conditions, as well as a set of structural, environmental, and visitor-related threats to the preservation of those finishes. An assessment of cultural significance, integrity, and visitor access was also determined while on-site. Recommendations for preserving this resource were made and entered into the database. Both documentation and conservation treatments were identified as specific preservation recommendations. Once the relative percentages of affected surface area for each condition were collected, this information and all of its associated point values were tabulated into a series of database reports. A standard set of reports was generated by this database to track elements of both conservation and archaeological interest.

Since this survey was primarily conducted to assess the condition of surface finishes, neither scaled elevations nor photographic montages were created. However, assistance from US/ICOMOS and Fort Lewis College interns enabled park staff to complete additional work, beyond the scope of a level 2 survey. Preliminary level 1 documentation was also conducted in the form of layer, iconographic, and schematic documentation.

Samples were obtained from the most significant finishes and, at the time of this writing, were being analyzed at the University of Nevada Department of Geoscience. This study seeks to use XRD analysis in conjunction with cross-sectional optical microscopy to determine the color and formulation of surface finish layers (Drohan 2004)[2]. Layer and scheme observations from this survey have already been entered into the ASCP database and made available to researchers.

An experimental application of GIS programming was conducted in conjunction with the Five Sites Condition Assessment Survey. The location, type, and extent of conditions known to affect the preservation of surface finishes were plotted on a plan map of Nordenskiold Ruin 12. This process aided park staff in visualizing how deteriorating surface finish conditions overlap and influence each other. The location of extant surface finishes was plotted within the context of previously mapped water drainages, wildland fires, and soil deposits. The absence of surface finishes at the east end of this site was found to coincide with water drainage patterns; the most common water-related condition at the west end of this site was surface finish delamination. This exercise generated some theories regarding the role of water drainage patterns and their relationship to surface finish detachment versus surface finish delamination. Architectural conservators will need to apply this method of graphic representation to additional sites in order to augment our understanding of these relationships.

The Five Sites Condition Assessment Survey brought these sites up to and exceeded the ASCP level 2 standard for archaeological site management. Each wall surface was assessed to determine the extent, condition, significance, integrity, visitor impacts, treatment needs, and time frame for implementing those treatments. The level 3 inventory and a level 2 assessment were completed, priority architectural spaces were identified, level 1 surface finish documentation was initiated, and digital analysis was conducted. Recommendations for conservation treatments have now been made. The data generated by this study will be used to direct the further monitoring, documentation, treatment, and visitor appreciation of this cultural resource.

Case Study 2: Spruce Tree House Documentation, Assessment, and Treatment

Spruce Tree House is one of the most heavily visited cliff dwellings in the Southwest. As the third-largest cliff dwelling in Mesa Verde National Park, Spruce Tree House is actively interpreted and visited by more than 400,000 individuals annually. This constitutes at least 75 percent of the park's total visitation. Early excavation and stabilization records for this site include contributions from Gustav Nordenskiold in 1893,

Jesse Walter Fewkes in 1909, and Stanley Morse, while working for the Public Works Administration in 1936. Constance Silver conducted a survey of Spruce Tree House surface finishes (1985), and a condition assessment was conducted in 1999 (Bass 1999), using a form package that predated ASCP procedures. This survey identified walls and architectural surface finishes that were in need of conservation treatments. Detailed architectural documentation of Spruce Tree House began in 2000 with funding from Save America's Treasures (Brisbin 2003).

In 2002, a grant from the Colorado Historical Society/ State Historical Fund supplemented federal funding to document eighteen rooms and one kiva. The purpose of this study was to document the structure and to enhance our understanding of the population dynamics at Spruce Tree House (Brisbin 2003). Stabilization reports and historic photographs were used to support field observations in an effort to identify the construction sequence at this site. The same year, documentation of surface finish application, iconography, and schematic interpretations were conducted in each of the priority spaces identified in the 1999 survey. Since 2000, isolated emergency treatments have been conducted on an annual basis.[3] To date, approximately half of this site has been recorded using the ASCP level 1 documentation system.

In 2003, sufficient funding was provided by a Vanishing Treasures grant to conduct conservation treatments. Two of the larger wall surfaces identified as a high priority in the 1999

condition assessment survey (Bass 1999) were selected. Architectural conservators from the University of Pennsylvania conducted condition mapping and conservation treatments. Conservation treatments included infilling of subsurface voids, edging with earthen materials, and isolated injection treatments. These treatments were intended to slow the rate of surface finish deterioration. An effort was made to bring blistered and displaced fragments of finish back in line with the plane of original wall surfaces. These treatments provided additional support to delaminated and detached surface finishes. The University of Pennsylvania Architectural Conservation Laboratory digitized all conditions and treatments for this project.

To monitor the impacts of site visitation and assess the general condition of this site, student interns produced scaled photographic images and documented this resource in its current condition. Room 116 was selected as a priority space for documentation and treatment due to the iconography displayed on its plastered surfaces. Close examination of the interior walls and archival descriptions of Room 116 reveals a complex design consisting of a tan floor band and red dado, both embellished with sets of triangles and dots. A red geometric design adorns the east-facing wall, and archival descriptions reveal the locations where bighorn sheep and other animals once decorated the north wall (Fig. 8). Conservation treatments have been recommended to preserve the paintings in this culturally significant room. The documentation

FIGURE 8 This iconographic design adorns the north wall of Room 116 of Spruce Tree House. Courtesy of ASCP Digital Archives, Mesa Verde National Park. Photo: Valerie Gomez and Kristin Kent.

conducted in 2004 will also provide a template for recording the location of future conservation treatments. By digitizing this data, site managers and future researchers can obtain a means to identify materials that might be lost, to monitor the impacts of visitation, to monitor other environmental factors that cause site deterioration, and to quantify changes over time.

Analysis of the building materials used to construct Spruce Tree House has been an interdisciplinary effort. Mesa Verde National Park has enlisted the aid of geologists, soil scientists, and architectural conservators to better understand this earthen architecture. The combined goals for this research were to (1) identify the mineralogy and particle size distribution of construction materials, (2) identify trace elements that may help us to locate sources for original materials, (3) assist in the formulation of compatible treatment materials, (4) support or dispel theories of construction sequence and occupational maintenance, (5) reveal the color and formulation of underlying surface finish layers and schemes, and (6) identify the presence of specific paint binders.

ASCP is interested in documenting and understanding how these dwellings reflect the communities that inhabited them. Archaeologists are often able to deduce the construction and remodeling sequence for Ancestral Puebloan sites using a combination of methods. Dendrochronology, wall abutment patterns, and infilled doorways each indicate a time frame for architectural modification. Geologist Mary Griffitts completed a study of Ancestral Puebloan mortar formulations in Mesa Verde National Park. The purpose of her study was to document differences in petrography and color between mortar samples from different construction episodes and different sites. One result of this study was a key to the mineral composition of the most prominent mortar types within Spruce Tree House. This data will aid archaeologists in determining which architectural modifications were constructed from the same source material.

The University of Nevada Department of Geoscience has also undertaken mortar analysis at Spruce Tree House, but has taken a different approach to the question of materials sourcing and interpretation of construction sequence. Building upon the work of Mary Griffitts, soil scientist Patrick Drohan is using X-ray diffraction/X-ray fluorescence (XRD/XRF), scanning electron microscopy/electron dispersion spectrometry (SEM/EDS), chemical spot testing, total elemental composition, and point counting to compare the source signatures of Ancestral Puebloan building materials to those found in the natural environment (Drohan 2004). Results of this analysis will be compared to Soil Survey Geographic (SSURGO) data

from previous soil surveys. This method may identify whether specific sources of construction materials are related to specific social groups.

Architectural conservators from the University of Pennsylvania Department of Historic Preservation have conducted extensive analysis on the mortar and plaster samples from Cliff Palace, and similar analysis is underway with samples from Spruce Tree House (Matero, Cancino, and Fourie 2002). Innovative analysis conducted by the University of Pennsylvania has already provided Mesa Verde National Park with a better understanding of the materials used to construct Ancestral Puebloan architecture and compatible materials for surface finish conservation treatments. Graduates from this program are conducting microscopic analysis of surface finish formulations and stratigraphy. This analysis will enhance our knowledge of the decay mechanisms that affect surface finish preservation. It will also provide insight into the Ancestral Puebloan cultural use of color and layering sequence for surface finish application.

The ASCP level 1 architectural documentation of Spruce Tree House is still ongoing. This project is a good example of the documentation, analysis, and treatment conducted at Mesa Verde National Park to ensure the preservation and cultural value of Ancestral Puebloan architecture. Funding has been secured to continue the documentation of Spruce Tree House in 2005 and 2006. This high level of architectural documentation provides a means for monitoring the effectiveness of conservation treatments and for tracking future changes in site condition.

Conclusion

A major strength of this program is that it incorporates the concepts and data collected from more than twenty years of survey work. The ASCP model standardizes a method for using this data as a management and research tool. Consistent data-collection techniques enable the park to build upon the previous research conducted through this program.

The following goals have been identified for the continuation of this program:

1   Incorporate all previous survey data into the current documentation system.
2   Identify which sites contain surface finishes and map them geographically within the park boundaries.

3   Survey the condition and research value of extant surface finishes that have not already been documented.

4   Bring the surface finish emergency treatment schedule up to date and eliminate the treatment backlog.

5   Bring the previous survey records, for all public sites, up to the current ASCP documentation standard.

6   Once all sites have been identified and entered into the ASCP database, use this information as the baseline data for a parkwide maintenance plan. This plan will structure the mapping, monitoring, and treatment of surface finishes with a special emphasis on the mitigation of visitor impacts.

7   Implement the maintenance plan.

This plan sets forth a method for establishing cyclic maintenance schedules for all sites where surface finishes have been identified. The approach that has been outlined in this paper consists of principles set forth by the Archeological Site Conservation Program of Mesa Verde National Park to inventory, assess, document, analyze, and maintain the value of this resource. Only through the continuation of this program—and an understanding of the contribution that surface finish preservation has made to this program—will preservation and interpretation of the park's cultural resources be furthered.

Notes

1   Funding for this survey was provided by the Colorado Historical Society/State Historical Fund and the National Park Service.

2   This research was begun by Rebecca Carr and Patrick Drohan. No formal report was published.

3   Emergency treatments were conducted in 2000 by Rynta Fourie, in 2001 by Rebecca Carr and Angelyn Bass Rivera, in 2002 by Rebecca Carr, and in 2003 by Rynta Fourie, Pietro Mangarella, and Kecia Fong.

Acknowledgments

Thank you to Larry Nordby, my supervisor at Mesa Verde National Park, and Frank Matero, my thesis advisor at the University of Pennsylvania. I also want to thank everyone who participated in these projects.

References

Bass, Angelyn. 1999. Architectural surface finishes treatment priority assessment, Mesa Verde National Park 1998–1999. Interim report, Division of Research and Resource Management, Mesa Verde National Park.

Brisbin, Joel. 2003. Personal communication.

Carr, Rebecca J. 2002. Evaluation of adhesive binders for the preservation of in-situ aboriginal surface finishes at Mesa Verde National Park. Master's thesis, University of Pennsylvania.

Dix, Linnaea A. 1996. Characterization and analysis of prehistoric earthen plasters, mortars, and paints from Mug House, Mesa Verde National Park, Colorado. Master's thesis, University of Pennsylvania.

Drohan, Patrick. 2004. Personal communications with author and research proposal, Mesa Verde National Park.

Griffitts, Mary. 2002–3. Personal communication.

Manning, Robert, William Valliere, and James Bacon. 2002. Research to support application of carrying capacity to Mesa Verde National Park. Internal report for Mesa Verde National Park, Park Studies Laboratory, School of Natural Resources, University of Vermont, Burlington.

Matero, Frank, Claudia Cancino, and Rynta Fourie. 2002. Conservation of architectural surfaces program for archeological resources: Cliff Palace, Mesa Verde National Park. Internal report for Mesa Verde National Park, Architectural Conservation Laboratory and Research Center, Graduate Program in Historic Preservation, University of Pennsylvania.

National Park Service (NPS). 1998. *NPS-28: Cultural Resource Management Guidelines.* Washington, DC: National Park Service, Department of the Interior.

Nordby, Larry V. 2001. *Prelude to Tapestries in Stone: Understanding Cliff Palace Architecture.* Archeological Research Series: Architectural Studies No. 4. Mesa Verde, CO: Division of Research and Resource Management, Mesa Verde National Park.

Nordby, Larry V., Todd Metzger, Cynthia L. Williams, and James D. Mayberry. 2002. *Mesa Verde National Park Archeological Site Conservation Program Guidelines, Volume I: Standards for Field Data Collection and Documentation.* Mesa Verde National Park, Division of Research and Resource Management. Mesa Verde National Park, CO.

Silver, Constance S. 1985. Summary of the results of the 1985 project survey of prehistoric plaster and rock art at Mesa Verde National Park. Internal report, Mesa Verde National Park.

Archaeological Site Conservation at Mesa Verde National Park

Part II   **Surface Finishes, Decoration, and Social Organization at Cliff Palace, Mesa Verde National Park**

Larry V. Nordby

This paper is an initial exploration into the relationship between the architecture of prehistoric Puebloan buildings, their architectural finishes and decoration, and the social organization of the people who inhabited them. The information presented here specifically pertains to Cliff Palace, one of the largest and most architecturally complex alcove sites at Mesa Verde National Park. At some level, it also generally applies to other alcove sites at Mesa Verde. Approximately 600 cliff dwellings of Mesa Verde were built and occupied between AD 1200 and 1300. Estimates based on tree-ring dating data suggest that most of the alcove sites were used for only twenty to thirty years during that century. Descendents of the ancestral Puebloan people still live in the southwestern United States, and oral traditions establish a strong connection with Mesa Verde and its sites.

From a sociological viewpoint, a fundamental assumption of spatial studies concerning cliff dwellings (or alcove sites) is that in relatively low-density agrarian societies people who are related to one another are likely to live near one another. Furthermore, adjacent groups of residential spaces are more likely than not to reflect kinship ties. Although there are exceptions to this assumption, Cosmos Mindeleff provides a basis for this approach in his publication *Localization of Tusayan Clans* (1900), which has also been reinforced with over a century of ethnographic study. Most researchers believe that deviations from this pattern are largely a product of living in the modern age, in which employment away from the various pueblos or reservations has changed residential models. The following discussion assumes the validity of this theory as a pattern, while recognizing that human social behavior is highly adaptable, often deviating from pattern.

Many of the cliff dwellings at Mesa Verde are small, only one or two rooms built in alcoves or shallow caves. Cliff Palace (Fig. 1) is a village of about 150 rooms and twenty-one to twenty-three kivas (circular underground rooms). Kivas may have been used as living spaces, but also as important social gathering areas or ritual locations. Though the varied use of kivas is enjoying renewed debate among archaeologists, we do know that at some level or some time, kivas were probably used as more than a single nuclear-family residence.[1] In addition to the circular subterranean kivas there are many rectangular surface rooms in Cliff Palace, as well as in Spruce Tree House and other large cliff dwellings.

This ancient village and others are being studied by staff members from Mesa Verde National Park's Archeological Site Conservation Program (ASCP), who collect and organize information using a tabular database known as ArkDoc. A custom Microsoft Access application, this database is "modularized." The data is organized into groups of observations on either the physical remains of prehistoric buildings (such as roof construction, stone masonry, or plasters) or on special research topics and issues (such as rock art, historical inscriptions, or structural engineering). The collection of field data is standardized by detailed instruction manuals (Nordby et al. 2002). All of the modules serve either as stand-alone or articulated products (see R. Carr, this volume). This paper explores the relationship between the three modules focusing on architecture, surface finishes/plasters, and decoration or embellishments.

FIGURE 1 This overview photograph of Cliff Palace shows the village's architectural complexity. Circular structures below grade are kivas.

The Hierarchical Social Interaction Model: Architecture, Social Organizations, and Surface Finishes at Cliff Palace

The Hierarchical Social Interaction Model (HSIM) developed for Cliff Palace (Nordby 2001) organizes architectural information and provides a framework to evaluate the social organization of its past residents (Fig. 2). The model is currently being applied at Spruce Tree House (Brisbin 2003) and Spring House (Nordby 2002), as well as at smaller sites in the park. For the purposes of this paper, I will focus on the courtyard complex to facilitate the study of Cliff Palace's (1) architectural units and the social organization that used these various

FIGURE 2 The Hierarchical Social Interaction Model (HSIM) developed during the work at Cliff Palace is applied to explain architectural relationships at other sites at Mesa Verde National Park.

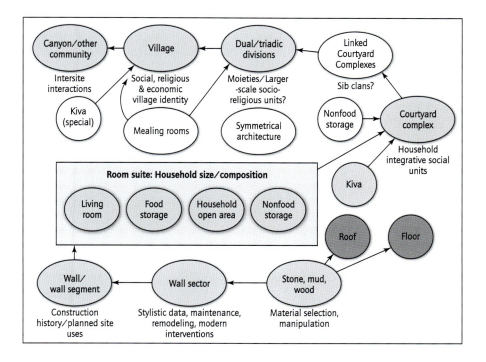

room/kiva groupings (recorded in the ArkDoc architectural module), (2) the extant surface finishes found on both the interior and exterior of the structures (recorded in the surface finishes module), and (3) the imagery associated with them (recorded as part of the rock art module). This approach reveals information about group or individual identity.

By using the architecture to infer social organization, we have estimated the numbers of nuclear and extended family households at Cliff Palace, as well as other complex social groupings. Through tree-ring dating it was possible, in some cases, to ascertain the arrival of a given household within a very precise period of time, and to track the building's development over the next decade or so (Nordby 2001: 102–5). The surface finishes and rock art modules are currently under analysis and will be integrated into the larger Cliff Palace data sets. The remainder of this paper describes the surface finishes and rock art found on different types of spaces in Cliff Palace and how surface finish and decorative signatures have proven useful in the analysis of social use and meaning in each category of space.

The Courtyard Complex

As suggested by the model, rooms are combined into suites where a single nuclear family probably lived. Some social unit more complex than the nuclear family, such as an extended family or clan, resided in the courtyard complex, an architectural unit shown in Figure 3. The role of the courtyard complex is shown graphically in Figure 4. The spaces that pertain to the courtyard complex are the kiva, the plaza or courtyard, nonfood storage rooms, and miscellaneous structures and/or retaining walls that delimit spaces. The units comprising the component room suites (living rooms, granaries, and household open areas) were used by component nuclear households lower on the model.

Architecture

Generally, the courtyard complex consists of room suites composed of a group of rooms clustered around a kiva's rooftop plaza. The exteriors of these room walls are often plastered and decorated with painted or incised designs. These decorated surfaces may have served to delineate group identity buildings for extended families or clans. Although the resident social unit for the courtyard complex is variable in size and composition, what is suggested here by the surface finishes and spatial configuration of a kiva with adjacent rooms is that it may have been used by a group larger than a nuclear family but no larger than a clan. Kivas lacking adjacent residential spaces probably are related to special-use buildings that reflect social organizations more complicated than the clan.

FIGURE 3 This photograph of Courtyard Complex M shows a kiva and its surrounding rooms. When Kiva M was roofed, the rooms would have opened onto a courtyard or plaza that was used as a gathering space for the clan. The walls of the courtyard would have been plastered white, and the exterior walls of Rooms 39 and 40 were then decorated with a panel of stamped handprints.

FIGURE 4 This model depicts a derivation of the HSIM showing the complexity of social structure and architectural units of each. The concept of borrowed buildings is shown by the arrows.

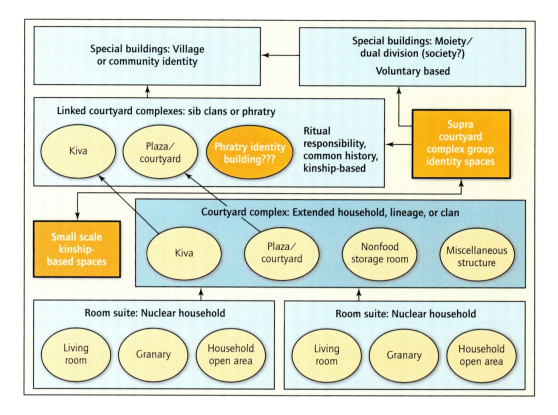

The Clan—The Fundamental Social Unit of Puebloan Society

Fred Eggan's (1950) work on social organization of Puebloan groups provides an excellent source of information on kinship and other social units.[2] In our research attempting to link social constructs with ancient architecture at Mesa Verde, we have centered our study on the Hopi. This approach does not disregard similar, albeit not identical, social structures for other modern-day Puebloan groups, but at this stage, this paper is but an initial foray into this type of social study, and other avenues of data will be explored as the work progresses. There is a large body of Hopi and other Puebloan ethnographic literature that undoubtedly applies and could be used to improve, what is of necessity here, a cursory summary.[3]

At the most fundamental level, clans are organized on matrilineal principles, and identified by a totemic name (Eggan 1950: 18). As Eggan notes, the following characteristics can serve as a point of departure for architectural studies (see also note 2):

- "The basic local organization is the extended family based on matrilocal residence, with a household of one or more rooms in common."

- Clans are grouped into exogamous phratries (a social group consisting of brother/sister or sibling clans that share a special relationship).
- Clans are the land-owning group.
- The clan is the basic ritual unit, insofar as the control of ceremonies and paraphernalia is in the keeping of certain clans.
- Each clan has a clan house, where the clan mother resides, caring for ritual objects that the clan needs to perform its duties for the welfare of the entire village.

Eggan notes that traditionally one may not marry within one's own household or clan, father's household, or phratry. Among modern Hopi, marrying within the father's clan and phratry is theoretically forbidden but tolerated.

Surface Finishes and Decorations

With these concepts in mind, we can turn to the courtyard complexes to examine what they might reveal about lineage or clan identity. Many of these courtyards have architectural surface finishes with contrasting color schemes.[4] Walls may have a cocoa brown or tan to beige base coat with a white to gray-colored wash covering part of it. These colors and schemes delineate dadoes, floor bands, fields, horizontal stripes, or auras around doorways or other openings. Some are decorated with painted geometric elements.

Unfortunately, many of the decorated surfaces are poorly preserved, and the schemes and embellishments or pictographs are difficult to identify. Fairly typical examples of embellishments are a panel of numerous stamped handprints above doorways and a series of zoomorphic (animal) figures painted onto plasters.

Handprint panels on banquettes or pilasters occur in some of these clan kivas (at least those with surrounding rooms) such as Kiva J at Cliff Palace. These are panels composed of several handprints, rather than only one or two. When the HSIM is applied, these handprint panels are consistent with expectations for clan kivas and courtyards. They are, in part, very personal, like signatures, and yet affirm the larger clan membership through inclusion within a group of similar units. Although there are exceptions, generally extended household/clan/lineage spaces may be identified by the presence of such panels.

Kivas also display embellishments. Kivas in alcove sites are usually plastered, often with many coats (possibly for refurbishment after extended use). Kiva K, built in 1271 (the same year as Kiva J) contains a unique type of embellishment, in both application method and subject matter. What have been identified as shields, shield figures, and perhaps masks are incised into the plaster.[5] Since clans generally have ritual responsibilities and social roles to perform, it is reasonable (but admittedly conjectural) to suggest that these images are relevant to those responsibilities, or to some event in the history of the clan. These images might relate to a warrior group or some kind of defense, even though there is little evidence of warfare at Mesa Verde.

Kiva N, again at Cliff Palace, shows a differing kind of decoration. The exposed surface plaster is incised with a band of small triangles, which overlays a scheme of painted anthropomorphic and zoomorphic figures. These images could represent the totemic nature of the clan or some event in the history of the clan, in contrast to ritual responsibilities. The point here is that clan membership and history are codified in the plasters and embellishments, especially for those kivas that have surrounding residential spaces.

To summarize these three examples at Cliff Palace, the courtyard complexes contain plaster schemes that may have contrasting colors and are sometimes decorated with imagery.

From the few poorly preserved examples, we see that the courtyards contain multiple small personal images such as handprint panels and geometric elements. Clan or extended-family kivas (with adjacent residential rooms) have similar handprint panels, but may also have images associated with clan social or ceremonial responsibilities, or perhaps totemic images.

Supracourtyard Complex Spaces

Taken together, the room suite and the courtyard complex are seen as small-scale kinship-based spaces, with kivas (enclosed) or courtyards (open spaces). Beyond these small-scale units are different kinds of group-identity spaces, collectively termed *supracourtyard complex spaces.* For the purposes of this initial exploration, these can be divided into two types:

(1) Linked courtyard complexes, perhaps representing "sib," or brother/sister, clans. This group represents association based on factors other than kinship, but reinforced by it. In Hopi society, this is a phratry.

(2) Dual divisions, representing voluntary societies. Membership in these organizations is often based on choice, rather than blood or marriage, and reinforced by kinship but not created by it.

In the larger picture, villages are created by these two groups, and communities are formed by more complex residential groupings that include people from other villages.

Phratries and Component Sib Clans

The phratry (Eggan 1950: 62) consists of linked or associated clans among the Hopi. Phratries are a unit formed by common experiences of the linked clans during migrations (as opposed to common ancestral totems that signify and supply names for the clans). It is the largest kinship unit and is exogamous. Its purpose is not explicitly ritual, economic, or political, but it serves to integrate clans into larger social units that can absorb ritual responsibilities in case the member clans become too small in population to carry out their responsibilities. (This has been known to happen during the modern era and has been codified in tribal oral traditions.[6])

Architecture Hopi society phratries do not normally have a separate name beyond some hyphenated version of the component clans, nor do they have specific ritual responsibilities beyond those of the clan; therefore, one would not necessarily expect them to have a specialized group-identity building. However, some buildings at Cliff Palace do appear to be group-identity buildings, as suggested by their placement between kivas built during the same year or linked to the kivas by tunnels. The interior surfaces of these units were not plastered or decorated, but the exterior walls were finished with schemes similar to those of clan units. An example is the circular two-story tower between adjacent Kivas J and K, which were built in the same year. This is a singular building with a well-finished exterior of pecked and ground sandstone blocks. The exterior was plastered, but only after other units were added to the outside. Doorways (one on each story) closed from the exterior, and there is no evidence of heating (hearth or sooting) on the interior, indicating that both stories of this building may have been used as storage. Doorway openings are oriented toward the Kiva K side.

Even in the absence of well-defined phratry buildings, there is archaeological evidence for the phratry system in the larger Mesa Verde alcove sites (Nordby 2001). The evidence includes: (1) kivas built during the same year, (2) collaboratively constructed residential architecture, (3) kivas linked by tunnels, and (4) kiva rooftop courtyards or plazas that share a traffic flow that is perpetuated even as surrounding spaces change and rooms are added. The key factor is that the kivas have surrounding residential architecture: rooms and room suites.

That kivas or other spaces of component clans were utilized or "borrowed" is a reasonable assumption and possibility—especially the larger, open kiva rooftop plazas that could have accommodated the larger groups of a phratry. Transmission or sharing of certain ritual responsibilities and intellectual property of component clans within the phratry might take place within clan kivas.

Surface Finishes and Decorations The surface finishes and embellishments of "borrowed" phratry buildings are nearly indistinguishable from the component clan kivas. Since the scheme preservation is often poor, and it is not possible to expose underlying decorative schemes without destroying the stratigraphy, we are currently unable to decode the synchronic schemes of clan organizations in kivas or courtyards. Perhaps future advancements in multispectral imaging will allow us to observe and record surfaces obscured by later surface finish applications. Without further examination of the full stratigraphy of plaster and decorative schemes, the identification of phratry-specific spaces or buildings will continue to be challenging.

Voluntary Groups or Societies

Eggan (1950: 28) notes that among the Hopi there are some groups whose membership has no explicit kinship ties, even though relatives are often involved. These groups often have ceremonial responsibilities throughout the calendar year. Collectively, and for the purposes of this paper, these are termed *societies*. Examples listed by Eggan (1950: 90–92) include the kachina cult; tribal initiation societies; societies focusing on rain, war, clowning, and curing; and the winter solstice ceremony. Membership involves complex interrelationships between clan, society, and kiva groupings, and often includes a ceremonial father rather than the biological father (Eggan 1950: 52–53). A man's membership in a kiva group is not controlled by lineage but by the males' continued involvement with their initiation kiva, a connection that is tied to a ceremonial father.

Architecture Not all Mesa Verde sites have definitive evidence of voluntary groups, societies, or similar structures. In some cases, clan, society, and kiva groups intermingle to produce a wide variety of buildings or spaces. In addition, these units might also borrow buildings as phratries do. As a result of the variety and combination of structures, a clear-cut description of the architecture and the archaeology is difficult. In terms of the hierarchical social interaction model, it is tempting to classify otherwise unexplainable spaces and constructs as belonging to those units.

Nevertheless, some Mesa Verde sites have convincing evidence of dual architectural divisions that may be tied to societies. These tangible architectural divisions are formed by walls and specialized buildings that divide the site into two distinct parts and restrict traffic flow between the two areas. When there are such divisions, they may represent moieties, which can contain more than one phratry and are exogamous. In other words, the architecture can physically separate two groups of people within a village, each of which is made up of related clans that marry outside of their moiety. Among the earliest recognized examples of this architectural division was Mug House, excavated by Rohn (1971). It also occurs in Cliff Palace.

Surface Finishes and Decorations At Cliff Palace, neither Room 59 nor 64, which are specialized rooms that spatially divide the site, have elaborately plastered interiors, although the stone walls are massively constructed. The exteriors of these buildings were plastered with monochromatic schemes, and the embellishments are generally limited to mudballs (patches of dried mud splatter) on the building fronts.

The symbolism of the mudballs is somewhat conjectural in ancient contexts. Hopi tribal members have suggested that they may be associated with marriage activities. The groom's female relatives engage in a mudball fight with the clan into which their brother is marrying and into which their nieces and nephews will be born. This idea reinforces the notion that these dual divisions may be moieties that integrate the two halves of the village through marriage, and further, that marriage associations helped to ensure an orderly transfer of land through the female line at the time these structures were built (AD 1200–1300). It should be noted, however, that mudballs are also found in contexts other than these dual buildings in both Cliff Palace and Spruce Tree House. Nonetheless, the distribution and nature of surface finishes and embellishments are critical components for future study of dual social units.

Village Identity

Architecture

Socially, villages consist of groups of people that probably see each other every day. It is reasonable to assume that, as these groups come together, specialized structures are built. At Cliff Palace, there are not enough residential spaces to account for all the storage rooms that are present (Nordby 2001), so it is possible that the village may have included other social groups outside the village residents. In this multiuse context at Cliff Palace, the major village-identity building is the Speaker Chief Complex,[7] which may have served the broader purpose of bringing together the resident dual divisions of the site. Its plaster and decorative elements are an important line of evidence that link room function and placement.

The Speaker Chief Complex (Fig. 5) is a three-story building with two rooms on each story, totaling six rooms. The doorways are sealed from the exterior, and the enclosed rooms lack hearths, indicating nonresidential use such as storage. Appended to the southeastern side are two single-story rooms that are not part of the original footprint. One of the appended rooms is a *mealing* (corn-grinding) room, which is a rare type of structure that may be linked with social or cer-

FIGURE 5 This ground plan shows the Speaker Chief Complex and Kiva Q, an example of a village-identity or integrative building. Illustration by Gregory E. Munson.

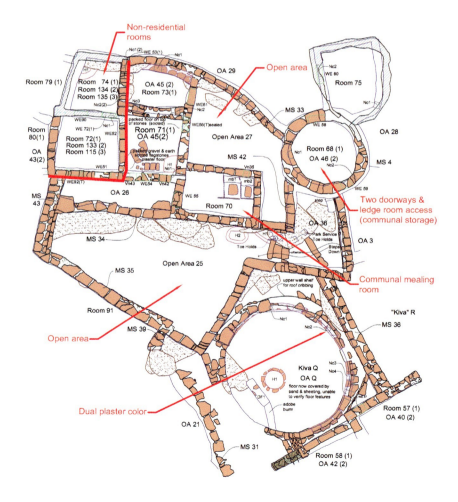

emonial events that united the various parts of the village. In front are two courtyards formed by partition walls linked by a single-slot doorway. Access to the symmetrically arranged storage buildings was from the roof of an adjacent circular tower with two doorways. (This is the only example of a surface room with multiple doorways.) At the foot of Speaker Chief Complex is Kiva Q, a large associated kiva with eight pilasters, rather than the usual six.

Integrative Surface Finishes and Embellishments

The plastered face of Speaker Chief Complex is the most visible decorated surface at Cliff Palace.[8] The white field above the doorway is associated with two ventilation ports that resemble eyes, and as a result, has been referred to by some as a mask or face.[9] The wall below is a tan color surrounded by a rectangular doorway that, if the analogy were continued, could be construed as a nose or mouth. Other embellishments include at least three handprints, mud splatters, and fingertip impressions in the plaster. Each of the two open areas has red paint—one area with broad, red, vertical stripes. One has mudballs, and the other has incised dots. One of the appended, enclosed rooms has a horizontal row of triangles coupled with several

birds and mudballs. On the interior of an unplastered room, a frog is carved into a building stone. As one might expect, since this building is the expression of a larger social group consisting of numerous component social groups, surface finishing techniques and formulations, as well as embellishment motifs and execution, are complex and difficult to interpret.

In Kiva Q, at the base of Speaker Chief Complex, a bilaterally symmetrical application of bichromatic plaster displays the connection of dual divisions (Fig. 6). Kiva Q introduces the concept of "two becoming one" where two plaster colors come together in the unbroken circle of the kiva walls. The margins of each color meet at a niche at the rear of the kiva, demonstrating that the application is tied to architectural details and not merely a coincidence.

One of the best-preserved examples of applied decoration at Cliff Palace is on the interior of the four-story tower. The basal unit of this tower, Room 11, is positioned between three kivas; one could have entered the tower from any of these kivas' rooftop courtyards. The painted rooms in this tower have been documented and conserved by the University of Pennsylvania and Mesa Verde conservators and archaeologists.[10] Room 121, on the third story of the tower, is the most

FIGURE 6 Coupled with the placement of Kiva Q, the symmetrical bichromatic application of plasters (indicated by the dotted black line) probably shows the integration of two social units becoming one. This building may have been the gathering space for dual societies.

elaborately plastered and painted. Malville (1989) has suggested that the paintings in this tower are linked with astronomical observations, and that its placement is linked to Sun Temple, a mesatop structure across Cliff Canyon. This is based largely on mathematics and positioning, rather than line-of-sight observations from buildings on the ground.[11]

The social role of this tower is still unknown; however, if one applies the concept of "two becoming one" from Kiva Q, this building makes some sense as both a village-identity building and a structure that joins component social parts. Could the painting on the tower's interior south wall, which resembles a mended blanket (Fig. 7), be another example of two becoming one in a context other than a kiva? Taken in this context, the other embellishments in this room, which include a multitriangle design, may indicate that this structure is indeed a village-identity building. Similar triangular designs from Spruce Tree House suggest that this kind of dado identifies public buildings.[12]

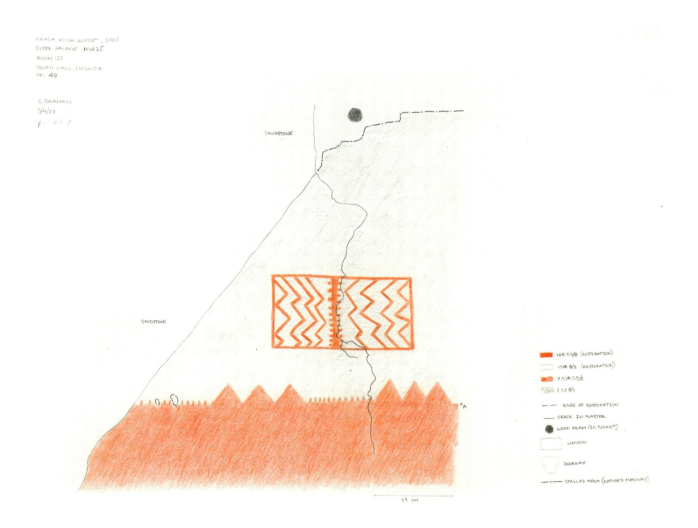

FIGURE 7 Located in Room 121, this painting resembles a mended blanket and suggests that this building may have served as an integrative space where two societies within the village merged. The dark red dado below, with its multiple contiguous triangle design, is believed to be a signature motif for Mesa Verde culture, even when it occurs in other parts of the Southwest.

Corroborating Evidence: Spruce Tree House

Integrative Architecture, Surface Finishes, and Embellishments

A second example of dual-division connectivity is found in the central building of Spruce Tree House. While comparable in size to Cliff Palace, Spruce Tree House has proportionately more residential spaces and room suites, albeit only eight kivas that were in use during its final footprint. In overall plan, the core unit of Spruce Tree House resembles an E, although the overall village plan is more complex. The middle leg in the E could be entered from either side through bilateral T-shaped doorways or subterranean tunnels from kivas.

Three rooms have substantial amounts of decoration, including a bichromatic plaster scheme. The dotted, three-triangle scheme shown in Figure 8, which can be combined with other symbols, is probably the most common in Mesa Verde public buildings, including the Cliff Palace tower. This motif has also been found in sites far from Mesa Verde. Sally Cole believes that where this occurs it is a signature of Mesa Verde cultural connection.[13]

FIGURE 8 This field drawing of one of the walls in an integrative building in Spruce Tree House shows the dark red dado with sets of three contiguous triangles, adding as well a row of dots above the dado. The wall above the dado has been painted or plastered black. Although the meaning of the multiple contiguous triangles is unknown, some believe that it is a group of mountains, such that the dado represents a skyline with landscape features.

The decorated T-shaped doorway in Spruce Tree House serves as the entry to a singular weaving room that is linked with other rooms in the building. The decoration is both incised and painted. The doorsill is embellished with a complex, incised pottery design, and the jambs are painted with a horizontal red stripe. Like the carved frog in the Speaker Chief Complex at Cliff Palace, these decorations are unique. The extent and craftsmanship of the decoration and the complexity of plaster schemes in this group of three rooms has resulted in this area being known as an "artists' guild."

Conclusion

The architecture of Mesa Verde cliff dwellings mirrors the social organization of the residents. Understanding the architectural and social context of the surface finishes and embellishments is important for two reasons: First, decorated surfaces are an expression of social-group identity within a space, and not just a display of artistry. As generations pass, these spaces are transformed into icons of social-group identity and imbued with power. Second, when they are present, surface finishes and embellishments help to identify the function of spaces and determine social relationships. The integrity of these decorated architectural surfaces must be conserved for future study.

With a few noteworthy exceptions, the interpretation of the architecture at Cliff Palace and other alcove sites in Mesa Verde emerged without the consistent application of surface finish or embellishment data; however, now that the archaeological value of the surface finishes has been recognized, this study will be incorporated in future research projects. Analysis of the decorated surfaces will not only allow us to present a more personal picture of life in these sites, but it may help us to better understand and preserve the evidence of past events in an architectural and social context.

Acknowledgments

While much of the foregoing is preliminary and conjectural, I am indebted to numerous colleagues who took the time to engage in productive, thought-provoking discussions regarding the subject matter of this paper. These include especially Joel Brisbin, Kay Barnett, Frank Matero, Gay Ives, Lloyd Masayumptewa, Lyle Balenquah, Kathleen Fiero, Carol Graham, and Sally Cole, who also supplied much of the project information on the ancient images. Christy Garrou scanned Sally's drawings for incorporation into the oral presentation, and Rebecca Carr helped with ArkDoc database searches for relevant data.

Notes

1   For additional information on the debate, see Lekson (1989).

2   Kinship and social terms used in this paper are largely congruent with Eggan's (1950) usage for the Hopi. Several general definitions are included here to assist readers unfamiliar with these terms, but interested scholars are directed to Eggan (1950) or other references listed for greater precision. A *phratry* is a group of two or more clans that share some experience or history that links them in a special way. Each *sib* or *sibling* clan forming a phratry thus has a special associative relationship that is not shared by other clans resident at the same village or site. Phratries have their roots in kinship relations, augmented by common events. A *voluntary society* is a group of people who have a special relationship based on interests, although those interests may be based on kinship. Among some Puebloan people, these groups tend to have different social and ceremonial responsibilities throughout the year (e.g., summer people and winter people). Archaeologically, a number of sites have dual architectural divisions that may reflect two major voluntary societies now present in modern pueblos. Cliff Palace is an example of this. In my view, these groups are probably *moieties*. Since members marry outside their own moiety (are *exogamous)*, the effect is to solidify a larger social group through marriage customs and relationships.

3   Additional perspectives on the Hopi and other Puebloan groups can be found in Fox (1967). Enhanced understanding of Hopi iconography can be garnered by looking at Bernardini (2002), Cole (1992), and Adams (1991), or by speaking with tribal members.

4   The terminology associated with plastering and decoration used in this paper was developed in collaboration between staff members from the University of Pennsylvania and Mesa Verde National Park for the purposes of ArkDoc, the park's Archeological Site Conservation Program (ASCP) database (Nordby et al. 2002). The purpose was to develop a standard lexicon and database-encoding process that interdisciplinary researchers could apply. The following terms were selected following several often-spirited discussions. A *scheme* attempts to enter the mind of the ancient plasterer and evaluate what the decorative or other objective may have been. It is the combination of various plaster applications and decorative elements listed below. In some cases, especially for kivas that were repeatedly plastered and decorated, the walls were covered with sequences of coatings and retain vestiges of each scheme. Understanding and decoding these schemes is difficult and complex, but the scheme supplies a unifying principle within which to organize the various plaster applications and constituent decorations or embellishments. Plasters at Mesa Verde follow several schemes, which most often consist of one or more of the following applications of plasters or washes: (1) *dado,*

an application to approximately the lower half or third of the wall; (2) *field,* an application to the upper portion of a wall; (3) *floor band,* an application to the wall immediately above the floor, usually extending about 10 to 20 cm above the floor; (4) *aura,* an application of contrasting color, usually white or light gray, around a doorway or other wall opening. Decorating the walls of ancient pueblo buildings is done both to plasters (commonly) and washes (infrequently), as well as to unplastered walls, where they are added to the surfaces of building stones. Some alterations result from painting, and some by incising/scratching or pecking/hammering the decorative elements. Some of these alterations may not have been purposeful, and it is not always easy to determine the relationship between the alterations and the overall scheme. We have applied the term *embellishment* to all of these alterations, whether painted (*pictographs*), pecked/hammered (*petroglyphs*), impressions made with the fingernails and fingertips (*punctations*), or incised/scratched. It also includes the remnants of mud and small stains left behind when *mudballs* were thrown at the wall but did not adhere.

5   Sally Cole, personal communication. (Sally Cole is a noted specialist on pictographs and petroglyphs of the southwestern United States who also gathers the views of Puebloan descendents on these images and articulates them in her studies. She works as a consultant to Mesa Verde National Park and other agencies.)

6   Eggan (1950) describes the interplay between clan and phratry in some detail.

7   The name "Speaker Chief House" was developed by J. W. Fewkes (1911); it was not used by tribal members. I have used the word "complex" here, since it was not a house but a collection of other kinds of rooms.

8   Several studies on the plaster and rock art decoration of Speaker Chief Complex have been conducted by Copeland and Ives (1973), Matero (2003), Connie Silver (unpublished); and Sally Cole working with Hopi elders (also unpublished).

9   Sally Cole, personal communication.

10   The University of Pennsylvania's Architectural Conservation Laboratory has worked at Mesa Verde National Park for the last decade. Their work has involved condition assessment, documentation, and treatment of many wall surfaces. Of these, the tower at Cliff Palace received the most attention because of the completeness of its scheme, its state of preservation, concerns over its ongoing decay, and the fact that it serves as an interpretive and educational focal point at Cliff Palace.

11   Advances in archeoastronomy prompted in part by the emergence and availability of global positioning technology, and the application of anthropological and social modeling to cliff dwelling proxemics have emerged during this same time frame. Room 11 and the rooms above it, especially Room 121, seem to sit at the conjunction of these various interests, even though their roles remain incompletely understood.

12   Following Fewkes's excavations in Spruce Tree House (Fewkes 1909), the site was opened for public visitation but saw little additional research until the year 2000. In the past decade, work at Spruce Tree House on the plasters by the University of Pennsylvania, the decorations or embellishments by Sally Cole, and the architecture and its social parameters by Joel Brisbin of the National Park Service has for the first time made it possible to systematically articulate these three lines of evidence.

13   Sally Cole, personal communication.

References

Adams, E. Charles. 1991. *The Origin and Development of the Pueblo Katsina Cult.* Tucson: University of Arizona Press.

Bernardini, Wesley. 2002. The gathering of the clans: Understanding ancestral Hopi migration and identity: A.D. 1275–1400. PhD diss. submitted to Arizona State University, Tempe.

Brisbin, Joel M. 2003. *Spruce Tree House Architecture, A.D. 1240–1250: Architectural Documentation in the Courtyard Complex E Area.* Archeological Site Conservation Program, Mesa Verde National Park, CO.

Cole, Sally J. 1992. *Katsina Iconography in Homol'ovi Rock Art, Central Little Colorado River Valley, Arizona.* Phoenix: Arizona Archaeological Society.

Copeland, J., and G. Ives. 1973. A survey of Cliff Palace wall decorations and kiva designs. Manuscript on file at Mesa Verde Research Center, Mesa Verde National Park, CO.

Eggan, Fred. 1950. *The Social Organization of the Western Pueblos.* Chicago: University of Chicago Press.

Fewkes, J. W. 1909. *Antiquities of Mesa Verde National Park: Spruce Tree House.* Bureau of American Ethnology Bulletin 41. Washington, DC: Smithsonian Institution.

———. 1911. *Antiquities of Mesa Verde National Park: Cliff Palace.* Bureau of American Ethnology Bulletin 51. Washington, DC: Smithsonian Institution.

Fox, Robin. 1967. *The Keresan Bridge.* New York: University of London, Humanities Press.

Lekson, Stephen H. 1989. Kivas? In *The Architecture of Social Integration in Prehistoric Pueblos,* ed. William D. Lipe and Michelle Hegmon, 161–67. Occasional Papers of the Crow Canyon Archaeological Center, No. 1. Cortez, CO.

Malville, J. McKim. 1989. *Prehistoric Astronomy in the Southwest.* Boulder, CO: Johnson Books.

Matero, Frank G. 2003. Managing change: The role of documentation and condition survey at Mesa Verde National Park. *JAIC* 42:39–58.

Mindeleff, Cosmos. 1900. *Localization of Tusayan Clans.* Bureau of American Ethnology, 19th Annual Report, 1897–98, Part 2, 635–53. Washington, DC: Government Printing Office.

Nordby, Larry V. 2001. *Prelude to Tapestries in Stone: Understanding Cliff Palace Architecture.* Archeological Research Series, Architectural Studies No. 4. Mesa Verde National Park, Division of Research and Resource Management, Mesa Verde National Park, CO.

———. 2002. Preservation and non-destructive research at Spring House (5MV1406). Manuscript on file at the Mesa Verde Research Center, Mesa Verde National Park, CO.

Nordby, Larry V., Todd Metzger, Cynthia L. Williams, and James D. Mayberry. 2002. *Mesa Verde National Park Archeological Site Conservation Program Guidelines, Volume I: Standards for Field Data Collection and Documentation.* Mesa Verde National Park, Division of Research and Resource Management. Mesa Verde National Park, CO.

Rohn, Arthur H. 1971. *Mug House, Mesa Verde National Park, Colorado.* Archeological Research Series, No 7-D 7/4. Washington, DC: National Park Service.

Museum Practice

Introduction

Susan Thomas

Many recent advances in the conservation of decorated surfaces on earthen architecture have allowed for in situ preservation; however, such was not the case for fragments excavated in the nineteenth and early twentieth centuries that are currently housed in museums around the world. This section on the conservation of decorated surfaces in the field of museum practice focuses on three case studies: the fourteenth- to seventeenth-century Hopi murals from Awatovi and Kawaika-a in the southwestern United States; Chinese wall paintings and architectural elements from the thirteenth, fourteenth, and seventeenth centuries; and the Nebamun wall paintings that were removed from an Eighteenth Dynasty Theban tomb. Although each example has distinct cultural affiliations and manufacturing techniques, and different methods were used to remove them from their original settings, they share a common thread: to provide adequate conservation or interpretation of detached murals, contemporary researchers must rely on the documentation that was generated at the time of removal as well as subsequent treatment documentation.

In the case of the Hopi murals and the Chinese wall paintings, meticulous attention was given to the early fieldwork aspects of the project, particularly the context of the wall paintings in situ and how they were removed. This information is most useful for research and interpretation because it provides the most accurate context for the detached decorated architectural surface. However, all three of the case studies, particularly the retreatment of the Nebamun wall paintings, also share the challenge of implementing modern conservation without thorough documentation of how they were previously treated in the lab. It can be difficult to determine how to reverse or remove old treatments without this type of documentation. Consequently, much of the lab time is spent analyzing the composition of the previous repairs to determine the requirements for retreatment. Also, there is often a disconnect between the maintenance of archaeological and curatorial files, which provide insight into the context and research aspects of murals, and the conservation files, which frequently focus on treatment procedures. These three papers demonstrate how different conservators approached the treatment and subsequent stabilization of detached decorated surfaces. Each case study provides new insights into the conservation of earthen materials, the use of historical records in assessing prior treatments, and the integration of field data and curatorial files with conservation documentation to ensure appropriate interpretation and preservation.

Out of Their Native Earth: The History of Excavation and Conservation of Ancient Hopi Murals from Awatovi and Kawaika-a

Angelyn Bass Rivera, Leslie Rainer, and Lydia Vagts

In 1935, a team of archaeologists from the Peabody Museum of Archaeology and Ethnology at Harvard University began excavation of Awatovi and Kawaika-a, two fifteenth- to seventeenth-century Hopi villages in the Jeddito Valley of northeastern Arizona. In 1936, they discovered fragments of a mural in a kiva (ceremonial room). Four seasons later, they had uncovered the remains of over two hundred paintings on the earthen plastered walls of approximately twenty kivas. The archaeologists, led by Watson Smith, exposed and recorded the murals layer by layer, and then removed fifteen painted fragments from the walls using the strappo technique. After removal, the fragments were transported to the Peabody Museum and remounted on a permanent backing for exhibition and study.[1] While the murals were at the Peabody, some of the foremost archaeologists and conservation scientists of the time conducted extensive examinations and investigations. Also at that time, painted reproductions of the murals were made from the field notes.

Today, the Peabody Museum and the Museum of Northern Arizona house the collection of mural fragments removed from Awatovi and Kawaika-a and other sites on Antelope Mesa. These fragments have been exhibited or in storage for over sixty-five years. In 1998, a collaborative project began between the two museums to assess the condition of the fragments and conserve them for possible future exhibition. The principal conservator on the project was Leslie Rainer, with collaboration from Angelyn Bass Rivera, Lydia Vagts, and others.[2] This paper briefly summarizes the history of excavation, investigation, and exhibition of the Awatovi and Kawaika-a murals, and then describes the recent conservation work.

Discovery and Significance of the Jeddito Murals

Harvard's Peabody Museum Expedition to the Jeddito Valley in Arizona in the 1930s was undertaken with the goal of studying the continuum of Pueblo and Hopi civilization from prehistoric times to the present.[3] The expedition focused on sites on Antelope Mesa located east of First and Second Hopi Mesa (Fig. 1). Atop the steep escarpment of Antelope Mesa were at least five large pueblos and hundreds of smaller villages and farmhouses that were built and occupied from about AD 500. One of the larger pueblos, Awatovi, was occupied from the mid-thirteenth through seventeenth centuries. In addition to the ancient pueblo structures, there were also numerous Spanish Franciscan missionary buildings constructed in the seventeenth century.

The excavations confirmed that Awatovi was a thriving aboriginal village until ca. 1630, when the Spanish Franciscan order seized control of the pueblos and established several missions in this and other Hopi villages. At Awatovi, the friars built a church and *convento* over the existing Hopi structures. In 1680, the missionaries there were killed and the church was razed during the Pueblo Revolt.[4] Twenty years later, when the Spanish attempted to reoccupy Awatovi, the Hopi resisted by destroying the entire village and its inhabitants, including both Hopis who had assisted the Spanish and the missionaries.

When archaeologists began excavations at Awatovi and the neighboring village Kawaika-a in 1935, they expected they would find painted kiva murals. This assumption came from knowledge of historic Pueblo practices, as well as from the discovery of fragments of kiva murals at neighboring sites on

FIGURE 1 Map of the Four Corners area of the Southwest United States showing the locations of Awatovi and Kawaika-a (underlined) and other sites, including Mesa Verde National Park. (Reproduced from Watson Smith, *Kiva Mural Decorations at Awatovi and Kawaika-a: With a Survey of Other Wall Paintings in the Pueblo Southwest*, Papers of the Peabody Museum of American Archaeology and Ethnology, vol. 37, 1952. Reprinted courtesy of the Peabody Museum of Archaeology and Ethnology, Harvard University. Redrawn by Nick Swarts, 2004.)

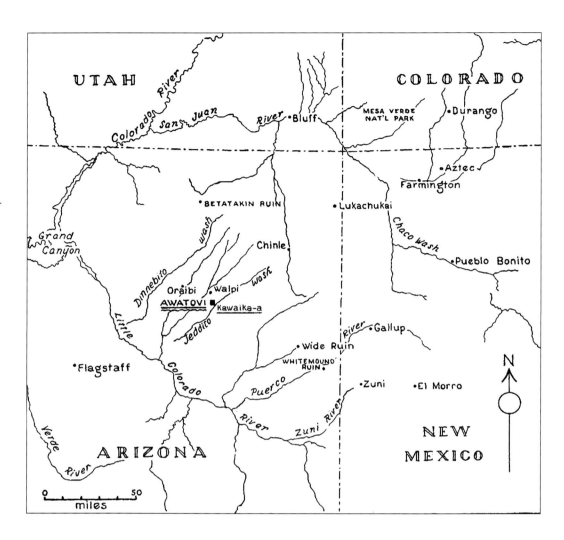

Antelope Mesa and at other Puebloan sites such as Lowry Ruin in Colorado and Kuaua in New Mexico.[5] They had no idea, however, of the wealth of material and information they were about to uncover.

The murals of the Jeddito are extraordinary. Their style ranges from geometric to abstract to detailed representational compositions showing humans, kachinas, supernatural beings, animals, and objects involved in ceremonies. Some murals were designed and executed in the Sikyatki style of decoration, named for the complex Hopi ceramic tradition from the same area, which is considered among the most elaborate and beautiful artistic achievements of the prehistoric Pueblo peoples (Fig. 2). Both Watson Smith and J. J. Brody, who studied the murals in depth, felt strongly that the murals were painted expressly for particular ritual observations and were to be seen by only a select few as part of a ceremony or special event. Smith stated that the elements portrayed in the paintings "were mimetic of the living scene that was acted out, whether in the kiva or at an associated dance in the village plaza" (Smith 1952: 46–47). Brody thought that the process of making and using these paintings in a ceremony may have been of greater importance and value than the physical paintings themselves (Brody 1991: 174). We can be assured that murals we see today are only a small, tangible part of a larger, complex experience that may have also involved sound, motion, people, time, and place.

Although the murals tell only a fraction of their story, we gain tremendous inspiration and intellectual insight from them. Within the context of other Pueblo mural paintings, they are among the finest discovered. They lay bare a longstanding Hopi wall painting tradition and demonstrate the sophistication of Pueblo mural painting from the fourteenth to seventeenth centuries. They are evidence of the long continuity of Hopi religious symbolism and practice. They provide

FIGURE 2 Reproduction of mural fragment from Awatovi (Room 3, front wall) showing the Sikyatki style of painting. (Reproduced from Watson Smith, *Kiva Mural Decorations at Awatovi and Kawaika-a: With a Survey of Other Wall Paintings in the Pueblo Southwest*, Papers of the Peabody Museum of American Archaeology and Ethnology, vol. 37, 1952. Reprinted courtesy of the Peabody Museum of Archaeology and Ethnology, Harvard University.)

information on animals and plants of that time, as well as clothing and textiles[6] (Fig. 3). They emphasize the intimately dependent associations between man and nature, reality and mythology, and represent a depth of emotion, belief, and extraordinary artistry that inspires us today.

Construction, Excavation and Removal History

Context

The first Jeddito mural was discovered early in the second field season of the Awatovi Expedition, in 1936. It was found in Room 218, which was a small rectangular kiva with over a hundred layers of earthen plaster on the walls. The plaster layers alone were over 10 cm thick. Of those hundred layers, twenty-six were painted with murals. Over the next four field seasons, Smith and others uncovered the remains of over two hundred individual paintings on the walls of about twenty kivas.

Some of the best-preserved Jeddito murals come from an intact kiva (Room 788) found under the main Franciscan church. Before the new church was built over it, the kiva was filled with fine, clean sand to prevent its collapse (Smith 1990: 47). This is unusual, as most subterranean structures were filled with their partially collapsed roof and walls and/or domestic trash. The clean sand helped insulate and preserve the murals from damage.

Construction Technique

According to Smith, the rectangular kiva walls that supported the paintings were built primarily of shaped sandstone blocks set in earthen mortar. Some walls were made from adobe

FIGURE 3 Mural fragment from Kawaika-a (Room 4) after conservation treatment in 2004. This fragment depicts frogs or lizards in various shapes and colors, a fish resembling a pike or gar, lightning, ears of corn, and ceremonial bowls. Inset shows the painted reproduction made from the field notes (2630 NA 1001.R.4.20, Museum of Northern Arizona). Photo: Angelyn Bass Rivera. (Inset reproduced from Watson Smith, *Kiva Mural Decorations at Awatovi and Kawaika-a: With a Survey of Other Wall Paintings in the Pueblo Southwest*, Papers of the Peabody Museum of American Archaeology and Ethnology, vol. 37, 1952. Reprinted courtesy of the Peabody Museum of Archaeology and Ethnology, Harvard University.)

bricks. The kivas varied in length from 4 to 6 m long and in width from 2.5 to 4 m, with an average height of approximately 2.5 m. Only two kivas in Awatovi had intact roofs at the time of excavation; most of the other roofs had collapsed, and the upper parts of the walls and the earthen plasters were destroyed. Covering the interior face of the masonry walls was a thin coat of grayish adobe mortar followed by numerous thin layers of fine-textured, reddish brown plaster, which form the ground for the painted schemes. Kiva paintings did not occur on every plaster layer, and did not necessarily cover the full extent of the four walls; however, they were a common feature of kivas throughout the occupancy of Awatovi and other villages on Antelope Mesa (Smith 1952: 21). Dwelling rooms were plastered in a similar manner, but they were not usually painted and generally had far fewer plaster layers than kivas (Smith 1952: 17).

Kivas, in both ancient and modern pueblos, are frequently renewed with successive layers of plaster. At Awatovi, the kivas have anywhere from twenty to a hundred layers of fine plaster. The frequency and reason for plaster renewal is not certain, but it may have been done for maintenance, renovation, or ceremonial practice. Ritual obliteration of painted decorations is a common ceremonial practice, both historically and in modern pueblos (Smith 1952: 20–21). Fortunately, the Jeddito murals were not destroyed after the conclusion of a particular event, but were covered with a coat of sandy clay plaster. This not only obscured the painted designs but also prepared the surface for a new painting and helped preserve the underlying murals.

Analysis of the mural paints revealed that the pigments were derived from readily available minerals such as iron oxides, red ochre, manganese, and kaolin, as well as azurite and malachite.[7] The only organic pigment identified was charcoal or bone black. The binder was not determined, but the pigments were probably mixed with a vegetable gum or animal fat mixed with water or saliva (Smith 1952: 30–31). The paints were applied on a dry plaster, probably with a stiff brush of yucca, cornhusk, or feather. Frequently, striations left by the brush were visible on the mural surface.[8] The mural designs appear to have been painted freehand, without a preliminary drawing.

Excavation and Removal

Though the discovery of painted kiva walls was anticipated, the large number of murals and their broad scope of subject matter were unexpected. Since it was clearly impractical to remove the walls intact and transport them to a laboratory for separation of the paintings layer by layer,[9] each mural was exposed in situ, and where possible, fragments of them were detached from the walls using the strappo technique. The project archaeologists under the direction of Watson Smith carried this out. The excavation and removal procedures are as follows:[10] First, the kivas were excavated from the center of the wall out to the corners, leaving a balk of fill approximately 50 cm from each corner to support the wall in place. Damaged upper portions of the kiva walls, large cracks, exposed plaster edges, and partially detached plaster layers were patched or stabilized with an earthen mortar by grinding original plaster fragments found in the room fill. Even in the 1930s, Smith knew very well the benefits of using compatible repair materials. He noted in his report that "pulverized, dampened and re-plasticized [original plaster] . . . provides a perfect patching compound . . . Both old and new plaster thus being equally damp, an even shrinkage occurred on drying, and a perfect bond was achieved" (Smith 1952: 35).

When the full extent of the mural was exposed and the damaged areas were stabilized, the mural surface was fine-cleaned with a penknife and small paintbrushes. Once the painting was dirt free, a grid was placed over the mural, and photographs and descriptive notes and scale drawings were made[11] (Fig. 4a–b). Samples of the paints were also taken for analysis.

After documentation, two coats of an adhesive solution (PVAc)[12] were applied to the mural with a brush. Overlapping sheets of unbleached muslin (measuring approximately 30 × 30 cm or 30 × 60 cm) were then pressed over the surface. When thoroughly dry, the muslin was peeled from the plaster, taking with it the paint film and a bit of the plaster, leaving most of the substrate undamaged (Fig. 4c–f). Although the description of this procedure sounds simple and quick, Smith noted that in each case, an "unsuspected galaxy of complicating factors was involved" (Smith 1952: 39). The adhesive was often modified to suit the physical condition, composition, and porosity of the individual plaster layers as well as the climatic conditions (ideally warm, dry, and windless). Various proportions of solvents and plasticizers were added to adjust the adhesive's speed of drying, degree of viscosity, flexibility, and ease of reversibility.

After detachment from the wall, the muslin-faced mural fragments were rolled or packed flat, and protected on both sides by newspaper to prevent the panels from sticking together.[13] The wall was then scraped again until the next mural was exposed, and the stripping process was repeated. Only sections from fifteen of the best-preserved murals were

FIGURE 4 Series of historic photographs showing (a) exposure of the murals, (b) field recording, (c, d) preparation of the mural surface with PVAc and muslin sheets, and (e, f) stripping of the paint layer from the wall. (Reproduced from Watson Smith, *Kiva Mural Decorations at Awatovi and Kawaika-a: With a Survey of Other Wall Paintings in the Pueblo Southwest*, Papers of the Peabody Museum of American Archaeology and Ethnology, vol. 37, 1952. Reprinted courtesy of the Peabody Museum of Archaeology and Ethnology, Harvard University.)

removed from the walls and remounted; the other fragmentary wall paintings were recorded, but not preserved.[14]

The excavations at Awatovi and other sites on Antelope Mesa concluded in 1939. Currently, these sites on the Hopi Reservation are closed to the public.

Laboratory Conservation

Once the mural fragments were removed from the walls, they were rolled and transported to the Peabody Museum of Archaeology and Ethnology, Harvard University, for analysis, conservation, and remounting. The fragments measured as large as 1.8 m long by nearly 1.2 m high, and as small as 10 × 10

cm. Considerations for the remounting were practical as well as aesthetic. Firstly, it was felt that "the prime essentials of the backing material must be durability, lightness, economy, and the ease with which the paint film could be affixed to it" (Smith 1952: 43). Secondly, there was a desire to remount the paintings in a way that was relatively true to their original appearance on the kiva wall. To meet these criteria, untempered Masonite Presdwood[15] was selected as the secondary support. Its high density, comparable color, and the ease with which it could be cut made it a suitable material. To prevent the panels from warping, both sides of the Masonite were coated with a glue size, and some of the larger panels were joined together with wood battens. To provide additional stability, wood frames with cross braces were added on the reverse of each piece.

Before the paintings were remounted, the face of the Masonite support was coated with an emulsion of crushed and reconstituted original plaster from the kiva walls mixed with a solution of Cologne glue in water.[16] This earth-based ground layer unified the appearance of the original fragments with their new support and replicated the color and texture of the original kiva walls. When the ground layer was dry, more Cologne glue was brushed on the reverse of the mural fragment, and the painting (with its facing still attached) was adhered to the Masonite. The facing was then removed by placing the panel upright and spraying the surface with acetone. As the solvent dissolved the adhesive, the muslin facing was peeled off in sheets, taking care not to remove any of the painted surface. Following removal of the facing, the exposed painted surface was sprayed with a 4 percent mixture of formaldehyde in alcohol to "harden the surface and render it damp resistant" (Smith 1952: 46). Three of the fragments were not remounted and retain the facing used in the stripping. These fragments remain intact as documentation of the detachment process.

Once the fragments were remounted, the murals were comparatively analyzed and studied in detail. In 1952, Watson Smith's monograph *Kiva Mural Decorations at Awatovi and Kawaika-a* was published. The monograph summarizes the excavation, removal, and conservation history of the murals. It also provides results of compositional and stylistic analysis and includes a comparative study of other wall paintings in the Pueblo Southwest. Smith spent decades researching and studying the murals. His documentation and analysis are invaluable for scholars today and greatly served the recent conservation work.

Since Smith's analysis and exhibition of the murals,[17] the fragments have been housed at the Peabody Museum of Archaeology and Ethnology at Harvard University and the Museum of Northern Arizona in Flagstaff, Arizona. The Peabody Museum has ten fragments; the Museum of Northern Arizona has five. Seven of the fragments at the Peabody Museum are stored vertically in a climate-controlled basement storage area alongside full-scale reproductions (Fig. 5). One small fragment and two others with their facings attached are in flat storage. At the Museum of Northern Arizona, four fragments are stored vertically in a climate-controlled area.[18] One small fragment with the facing attached is in flat storage. At one time, four of the mural fragments were on exhibit at the Museum of Northern Arizona in a spe-

cial gallery created to resemble an ancient kiva. The exposed Masonite supports of this set were whitewashed.[19] Currently, only one fragment, which is behind Plexiglas and delimited with off-white fabric surrounding the fragment, is on display.[20]

1998–2004 Conservation Project

In 1998, a collaborative project was initiated between the Peabody Museum and the Museum of Northern Arizona to assess and conserve the mural fragments for possible future exhibition. The conservation project was completed in phases, starting with documentation, condition assessment, and materials analysis, followed by conservation treatment and attachment of secondary structural supports to some of the larger fragments. Between 1999 and 2004, conservators

FIGURE 5 Steven Leblanc, Director of Collections, Peabody Museum of Archaeology and Ethnology, Harvard University, examining mural fragments and reproductions in the storage area. Original mural fragments and reproductions are stored vertically for ease of access and study. Photo: Leslie Rainer, 2004.

reexamined and treated the fragments at both museums. Following is a description of the recent work.

Condition Survey and Results of Examination

Prior to treatment, graphic, photographic, and written documentation of all fragments was completed at each museum (Rainer 1999). Graphic documentation involved recording conditions and previous treatments on acetate sheets overlaying black-and-white photographs of the fragments. In addition to the photographs, 35 mm slides and digital images were taken of the fragments before, during, and after treatment. Written condition assessments of each fragment, as well as details of the treatments, were entered into a customized database.[21] Standardized methods of examination and documentation made it possible for different teams of conservators working in separate locations to assess and record conditions and treatments similarly. It also helped conservators to determine if deterioration or damage was an isolated occurrence or common among all fragments, and to design and implement appropriate treatments.

In general, the mural fragments were found to be in fair condition. The condition assessment revealed that the common deterioration problem was air bubbles or voids between the original paint layer and the added substrate. These voids may have been preexisting or have occurred during detachment and remounting. Another common condition was overfilling of repairs made during excavation and remounting. Fills ranged in color, texture, and level. In some areas, fills obscured the original paint.

Examination revealed that storage of the fragments often affected their condition. Storage methods differed at the two museums over the years, and as a result, the condition of the fragments also varied. The fragments stored horizontally on top of cabinets at the Museum of Northern Arizona often showed sign of stress, such as large cracks along the seams where the Masonite panels were joined. These cracks probably occurred when the fragments were moved for access or study. In addition, the fragment edges were clearly worn from handling or accidents during transport, and there was a substantial accumulation of dust and grime on the surface.

Recent Analysis

Instrumental analysis was carried out to identify the various repair materials on the fragments, to confirm Smith's records, and to develop appropriate conservation treatments. Analyses included Fourier-transform infrared (FTIR) and scanning electron microscopy (SEM-EDS).[22] FTIR confirmed the presence of polyvinyl acetate (the adhesive Smith used for the muslin facing) and protein (likely the Cologne glue used to remount the fragments to the Masonite). Other results from FTIR revealed the presence of quartz and clay, components of the earth-based plaster ground that was applied to the Masonite prior to remounting the fragments. Kaolin was identified as the primary component of the whitewash found on the Museum of Northern Arizona fragments. SEM-EDS further detected the presence of titanium and iron in the whitewash, which may have been added as bulking agents.

Conservation treatment materials were also tested. Soil samples were analyzed for use in filling voids between the mural fragments and the Masonite support. Soils were collected from sand and gravel yards in the Flagstaff area and from the Hopi mesas.[23] Analysis was performed to characterize the soil (percentage and ratio of sand, silt, and clay, as well as alkalinity and soluble-salts content) and to determine which soils were similar in composition to the original mural plaster.[24] Additionally, conservators carried out on-site empirical testing to determine solubility of previous conservation materials, and methods to remove or reduce inappropriate repairs.

Smith's documentation of the treatments carried out in the field and records of the materials used were invaluable for the recent conservation work. Designing our treatments was simplified because Smith's reports confirmed most of the repair materials used on the fragments. Unfortunately, there was very little written documentation and no photographs of the remounting and subsequent treatment done in the laboratory during the 1940s.

Conservation Treatment

Treatment of the mural fragments was carried out at both the Peabody Museum and the Museum of Northern Arizona from 2003 to 2004 (Rainer, Bass Rivera, and Vagts 2004). In 2003, a model treatment was performed on one of the fragments at the Museum of Northern Arizona to test various conservation materials and techniques and to develop standard treatment procedures (Rainer and Bass Rivera 2003). Since the condition of the fragments varied, the treatments were a combination of those tested on the model and specialized treatments tailored to the specific needs of each fragment. Following is a general description of the treatments performed.

Structural Support

Six of the larger mural fragments (two at the Peabody Museum and four at the Museum of Northern Arizona) were structurally unstable because the Masonite support was heavy and pliable. As a result, the fragments flexed when they were lifted, causing large cracks through the mural and numerous small cracks on the surface. To stabilize the fragments, custom secondary-support panels were added to the back of the Masonite (Fig. 6). The panels were made of a honeycomb aluminum core sandwiched between two aluminum sheets reinforced along the edges with wood strips.[25] Together, these materials form a rigid and lightweight stress-skin panel. Aluminum was chosen as the support material because of its high strength and light weight.

Prior to installing the secondary supports, each fragment was cleaned on the reverse with a HEPA vacuum. Some of the unnecessary battens were removed. The aluminum honeycomb panels were attached to the reverse of mounted mural fragments with screws and cup washers. The screws fit into holes predrilled into both the aluminum honeycomb panel and the wood frame around the Masonite. Short screws were used so they would not break through the front of the Masonite. This new, rigid, lightweight secondary support helps prevent the fragments from flexing when moved.

Plaster Layers

A frequent treatment was filling of voids and cracks in the plaster. The voids were often more extensive than they appeared on the surface, and were fragile and susceptible to collapse (Fig. 7). A mixture of finely sieved earth (generally three parts Hopi soil to one part topsoil) and water,[26] with a small amount of rabbit skin glue, was used to fill the voids and cracks.[27] The ratio of soils in the mixture varied slightly from fragment to fragment to match the color of the surrounding original plaster.

FIGURE 6 Schematic drawing showing orthogonal view and section of the aluminum-composite secondary support attached to the reverse of the mounted mural fragment. Drawing by Robert Rivera and Leslie Rainer.

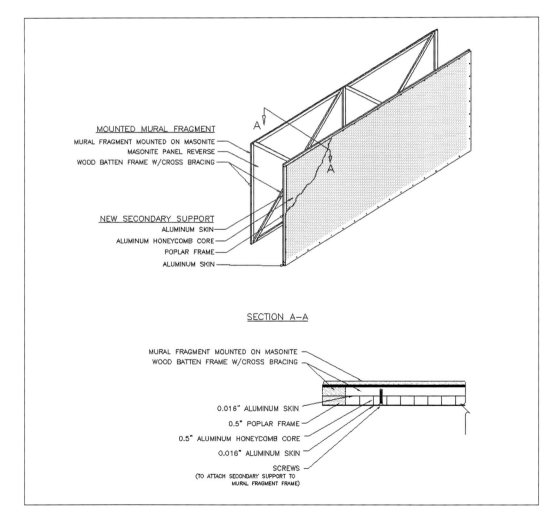

FIGURE 7 Lydia Vagts conserving a fragment at the Peabody Museum (39-97-10 / 23055b Peabody Museum). Inset shows an example of void behind the plaster layer. Recent conservation treatment included surface cleaning, removal of previous inappropriate fills, crack and void filling, and plaster reattachment. Photo: Leslie Rainer.

Prior to filling, the treatment areas were prewet with a 50 percent solution of isopropyl alcohol in water. Then the earthen mortar or grout was placed into the void with a small spatula or injected with a syringe. In some cases, where the air pocket was extensive, the plaster was lifted[28] so that the earth fill could be placed deep into the void. When the void was too narrow to inject the earth as a grout, only the rabbit skin glue was used. After filling, the treatment areas were blotted with a damp cosmetic sponge to prevent staining from moisture in the fill migrating to the surface. If needed, a small sandbag was placed on top of the treatment area to prevent the plaster from lifting while drying.

In addition to void filling, another frequent treatment was reduction and removal of previous fills and repairs. These fills were often higher than the surrounding original material, and varied in texture and color. Sometimes the fills covered original plaster and paint. To reduce and remove fills, they were softened with a moist, warm cotton compress. Then they were shaved with scalpels and gradually reduced in height until flush with the surrounding surface or entirely removed.

Frequently, original paint and plaster were exposed when the fill was removed.

Paint Layer

The paint layer was in good condition. No consolidation or emergency treatment was needed. While there was no retouching of the original painting, some toning of both new and previous repairs was carried out. This was done with commercial watercolors and/or dry pigments in water.

Surface Cleaning

Cleaning was relatively straightforward and involved primarily removal of grime and dust from the surface. To remove the accumulation, the fragments were surface-cleaned with a cosmetic sponge dampened with deionized water (Fig. 8). In addition to the grime, some of the fragments were dotted with isolated thick, glossy patches of PVAc adhesive. These patches were removed by swabbing acetone over the adhesive.

One fragment at the Peabody Museum had a large patch of adhesive on the surface. To treat this, conservators applied

FIGURE 8 Angelyn Bass Rivera and Leslie Rainer conserving fragments at the Museum of Northern Arizona. Note that the fragment at lower right is partially cleaned and the whitewash background has been partially removed. Photo: Angelyn Bass Rivera.

compresses of cotton impregnated with acetone to the area, and left it under foil until the PVAc adhesive softened. Swabs were then used to remove the excess adhesive, although some still remains on the surface because it could not be removed without damage to the underlying original paint and plaster layers.

Modern whitewash borders on three of the Museum of Northern Arizona fragments were removed to expose the Masonite support. The whitewash, determined to be kaolin based, had been applied for a past exhibition and was no longer aesthetically appropriate. It was easily removed with a scalpel, after which the Masonite surface was cleaned first with gum erasers and then a damp cosmetic sponge.

The three mural fragments with the facing still attached were surface-cleaned using moist cosmetic sponges on the plaster surface. The illustration board was vacuumed, and dry erasers were used to remove scuff marks on the surface. Raised edges were tacked down with rabbit skin glue. These pieces were rehoused and stored as before, in flat storage.

Conclusion

The impetus for the recent condition assessment and conservation treatment of the Jeddito mural fragments was a potential traveling exhibition planned by the Museum of Northern Arizona and the Peabody Museum. At this time, the exhibition has been postponed. Fortunately, the fragments received much-needed conservation assessment and treatment. The fragments are presently in stable condition, and the largest fragments have new secondary supports that significantly increase their rigidity and stability during handling. Also, the mural fragments at the Museum of Northern Arizona have been moved from horizontal to vertical storage, which will help protect them for the long term. The conservation treatments, specifically the reduction of overfilled repairs and cleaning, have improved the appearance of the fragments and have helped to make them more legible for examination and research (Fig. 9). In recent years, there has been a renewed interest in the study of kiva murals, especially the relationship of their iconography and design to ceramics and textiles from the same period.

Most notable in the recent history of these murals is the documentation and research accomplished by Watson Smith in the mid-twentieth century. The complex conservation treatments performed at the time, as well as his intelligent approach and thoughtfulness to documentation, analysis, and treatment, have helped to preserve the tangible mural fragments and, most importantly, aspects of their significance. Smith's work not only provided the conservators with guidance in the retreatment of the fragments, but it is an example of the value of collaboration between archaeologists and conservators and of the vital link between excavation, site conservation, and museum practice.

FIGURE 9 Fragment from Awatovi (Room 529) after treatment in 2004 (2630 NA 820.R.529.20, Museum of Northern Arizona). The two principal figures depicted in this fragment are an anthropomorphized squash maiden with leafy arms (center) and a warrior figure wearing a head-dress, kilt, and quiver with arrows and holding a banner or shield (right). It was not possible to completely remove from the Masonite the glue stains (at bottom left and upper right) from exhibition labels. Photo: Angelyn Bass Rivera.

Acknowledgments

Over the span of the recent conservation project from 1999 to 2004, numerous individuals have been involved in planning and implementing the work. The authors wish to thank the collaborators and assistants who worked on the project with us, and everyone on the staff at the Peabody Museum of Archaeology and Ethnology, Harvard University, and the Museum of Northern Arizona. We gratefully acknowledge the Peabody Museum, Harvard University, for permission to use their images.

Notes

1 Twelve of the fragments were mounted on Masonite Presdwood supports for display. Three fragments with the strappo facing still attached were mounted on illustration board for didactic purposes.

2 Louise Groll, Arlen Heginbotham, Craig Keller, Margaret Kipling, and Irene Sen.

3 The information on the Awatovi Expedition and analysis of the murals is described in detail in Watson Smith's *Kiva Mural Decorations at Awatovi and Kawaika-a* (1952), and his later publication *When Is a Kiva?* (1990).

4 The Pueblo Revolt of 1680 was an uprising of the Native American Pueblos and the Hopi against the Spanish. The rebellion, which took place throughout the southwestern United States, drove the Spanish south to El Paso (now Texas) and temporarily reestablished Pueblo Indian and Hopi independence.

5 For more information on these Pueblo murals see Dutton (1963) and Martin (1936).

6 Textiles are illustrated as clothing on the human and anthropomorphic figures. Commonly portrayed are woven shirts, braided sashes, and kilts with elaborate tassels, scarves, and headdresses.

7 Paint samples taken from the mural fragments were analyzed by some of the leading scientists of the time, including microscopic examination by Rutherford Gettens and Dr. Harry Berman at the Fogg Museum, chemical analysis by Dr. Harriet Greene at MIT, and spectrographic analysis by Dr. Rockwell Kent at Harvard (Smith 1952: 22).

8 This subtle evidence of painted striations was largely lost when the murals were removed from the walls.

9 Kiva walls with murals from Kuaua were lifted en masse and transported to a conservation laboratory where the paintings were separated layer by layer.

10 The details of excavation and mural removal are taken directly from Smith 1952: 33–52, unless noted.

11 The original field drawings with notations are in storage at the Museum of Northern Arizona in Flagstaff.

12 The adhesive solution was composed of Alvar 7-70 polyvinyl acetate (PVAc) in various combinations of solvents, with an added plasticizer (dibutylphthalate). Solvents tested included

toluene, ethyl alcohol, ethylene dichloride, acetone, cellosolve, and cellosolve acetate. Watson Smith received advice and assistance in formulating the adhesive from Frederick P. Orchard, assistant curator of Archaeology at the Peabody Museum, Harvard University, and Rutherford J. Gettens of the Fogg Art Museum.

13 Bits of newspaper adhered to the fragments were removed where possible during the recent conservation treatment.

14 Since the 1930s, when Watson Smith and others excavated and removed the murals from the walls, the fields of archaeology and conservation have evolved in their methods and techniques of excavation and study, especially in the area of ancestral Pueblo sites. Exposure of successive layers of wall paintings, and removal of murals or other features from their architectural context is no longer acceptable practice. Archaeologists, curators, and others who work with Pueblo artifacts are becoming increasingly aware of the sacredness of both movable and immovable artifacts (including mural paintings) and the need to respect the cultures and beliefs associated with them.

15 Masonite Presdwood (Masonite Corporation) is a hard composition board made of wood fibers heat-compressed into a rigid sheet.

16 The original plaster was washed, sorted, and dried to remove some of the darker particles, which made it too dark when saturated with the Cologne glue. Cologne glue is an animal glue made from leather scraps. According to Watson Smith, the mixture used was made by soaking one part dry Cologne glue in two parts water (both by weight) overnight, and then dissolving it in a double boiler. For each quart of glue produced, the following proportions of antibacterial additives were added: 1 cc oil of cloves, 1 cc carbolic acid, 1 cc thymol in a 50 percent alcohol solution, and 10 cc santophen in a 10 percent water solution (Smith 1952: 45).

17 Some of the fragments were loaned to the Museum of Modern Art in New York and other institutions for temporary exhibition.

18 Until 2004, the fragments were stored horizontally atop storage cabinets.

19 The remainder of this whitewash, which was determined to be kaolin, was removed during the recent conservation treatment.

20 Additionally, the Museum of Northern Arizona houses most of the collection of over two hundred half-scale reproductions made from the field notes, as well as the full-scale field drawings with annotations. The reproductions were executed on illustration board or Masonite using paints custom made from mineral pigments, gypsum, and casein.

21 FileMaker Pro version 5.5.

22 This analysis was carried out at Williamstown Regional Conservation Laboratory, Williamstown, Massachusetts.

23 It would have been preferable to use soil from Antelope Mesa, but this was not possible due to restricted access. Leland Dennis, Hopi community liaison for the mural project, provided us with samples of soils from nearby Hopi lands that are commonly collected and used to make modern plasters.

24 Green Analytical Laboratories in Durango, Colorado, carried out the soil analysis. Testing included soil texture, organic matter, pH, and quantitative and qualitative soluble salts. The soils used for the recent conservation (approximately three parts Hopi soil to one part topsoil) had an approximate composition of 8 percent clay, 9 percent silt, and 83 percent sand. This is comparable to the original finish plaster, which, according to Smith, had approximate proportions of calcareous material and quartz sand of 10 percent clay, 12 percent silt, and 88 percent sand. Although the material constituents of the original finish plaster varied slightly from kiva to kiva, the end product was fairly homogeneous (Smith 1952: 18).

25 The aluminum panels were custom made by SmallCorp, Greenfield, Massachusetts.

26 Deionized water was used for all conservation treatments.

27 Rabbit skin glue is a natural, nontoxic, water-soluble adhesive. It was added to the soil fill when needed to give it additional cohesion and bond strength. It was also used in a dilute solution (less than 5 percent) to reattach the plaster to its support. Rabbit skin glue was selected for use because of its moderate adhesive strength, high degree of elasticity and flexibility, strong initial bond, fairly neutral pH, and light color and translucency, which helped prevent discoloration of the treated area. An advantage of using the rabbit skin glue is that it is soluble only in water (insoluble in organic solvents and alcohol). This makes it highly compatible with the ground layer (Cologne glue and earth), providing good readhesion, while not adversely affecting the stability of the PVAc-saturated mural. In addition, the rabbit skin glue was ideal because its viscosity can be controlled by adjusting its temperature: it becomes liquid when warmed and gelatinous when cooled. Application of it as a gel helped minimize water migration and surface staining.

28 In some areas, the fragment was impregnated with PVAc and consequently was so plastic that the plaster could be lifted and replaced easily, without cracking or other damage.

Materials and Suppliers

Dry pigments: Utrecht Paints, 1030 Massachusetts Avenue, Cambridge, MA 02138; (800) 223-9132.

Hopi soil: Local Hopi source.

Local soil: Flagstaff Cinder, 6500 East Old Highway 66, Flagstaff, AZ 86004; (928) 526-0801; fax (928) 526-6580.

Primal AC33 (acrylic emulsion adhesive): Manufactured by Rohm & Haas and supplied by Talas, 20 W. 20th Street, 5th Floor, New York, NY 10011: (212) 219-0770.

Rabbit skin glue: Talas, 20 W. 20th Street, 5th Floor, New York, NY 10011; (212) 219-0770.

SP 1 Aluminum honeycomb supports: SmallCorp, P.O. Box 948, Greenfield, MA 01302; (413) 772-0889.

Winsor and Newton Watercolors: Graphaids, 3030 South La Cienega Blvd., Culver City, CA 90232; (800) 866-6601.

References

Brody, J. J. 1991. *Anasazi and Pueblo Painting.* Albuquerque: University of New Mexico Press.

Dutton, B. P. 1963. *Sun Father's Way: The Kiva Murals of Kuaua.* Albuquerque: University of New Mexico Press.

Martin, P. S. 1936. *Lowry Ruin in Southwest Colorado.* Field Museum of Natural History, Anthropology Series, vol. 23. no. 1. Chicago: Field Museum of National History.

Rainer, Leslie. 1999. Hopi kiva mural fragments at the Museum of Northern Arizona and Peabody Museum, Harvard University: Condition assessment report. Unpublished report.

Rainer, L., and A. Bass Rivera. 2003. Hopi kiva mural fragments at the Museum of Northern Arizona and Peabody Museum, Harvard University: Conservation Treatment Phase I. Unpublished report.

Rainer, L., A. Bass Rivera, and L. Vagts. 2004. Hopi kiva mural fragments at the Museum of Northern Arizona and Peabody Museum, Harvard University: Conservation Treatment Phase II. Unpublished report.

Smith, Watson. 1952. *Kiva Mural Decorations at Awatovi and Kawaika-a: With a Survey of Other Wall Paintings in the Pueblo Southwest.* Papers of the Peabody Museum of American Archaeology and Ethnology, vol. 37. Cambridge: The Peabody Museum of Archaeology and Ethnology, Harvard University.

———. 1990. *When Is a Kiva? And Other Questions about Southwestern Archaeology.* Tucson: University of Arizona Press.

Paradise: To Intervene or Not? A Review of Some Past Conservation Approaches for the Treatment of Clay-Based Chinese Wall Paintings and a Set of Seventeenth-Century Chinese Gate Panels

Kathleen M. Garland and Joe C. Rogers

In 2001, the Nelson-Atkins Museum of Art in Kansas City, Missouri, received a generous grant from the Getty Foundation to conduct a condition survey of three of its most important works of Chinese art: the wall painting of the *Paradise of the Tejaprabha Buddha,* ca. 1300–1324, the *Zinhua Ceiling,* ca. 1444, and the *Gate Panels,* mid-seventeenth century. These works were acquired by the Chinese dealer C. T. Loo and installed in 1932 for the opening of the Nelson-Atkins Museum in a room constructed to provide the atmosphere of a Chinese temple (Fig. 1). Both the wall painting and the gates have earthen components that have largely contributed to past treatment choices and their present condition. This paper focuses first on the gates and then on the wall painting, and compares the condition of this painting to other detached wall paintings that have had a similar conservation history, reflecting past museum practices in the United States.

Gate Panels

The original provenance of the gates is unknown, but their high quality suggests that they may have had some imperial connection and are probably from Beijing. The gates were originally intended to provide a decorative screen on a building in the summer months to allow privacy while cooling breezes circulated through the building. In the winter the latticework would be pasted over with paper to keep some warmth in the building. Gates of this type—especially those with little modern restoration—have become rare. It has always been assumed that the Nelson-Atkins gates were painted with Asian lacquer, which is quite weather resistant, over an earthen ground layer.

The gates have a China fir wood substrate[1] with joins covered with a woven textile interleaf. The original pink ground layer was identified by John Twilley[2] as calcite and talc in a glue binder (Twilley 2003a). This often incorporated a matted layer of fibers on the back of the panels. Vermilion paint in an oil binder was applied over this. A subsequent repainting, probably done in the twentieth century, involved a gray ground with calcite, talc, and glue binder and a red lead paint in a drying oil binder (Fig. 2). No Asian lacquer is present, and visiting Chinese scholars have indicated that tung oil was frequently used as a binder for clays and paints. The applied carved roundels were originally gilded with leaf. The desiccated textile, matted fibers, and dry ground layers were the primary source of deterioration on the gates. Flaking and delamination has occurred on most surfaces, particularly on the back, or inside, where a thick mat of unidentified plant fibers was applied with the gray ground material.

Securing these layers was challenging. Most commonly used adhesives, such as cellulose ethers, acrylics, or animal glues, were unsatisfactory, primarily because the adhesives darkened the ground layer, plant fibers, and the degraded paint film, or were not strong enough. The paint film was somewhat to very soluble in those solvents safe to use in public spaces (the conservators were on display for the project), while water-based adhesives significantly swelled the ground layers. Gentle heat softened the paint and usually resulted in a burnished surface.

After much consideration, we adopted the following steps. The matted fibers and powdery exposed ground layers were consolidated with repeated applications of thick wheat-starch paste. This was sometimes pushed in with some force

FIGURE 1 The *Paradise of the Tejaprabha Buddha* and the *Gate Panels* in the "Chinese Temple" at the Nelson-Atkins Museum of Art, Kansas City, Missouri.

using fingertips or spatulas. The wheat-starch paste did not darken the ground or fibers to any remarkable degree yet secured them to the clay-and-wood substrate. The paste was dry enough to avoid significant swelling.

Subsurface delamination of the paint layers was reattached with a solution of Paraloid B-72 at about 1:3 in acetone. The solution had to be very carefully injected, and every attempt was made to control it so that excess did not run over the red paint. Excess could be quickly wiped off with one roll of acetone on a swab, but anything more darkened the degraded paint. No visual compensation was done.

Paradise of the Tejaprabha Buddha

The wall painting *Paradise of the Tejaprabha Buddha* (Fig. 3) is from the Guangsheng Lower Monastery, located in southern Shanxi Province. The monastery may date to the Tang

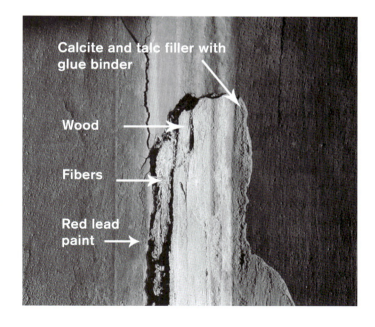

FIGURE 2 Detail of the *Gate Panels.*

FIGURE 3 *Paradise of the Tejaprabha Buddha*, at the Nelson-Atkins Museum of Art.

Dynasty, but was rebuilt after an earthquake in 1303. The monastery had close ties with the Yuan imperial court. In the 1930s the monastery was visited by scholar Laurence Sickman and others, who noted that paintings from the gable walls in the main hall had been sold to C. T. Loo in 1927 in order to make repairs to the clay and wood buildings. Two other paintings had been removed from the front hall before 1927. The two paintings believed to be from the front hall are now in the University Museum of the University of Pennsylvania. Of the two believed to be from the main temple, one is now in the Nelson-Atkins Museum, while the other is located at the Metropolitan Museum of Art in New York (Lippe 1965; Steinhardt 1987). All of these paintings were damaged by the removal process.

Scholarly study of the Nelson-Atkins painting has been impeded by poor-quality photography resulting from awkward architectural spaces in the gallery. The 2001 conservation survey and new developments in digital photography provided an excellent opportunity to document and study the painting (Miller et al. 2003). Some eighty-eight separate digital images were taken of the wall that were then assembled to make a complete image of the wall painting. The survey was documented using Adobe Photoshop 7.0 on each of the eighty-eight images. Each image represents an area of about 127 cm square on the painting. There is also a corresponding raking light image to better understand the condition of the surface. Though fragile, the wall painting appears to be in good condition and no treatment is necessary, though a monitoring program has been established.

Installation and Previous Treatment

Research in the museum archives and at other museums suggests that the wall paintings collected by C. T. Loo were detached from buildings in China in small sections that were then reassembled by restorers in Paris. It is likely that the Nelson-Atkins painting was pasted with paper and possibly a peach gum[3] (*Zhongguo wenwu bao* 2003; Twilley and Garland 2003) then cut up into small sections roughly 40 cm square. These small sections were shipped to Paris and reassembled by Loo's restorers onto larger plaster of paris blocks, which were then shipped to Kansas City. Records in the archives indicate that the museum consulted with Rutherford Gettens and George Stout during the installation process. There are also written recommendations for the mounting process and several black-and-white negatives at the Harvard University

Art Museums' Straus Center for Conservation. Correspondence suggests that the Nelson-Atkins's director, Paul Gardner, may have been personally responsible for some of the repairs. It seems likely that the proper left side of the painting was trimmed to fit into the architectural space. No further treatment has been recorded since the 1932 installation.

The survey determined that the larger plaster of paris blocks were installed following Gettens's recommendations. Metal angle braces were used to support each of the restored plaster blocks separately on the museum's brick tile wall, leaving a 4-inch gap between the brick wall and the painting. Metal ties, located in the corner of each block, were encased in "pillars" of plaster and used to align the blocks. The metal ties actually go through the wall painting; their location can be seen as 2-inch circular deformations in the corners of each of the plaster of paris blocks. The holes for the ties were filled with plaster, and the original painted surface was replaced over the holes wherever possible. Vinylite A, a Dupont polyvinyl acetate, was the recommended adhesive for friable areas, although it has not been identified in the survey. Gettens had previously published on the use of polyvinyl acetate adhesives for paintings on clay or earthen supports, and it became a preferred material in subsequent wall painting treatments in North America (Gettens 1932).

Although heavily restored, the original section lines used to cut the painting from the temple wall are still quite visible, as are the gaps between the larger blocks of plaster of paris. These gaps may have been filled with a 5–10 percent shellac mixture with 1:2 parts of clay (unspecified), toned with earth pigments, as suggested by Gettens.

The painting and remaining earthen support is about 1–2 cm thick now. Conservation scientist John Twilley analyzed some forty samples of the wall painting (Twilley 2003b, Twilley and Garland 2003). It is made of a layer of tempera paint over a white ground, usually kaolin, and a thin clay layer consisting of straw and dried mud. Original pigments include white kaolin clay, gypsum white, lead white, blue azurite, red lead, cinnabar red, dark red hematite, iron oxide yellow, lamp black, charcoal black, and green atacamite. The medium could not be identified.

It is possible that the green atacamite is actually manmade from corroded bronze, not the naturally occurring copper ores (Twilley 2003b, Twilley and Garland 2003). Crystals of tin oxide can be seen in scanning electron microscope (SEM) images. These were found only in the green pigments, and both copper and tin are components of bronze. The structure of the tin compounds did not show any cleavage or fracturing,

as might be expected had they been present in minerals undergoing pulverization for pigments. The lead white and the gypsum crystals are very small and have undergone considerable dissolution. There is also a thin, unidentifiable coating on the top surface. Infrared spectroscopy did not clearly identify the material, but the spectra are not incompatible with plant gums. This layer could be the remains of the facing adhesive used when the painting was cut from the earthen wall in the temple. It may also be related to the Vinylite A recommended by Gettens.

The restoration colors are easy to distinguish and include viridian green, copper arsenate colors, synthetic green malachite, red lead with red lake, iron oxide, and white lead. Careful visual observation suggests that about 10–15 percent of the painting has been painted or overpainted by Loo's restorers. This overpaint corresponds to the areas around each of the small sections originally cut out of the wall.

Notes on Some Other Chinese Paintings on Clay Supports

The Nelson-Atkins Museum has a number of other detached wall paintings on clay or earthen supports. Until recently the museum had a hands-off policy toward conservation of Asian material, while actively encouraging the treatment of Western painting, with two notable exceptions described below.

Two Bodhisattvas Preparing Incense

Two Bodhisattvas Preparing Incense (accession no. 50–64a) was acquired from Loo in 1950, and he was probably responsible for the painted fragment's being mounted on a plaster of paris block. Some damage occurred in transit, and another painting was detected underneath the first painting. These two paintings were separated and have been dated to AD 951 and 937 (Sickman and Roth 1952; Landau and Muller 1991; Ho n.d.). These two paintings, believed to have come from a temple in Henan, China, were separated by the museum's paintings conservator, James Roth, in 1952, using techniques that were probably close to the ones used by Loo's restorers in the 1920s and 1930s.

Separation Treatment 1952

This treatment was highly publicized in *Time* magazine, the *Kansas City Star*, and other publications,[4] as well as recorded by Roth (Roth n.d.), so we have a good documentary record of the treatment (Fig. 4). Roth applied a facing of Tosa Japanese paper to the front of the later wall painting with polyvinyl acetate (concentration and solvents not mentioned) and then cut through the paper and painting to a depth of 1/8 inch. The clay backing of the top painting was sliced through horizontally to separate the top painting from the one underneath. The clay ground was then thinned down, leaving "a certain amount to preserve the texture of the painting." The clay still attached to the back of the transferred painting was sized with gelatin and dried under slight pressure. A piece of thin silk netting was then applied to the back of the mud, and thin gesso was used to level the package so that all sections would be in the same plane. A sheet of Masonite was sized with rabbit skin glue, and a layer of gesso composed of gelatin and whiting was applied. The section was then pressed and leveled into the wet gesso. When dry, the facing was removed with toluene. The losses between the cut lines were filled with more gesso and inpainted using an unspecified technique. The remaining paint is in excellent condition, with little Loo

restoration, unlike the "skinned" surface found on many other detached paintings.

The paint on the concealed painting, *Kuan-Yin Bodhisattva* (50-64b) was "soft and chalky," but Roth was able to remove the clay mechanically, except for a final film. Brushing this remaining layer was "injurious," but the problem was successfully solved using an Electrolux vacuum cleaner. The conservator stresses the benefits of the vacuum cleaner, which suggests that this was an early and revolutionary use in our field. Everything was then coated and impregnated with a 5 percent Vinylite solution (solvent again not specified). The losses were filled with plaster of paris (Roth n.d.).

Inpainting of the early painting was closely supervised by the curator, Laurence Sickman. A preliminary study was done on a large photograph after studying related Chinese material; in fact, the missing left hand was modeled on the later painting of *Two Bodhisattvas Preparing Incense*. Dry pigments and gelatin were used. The image was made as com-

FIGURE 4 James Roth, the Nelson-Atkins Museum's paintings conservator, in 1952, separating *Two Bodhisattvas Preparing Incense* from the underlying painting: (a) applying a facing; (b) cutting through the paper, paint, and clay layers; (c) separating the two paintings at the clay interface; (d) attaching a section of the painting and facing to the Masonite board using gesso. Photos courtesy of the Conservation Department, the Nelson-Atkins Museum of Art.

(a)

(b)

(c)

(d)

plete as possible, and the large losses were painted with cross-hatching.

The cut lines are still quite visible on the top painting, especially in raking light. Other than this inevitable damage, the 1952 treatment was generally a success. The painted surfaces on both paintings are still stable and visually well integrated. The Vinylite coating is perhaps not what conservators would apply now, but the appearance is pleasing, and the resin does not seem to have yellowed to any great degree.

The original 1930s plaster support is more of a problem, since there is interior iron reinforcement that may be causing a few fine cracks on the front plaster layers. Roth's Masonite panel has worked better than the original plaster, although conservators today would avoid thinning any original clay ground layers.

Treatment 2004

The plaster of paris support under the bottom painting has numerous cracks, and a metal detector indicated the presence of ferrous material. The cracks were consolidated with repeated applications of Paraloid B-72, 25 percent w/v in acetone (after testing that the solution would not bleed through to the front and that the paint would not be altered by the solvent). This resin should not interfere with any future treatments should they be necessary.

In order to prevent any flexing of the plaster of paris, a backing was applied. The reverse of the plaster support was first sealed with an isolating layer of Paraloid B-72, 1:4 in acetone. A sheet of Japanese mulberry paper was adhered over the cracks on the back with the same resin, to prevent any structural adhesives from migrating into the cracks in the plaster and creating a difficult-to-reverse mechanical bond. An aluminum honeycomb panel was prepared by roughening the surface of the metal and drilling small holes through the panel in selected areas. The panel was adhered to the back of the plaster support using dabs of Epotek 370 epoxy. A discreet steel frame will replace the wood frame. The panel and frame should prevent the painting from flexing. The holes will serve as solvent ports to dissolve the isolating layer of B-72, should it ever become necessary to remove the panel. A steel frame will also be applied to Roth's Masonite panel to prevent the top painting from flexing.

Bodhisattva Seated on a Lotus

Bodhisattva Seated on a Lotus (52-6) is a fragment from the same temple in Henan as the two separated paintings. It also was acquired through Loo and is featured in his 1949 publica-tion *Chinese Frescos of Northern Sung.* Two painted elements visible in the upper corners of the black-and-white image are no longer visible in the painting. It may be that the figures in the corners were added to the composition by Loo, and then removed, since there is no trace of them now in ultraviolet radiation or X-radiography.

This fragment is typical of the type of restoration found on paintings that have been through Loo's hands. Under magnification, the uppermost layers of pigment look "skinned" from overcleaning or overtreatment. The upper surfaces of the black outlines are often lost. Overpainting is limited to damaged areas and to strengthening the original black outlines. The cut lines, however, are heavily restored. In this case the surface does appear to have a disfiguring yellow coating.

The plaster of paris supports have numerous iron rods. The iron used in Loo-period restorations has usually rusted, which results in cracks and losses in the plaster. The plaster support, often with incorporated textile, seems to have been the preferred mount for every fragment we have seen; obviously this is not a suitable material by today's standards. Surprisingly, we have not seen any soluble-salt problems from the plaster. The most common problem is flaking due to poor adhesion to the clay layers or from plaster fills that pull at the original paint.

James Roth treated the fourteenth-century *Illustration to the Travels of Sudhana* (47-88) in 1967–68. It may also come from the Guangsheng Monastery. Roth's records indicate that there was an insoluble coating and numerous old restorations.[5] An early image indicates that the painting consists of three fragments. The surface was faced with Tosa tissue and an unspecified methacrylate. The mud on the back was thinned to 3/16 inch, then leveled with gelatin and "Honan mud." This jar of silt is still in the conservation lab and is purported to have been collected in China to do Chinese-style "restorations."

The painting fragments were placed under weights for twenty-four hours to flatten them. PVA Vinac B7 in methanol and toluene was used to infuse the back, another leveling layer of plaster was added, and it was then sealed with PVA AYAF. The sections were then adhered with microcrystalline wax, Bareco V155W, to a Masonite panel on a hot table. The fills were made of Honan mud and gelatin. The whole painting was coated with Lucite 44[6] and the losses extensively inpainted with PVA AYAF in methanol. A final coating of Lucite was applied.

The painting is in good condition, although with a rather shiny and varnished appearance. The use of a wax adhesive, the emphasis on flattening and thinning, and the use of synthetic varnishes suggest techniques that were in use for European panel painting treatments at the time. This is more the case than with the 1952 treatment of the separated murals.

The Metropolitan Museum of Art, New York

The *Pure Land of Bhaisajyaguru* (65.29.2) is believed to have been located opposite the Nelson-Atkins painting in the temple in Shanxi. It too was removed from the temple by Loo in 1927, but was given to the Metropolitan Museum in 1954, almost thirty years later (Jing 1991, 2002).

European painting treatments also influenced the 1957 conservation of this work. Fortunately the treatment was documented (Metropolitan Museum 1957), although not signed. Five panels had been previously treated at the Fogg Conservation Center by Elizabeth Jones (in 1949) before Loo "decided that the treatment would be too great of an investment at the time" (Jones 1955). At that time they were cleaned with naphtha, infused with 40 percent polyvinyl acetate (unspecified) in ethanol and diacetone alcohol. The black lines were reinforced with 10 percent PVA in ethanol. Soap, water, and naphtha removed some of the "yellowish discoloration" from the flesh tones. The fills were inpainted with pastel and size, and a "coating" was applied using PVA and Santocel "C," an early aerogel matting agent marketed by Monsanto (Jones 1955).

The painting arrived at the Metropolitan Museum of Art in three major units, the small sections having already been assembled into 56 larger blocks, similar to those in the large Nelson-Atkins painting. The plaster of paris on the back of the three units was penciled with "P. Camerre"—the master mason's initials. Scraps from a Paris newspaper were found around the iron mounts; they dated to October 1931. A small piece of the original Asian paper facing was also discovered; it became sticky when wet. Previous restorations had been done with a water-soluble tempera (none of the 1930s restorations we have encountered have resolubilized). The original clay ground layers were identified as loess, sand, rice chaff, broken bamboo, wild oats, some charcoal, paper, cloth, hair, and snail shells.

To briefly outline this massive treatment (Metropolitan Museum 1957): The fills were removed with various solvents, detergents, and water. The front was infused with a 5 percent PVA solution (Dupont Vinylite AYAF) in slow-drying solvents such as toluene, alcohols, and ethylene dichloride, followed by applications of diacetone alcohol until no more was absorbed. This was repeated with 10, 15, and 20 percent solutions by

weight. The front was faced with another layer of PVA in methanol to "insulate the surface." Two layers of paper and one of muslin were then attached with rabbit skin glue. The units were turned over, and the plaster mount was removed by "striking with a mallet or a hammer." The coarsest layer of clay was removed, and the remaining clay was infused in the same manner as the front.

The units were attached to wire-mesh and steel channeling using inserted tie wires and a "molten mortar" of beeswax, damar, and gum elemi (7:2:1 by weight), with kaolin and jute fibers added. Heat was maintained using a heat blanket at 150°F (66°C). The facings were then removed. The inpainting is not described, although it was done to blend with surrounding areas. All the section lines are pleasingly toned and somewhat lower than the surface. The whole has an integrated appearance without looking "restored." The coatings do not seem to have yellowed significantly, and the wax lining adhesive was examined several years ago and was felt to be secure, even though this gallery was not air-conditioned for many years (Stone 2003).

It is interesting to compare this treatment with the Nelson-Atkins painting where the Loo fills and overpaint are extensive and quite obvious, and no attempt has been made to integrate the section lines.

University Museum, University of Pennsylvania, Philadelphia

Two paintings also from the Guangsheng Monastery are now in the University Museum in Philadelphia. Both were acquired from Loo in the early 1930s and have been attributed to after 1472, nearly two hundred years later than the two from the same temple discussed above (Jing 1991). The University Museum paintings are very similar in style and composition to those at the Nelson-Atkins Museum and the Metropolitan Museum, although the heavy black lines in the Philadelphia paintings suggest that considerable reinforcing may have taken place at a later date. The two paintings have a thick yellow varnish with a marked sheen. The artist who worked on them left a note in the University Museum files dated 1928 indicating that she had used white shellac as the varnish, then Weber's Matvar to "preserve and protect" the painting. In a transcribed letter dated 1956 she also states that she used Matvar, "a transparent harmless, protective solution" found at art stores. However, she then states that she did not use shellac because she was worried about deterioration and the effect on color. There is no record of any other treatment.[7]

Conclusions

These wall paintings, particularly those from the Guangsheng Monastery, need further technical study to complement the stylistic and architectural studies (Jing 1991; Steinhardt 1984, 1987). Has dating been influenced by different approaches to restoration? Buddhist temple painting is conservative, and strong black outlines are part of the traditional style of these paintings. The black outlines on faces, hands, and feet of the Nelson-Atkins painting seem to have been reinforced with black paint and coated with a shiny resin in the twentieth century to improve the visual coherence of the damaged image. The Metropolitan Museum's black lines have a confidence and artistry that seems lacking in much of the Nelson-Atkins painting (Fig. 5). The black outlines on the University Museum paintings are very dark and pronounced. How much of this is due to workshop differences, style, condition, or later restoration?

This outline of museum practices began as an investigation of the materials used by C. T. Loo's restorers and subsequent conservators as part of a conservation survey. We needed to better understand any deterioration mechanisms that may have taken place and what problems we might expect in the future. However, we have become increasingly interested in the past treatment history, in what has actually happened to the surface of the wall paintings in early restorations and how that is affecting interpretation and dating. There are numerous other detached Chinese wall paintings in museum collections that should be included in a more comprehensive study. More technical analysis is needed, and it should be integrated with the work of art historians to better understand how past treatments may or may not be affecting stylistic studies of these and other Chinese wall paintings. Related paintings still in situ should be documented and compared by scholars, conservators, and conservation scientists so that

FIGURE 5 Comparison of the feet of the central figures: (a) *Paradise of the Tejaprabha Buddha.* Photo courtesy of the Nelson-Atkins Museum of Art; (b) *Pure Land of Bhaisajyaguru.* Photo courtesy of the Metropolitan Museum of Art, New York.

damage caused by the transfer process and subsequent restoration can be fully understood. Nevertheless, our preliminary examination of these detached wall paintings has made one thing clear: removing these delicate structures causes irreparable damage and loss, and should only be considered as a very last preservation measure.

Acknowledgments

Financial assistance: The Getty Foundation.

Art historians: Marc Wilson, Yang Xiaoneng, Lu Ling-en, Jason Stueber.

Conservators and scientists: Steve Bonham, Elisabeth Batchelor, John Twilley, Jerry Podany, Zhang Zhiping, Eric Gordon, Dale Benson, Paul Benson, Christine Downie, Cary Beattie Maguire, Richard Stone.

Administrative assistance: Dinah Henderson.

Notes

1   Wood identification provided by botanist A. Wiedenhoeft, United States Department of Agriculture, for Wood Anatomy Research, March 2004.

2   John Twilley is an art conservation scientist whose business, Analysis and Materials Science for the Preservation of Cultural Property, is located in Hawthorne, NY.

3   Polysaccharide exudate of *Prunus persica*. In 1955, Ru Anshi briefly described the methods used for detaching the Tang Dynasty tomb paintings at Zhangjiawan, Xianyang, Shaanxi province in 1952. The steps were: (1) cleaning the mud on the wall surface with water from top to bottom, (2) drying the wall with coal fire, (3) attaching fabrics to the painting with peach gums, (4) detaching the painting with a thin-bladed knife from bottom to top, and (5) sandwiching the painting with wood blocks for shipping. (*Zhongguo wenwu bao*. 2003; translated by Ling-en Lu.)

4   *Time*, March 6, 1953; *Kansas City Star*, March 1, 1953; *Life*, October 5, 1953.

5   The Nelson-Atkins Museum archives.

6   N-butyl methacrylate, also known as Elvacite 2044.

7   University Museum, University of Pennsylvania, Philadelphia. Correspondence in the Registration Department.

Materials and Suppliers

Bareco V155W microcrystalline wax (apparently no longer manufactured): Baker Hughes, 2001 Rankin Road, Houston, TX 77073; (713) 625-6010.

Beeswax (beeswax contains about 10%–14% hydrocarbons, in addition to alcohols, fatty acids, and esters; the primary component is myricyl palmitate): Talas, 20 W. 20th St., 5th floor, New York, NY 10011; (212) 219-0770.

Damar (triterpenoid resin): Conservation Support Systems, P.O. Box 91746, Santa Barbara, CA 93190; (800) 482-6299.

Gum elemi (soft, sticky natural resin derived from trees of the family *Burseraceae;* used as a plasticizer for modifying consistency of varnishes in combination with waxes for relining): Talas, 20 W. 20th St., 5th floor, New York, NY 10011; (212) 219-0770.

Lucite 44 (now Elvacite 2044; polymethacrylate or n-butyl methacrylate): Talas, 20 W. 20th St., 5th floor, New York, NY 10011; (212) 219-0770.

Masonite is a type of hardboard building material first made in 1924 by William H. Mason, a wet-process fiberboard composed of fine wood fibers compressed into a rigid sheet using heat. The fibers are held together by the natural binders from the pulp. Masonite boards do not warp easily but may break under pressure. Standard Masonite Presdwood is brown and has one very smooth surface; the other has a wire screen impression (www.mfa.org/ _cameo; accessed December 2004).

Paraloid B-72 (ethyl methacrylate/methyl acrylate copolymer): Manufactured by Rohm & Haas Co., Philadelphia, PA; supplied by Conservation Support Systems, P.O. Box 91746, Santa Barbara, CA 93190; (800) 482-6299.

PVA AYAF (low-molecular weight thermoplastic polyvinyl acetate resin; AYAF was previously sold as Vinylite A) Manufactured by Bakelite, Union Carbide; supplied by Conservation Support Systems, P.O. Box 91746, Santa Barbara, CA 93190; (800) 482-6299.

Vinylite (low-molecular weight thermoplastic polyvinyl acetate resin; the name was formerly a trademark for polyvinyl acetate resins currently sold under the names AYAC, AYAB, AYAA, AYAF, and AYAT): Manufactured by Bakelite, Union Carbide; supplied by Conservation Support Systems, P.O. Box 91746, Santa Barbara, CA 93190; (800) 482-6299.

Weber's Matvar (may be similar to Martin Weber Matvar 53 Varnish, which is a multipurpose varnish containing turpentine and naphtha according to the MSDS): Manufactured by Martin F. Weber Company; distributed by Dick Blick Art Materials, P.O. Box 1267, Galesburg, IL 61402.

Wheat Starch Paste No. 301: Talas, 20 W. 20th St., 5th floor, New York, NY 10011; (212) 219-0770.

White shellac (transparent, colorless shellac): White shellac is decolorized with bleach and available from hardware stores.

References

Garland, K. 2004. Surveying Paradise: The conservation survey of a clay-based Yuan Dynasty wall painting. Paper presented at Second International Conference on Conservation Along the Silk Road, Dunhuang, China, June.

Gettens, R. 1932. Transport des fresques orientales sur de nouveaux supports. *Mouseion* 17–18:107–12.

Ho, W. n.d. A Five Dynasties date (951–953) group of esoteric Buddhist paintings from Cisheng-si, Wen Xian, northern Henan province. Unpublished paper.

Jing, A. 1991. The Yuan Buddhist mural of the paradise of Bhaisajyaguru. *Metropolitan Museum Journal* 26:147–66.

———. 2002. *The Water God's Temple of the Guangsheng Monastery: Cosmic Function of Art, Ritual, and Theater.* Leiden: Brill.

Jones, E. 1955. Correspondence. Straus Center for Conservation, Harvard University Art Museums, Cambridge.

Landau, A., and N. Muller. 1991. The Chinese Buddhist mural at Princeton. Seminar paper for ART401, Princeton University.

Lippe, A., 1965. Buddha and the holy multitude. *Metropolitan Museum of Art Bulletin*, May.

Loo, C. 1949. *Chinese Frescos of the Northern Sung.* New York and Paris: C. T. Loo.

Metropolitan Museum of Art. 1957. Conservation report. Sherman Fairchild Center for Objects Conservation, The Metropolitan Museum of Art, New York.

Miller, J., L. Meluso, and K. Garland. 2003. Digital imaging solutions for the reproduction and conservation documentation of a Yuan Dynasty mural painting, *Tejaprabha Buddha and Attendants* (c. 1300), at The Nelson-Atkins Museum of Art. *CIDOC/ADIT-2003*:83.

Roth, J. n.d. The discovery and subsequent separation of two layers of ancient Chinese wall painting. Report or draft for presentation, Conservation Department, The Nelson-Atkins Museum.

Sickman, L., and J. Roth. 1952. The separation of two layers of ancient Chinese wall-painting. *Artibus Asiae* 15:145–50.

Steinhardt, N. S. 1984. The Yuan Dynasty main hall: Guangsheng-si Lower Monastery and Yongle Gong. In *Chinese Traditional Architecture*, eds. N. S. Steinhardt et al. New York: China Institute in America, China House Gallery.

———. 1987. Zhu Haogu reconsidered: A new date for the ROM painting and the Southern Shanxi Buddhist-Daoist style. *Artibus Asiae* 47:5–19.

Stone, Richard (conservator, Metropolitan Museum of Art, New York). 2003. Personal communication.

Twilley, J. 2003a. Analysis of decorative layers from 17th century temple gates. Unpublished report, Nelson-Atkins Museum of Art, Conservation Department.

———. Painting materials and deterioration phenomena in the Yuan Dynasty wall painting from the Guangsheng-si Lower Monastery, Nelson-Atkins Museum Art. Unpublished report, Nelson-Atkins Museum of Art, Conservation Department.

Twilley, J., and K. Garland. 2003. Painting materials and deterioration phenomena in a Yuan Dynasty wall painting. Second Forbes Symposium, Freer and Sackler Galleries, Smithsonian Institution, Washington, DC, September.

Zhongguo wenwu bao. 2003. Ke zai chuli xing fanyin chu de dongtai baohu linian (A dynamic concept of conservation as seen from the re-installable [wall painting]). *Zhongguo wenwu bao*, Sept. 9.

The Nebamun Wall Paintings of the British Museum

Eric Miller

The Nebamun Wall Paintings, a collection of Eighteenth Dynasty tomb paintings from Thebes in ancient Egypt, are among the most treasured possessions of the British Museum. They are exquisite works of art (James 1985: 26–33). A curatorial plan to display them in a new setting that will do justice to their magnificence has been in existence for some time. However, a condition survey carried out in March 2000, revealed that most of them are in urgent need of conservation. These two issues combined gave the impetus for the launch of a major program of archaeological reevaluation involving scientific analysis to underpin and support the conservation of the paintings.

The conservation project, begun in November 2001, is complex and wide ranging, and it has not been possible to cover all of it in this paper. A brief description of the historical background of the paintings is followed by details of the condition of the paintings encountered during the initial examination, the conservation issues raised, and the treatments that are currently in progress. A fuller account is planned, however, drawing together all of the work carried out by curators, scientists, and conservators; that publication will appear after completion of the conservation, which is scheduled for 2006.

There are eleven wall painting fragments in the British Museum's collection[1] and they are referred to informally according to theme. The following is a list in inventory number order:

Census of Cattle	EA37976
Fowling in the Marshes	EA37977
Census of Geese	EA37978
Tomb Owner	EA37979
Bringing Produce	EA37980
Banqueting Scene with Musicians	EA37981
Harvest Scene	EA37982
Garden Pool	EA37983
Banqueting Scene with Dancers	EA37984
Offering Table	EA37985
Banqueting Scene with Guests	EA37986

The themes are standard for the decoration of tomb chapels of the period. They fill the space for the cult of the tomb owner with images evoking his wealth and status and the life he wishes to contrive after death. The themes are treated with individuality and are chosen and adapted to suit the tomb owner's career. Others are unique to the tomb owner's life, and together their purpose was to magically shape a world for him in the afterlife. *Fowling in the Marshes* is an example of a traditional iconic motif; it shows an idealized episode in which Nebamun is seen hunting birds as a leisure pursuit. It was originally half of a symmetrical composition, which also showed Nebamun spearing fish. Here he is holding caught birds, while he takes aim with a throwing stick in the form of a serpent. The scene is also charged with eroticism and symbolism, primarily concerned with the concept of rebirth, while certain elements can be read as symbolizing his triumph over chaos (Miller and Parkinson 2001).

The banqueting scenes are a very standard motif, showing a feast in honor of the tomb owner, and the *Offering Table* is a gift of food to Nebamun from his son and heir; traces of two figures representing the two protagonists are visible at either side. The *Garden Pool* shows his estate, inhabited by the goddess of the sycamore tree who presents him with fruit.

One wall was decorated with farm animals being presented to Nebamun from his estates. The hieroglyphic text in *Census of Cattle* relates the herdsman's remark to the other attendants as the cattle are being assembled for Nebamun. He is saying, "Come on! Get away! Do not speak in the presence of the praised one. He detests people talking. He does what is right. He will not ignore any complaint. Pass on in quiet and in order. He won't take anyone's side. He knows all the affairs, does the scribe and counter of grain of [Amun], Neb . . ." (Manniche 1988: 136–57).

The *Harvest Scene* is a standard motif, but one that was very relevant to Nebamun's job as a grain accountant. The caption/hieroglyphic text here relates the inspecting official's assistant's remark: "As the great god who is in the sky endures, the stela is correct, standing in its [place]"[2] (Manniche 1988: 136–57).

Historical Background

Nebamun was a member of the elite class. He was a grain accountant of the temple, which owned and irrigated major areas of the land under cultivation. His title appears in the tomb; it is "scribe and counter of grain" and sometimes includes "in the granary of divine offerings of Amun" (Manniche 1988: 136–57), which refers to the temple estates of the state god of Egypt.[3] He lived in Thebes in the Eighteenth Dynasty, and the style of painting dates him to the reign of Amenhotep III–IV—that is to say, around 1400 BC. At that time, Egypt was enjoying a long period of security as a consequence of its acquisition of wealth and power, and in the ensuing domestic climate, art and architecture flowered. Painting had had an important role in tomb decoration for millennia, but the creation of royal tombs at Thebes in the Eighteenth Dynasty turned tomb building into a well-organized local industry.

At that time, the tombs of the pharaohs and people of high rank, such as Nebamun, were cut into the rock of the hills of the west bank at Thebes. Teams of masons excavated the tombs, and sculptors carved decorative themes into the walls in low relief. Where the limestone was not of sufficient quality to accept fine carving, as in most private tombs including Nebamun's, walls were left rough for plastering and painting. A mud plaster *arriccio*[4] was prepared using Nile alluvium mixed with chopped straw, and this was used to make the walls flat and regular. One or two coats of a setting plaster made by heating gypsum were applied over the mud plaster to provide smooth surfaces suitable for painting. Analysis performed on a sample of the *intonaco* of *Geese* identified it as gypsum (Dinsmore and Howard 1988).

One or more draftsmen drew the imagery in outline, using a thin red wash, and color was applied to this by painters working in teams (Bryan 2001: 63–72).

Modern History

The Nebamun wall painting fragments were removed from the tomb chapel in 1820 by Giovanni d'Athanasi (1798–1854), acting on behalf of Henry Salt (1780–1827), who took up the position of British proconsul in Egypt in 1816. Salt sold the paintings to the British Museum, and they arrived there in 1821. At that time, archaeology was not an organized discipline; antiquities were simply removed from sites by collectors, and provenances were often not recorded. No record survives of the precise location of Nebamun's tomb. It is thought to be in the northern part of Dra Abu el-Naga, which is occupied by tombs of the elite. But a village has since sprung up in part of the area, and it may be that the site has been built over (Parkinson 2004).

At the British Museum, the wall paintings were placed in molds and mounts were cast around them in gypsum plaster. No account of this process was made at the time, but the task would have been made difficult by their fragile nature and the uneven depth of the mud plaster. During the recent removal of the mount attached to *Garden Pool*, fragments of newspaper were retrieved. They may have been used in a piecemeal casting process. One of them contains a date of May 1832, which is the first indication of when the paintings were mounted.

The water used in these mounting systems has been the cause of most of the woes suffered by the paintings since then, and as explained later, subsequent attempts to remedy them have often caused more damage (see "Past Treatments").

Technical Examination

Part of the examination process is to look analytically with the aid of magnification at the painters' and plasterers' work. The painters clearly were not simply blocking in color in a purely mechanical way. On the contrary, they were highly skilled colorists (James 1985: 26–33; Bryan 2001: 63–72), and in the interests of a greater understanding of their skills, records are being kept of observations that elucidate some of their techniques. The Eighteenth Dynasty was a stylistically developmental period, and it may be that some of these techniques were also innovative.

At the same time, a scientific investigation is being conducted to identify the materials used by the painters: pigments, paint media, and varnishes. The plaster layers are also the subject of a detailed scientific study, and as well as increasing our understanding of the plasterers' techniques, this is expected to resolve the issue of a common provenance for the fragments. Study has been concluded so far only on stylistic grounds (Manniche 1988: 136–57), and verification will be sought from statistical comparisons of types of aggregates and their ratios. Additionally, as the mud plaster layers are made accessible, it will be possible to make a comprehensive scientific survey of the plant material that was used as an additive.

Present Condition

The other part of the examination process is to assess and record the condition of the paint and plaster and the degree of separation between them, in order to inform a conservation strategy. To give a formal structure to this process, two paintings were selected as representative of the collection and examined in order to identify categories of impairment, for example, loss of paint, flaking paint, impact damage, and the like. Depending on each painting's size, between thirty and seventy-five hours is devoted to a detailed microscopic survey, and each category of impairment is mapped on a black-and-white image using a marker pen (Fig. 1). These maps will ultimately be scanned and saved as layers in Adobe Photoshop and filed in a subdirectory dedicated to that painting.

As stated earlier, the wet plaster cast directly onto ancient mud plasters in the nineteenth century to form mounts was the single most important cause of impaired condition. Water was released into the mud, and it permeated the ancient *intonaco* to a distance of about 10 cm from the edges before evaporating. The most serious consequence of this was that a great deal of paint was loosened in these outer zones, and much of this loosened paint has since fallen away (Fig. 2).

The paint layer itself remains cohesive, with the exception of the paint applied as background, which is prone to disintegration through failure of the medium. This may be because it was applied as a weaker, more watery paint, owing to the greater area it had to cover. A regular pattern on some paintings of bare *intonaco*—not confined to perimeter zones—seems to indicate a history of powdering and spalling

FIGURE 1 *Census of Cattle* (EA37976): Instances of flaking paint were recorded on a gray image. Photo: Compass.

FIGURE 2 *Banqueting Scene with Dancers* (EA37984): Detail of paint losses in the perimeter zone. Photo: Corinna Kenyon.

of background paint overall; nevertheless, the condition has been made considerably worse in the perimeter zones because of the plaster mounts.

The condition of the paint inside the perimeter zones is generally good. There are exceptions to this, however, particularly in areas painted with Egyptian blue and green. The coarse pigment particles and heavy paint applications frequently result in catastrophic loss of the whole detail, but occasionally the outer crust fractures, exposing a spongy interior, and from this it appears that the loss of pigment is gradual.

The paint layer of *Bringing Produce* was severely disrupted by the growth of sodium chloride crystals (Miller, Lee, and Ellam 1987: 289–95), but sodium chloride damage has not been found on any of the other paintings.

The condition of the *intonaco* in the perimeter zone of *Harvest* was reported as extremely friable. The scientific conclusion for the most likely cause of this is pressures generated within the *intonaco* by calcium hemihydrate migrating in water from the plaster mount and crystallizing as gypsum (Thickett 2002; Fig. 3). While this extreme friability has not been encountered elsewhere, the removal of nineteenth-century fills from cracks and lacunae of other paintings, particularly *Owner* and *Cattle*, and the exposure of *intonaco* edges after cutting back the plaster mounts (see "Remounting"), has revealed incidences of sponginess and fragility of the gypsum plaster in perimeter zones, indicating general weakness there. The cause of this weakness has not been established, but the expectation is that it is also from pressures exerted by the newly formed gypsum.

Fragmentation of the *intonaco* and separation from the mud substrate around the edges is a feature common to all the paintings. Whereas much of this probably occurred while the fragments were being prized off the tomb chapel walls, a great deal of the separation appears to have been caused by lateral compression by the plaster mounts during setting. Compression damage is identifiable by bulging and cracking of the layer (Fig. 4).

Impact damage occurred when the paintings were still in the tomb. These are not confined to perimeter zones, and unlike scratches and abrasions, they appear as small rounded lacunae; sometimes crushed paint and plaster have been found in the damaged areas.

Past Treatments

During the examination of the fragments it was observed that several attempts to secure the paint had been made. The archive mentions some of these, and they all appear to date to the late 1940s and the 1950s. It would seem that the approach

FIGURE 3 *Harvest Scene* (EA37982): Detail showing friable *intonaco* caused by crystals of gypsum forming in the layer from calcium hemihydrate solution from the mount. Photo: Trevor Springett.

FIGURE 4 *Banqueting Scene with Dancers* (EA37984): Detail from Figure 2 of bulging and cracking of the *intonaco* caused by compression. Photo: Corinna Kenyon.

to treatment involved applying adhesive over the deteriorated paint layer, which also had the effect of displacing paint. Analysis carried out during conservation treatment on *Geese,* in 1987, identified two treatment campaigns of this type using animal glue (Dinsmore and Howard 1988: 61–68; Fig. 5). However, in this case there is no record of these treatments having been applied.

A varnish applied to most of the painted surfaces of *Cattle,* in 1947, and *Owner,* in 1948, has been identified as cellulose acetate (Parker 2004a, b; Robinet 2002). On *Owner* it had been applied thickly in certain areas, particularly at the bottom, where it had turned milky. Otherwise, it had remained transparent but had shrunk, pulling up flakes of paint, and in places the cellulose acetate film had separated from the paint, creating optical opacity. In addition, dust and dirt that had found its way onto the surface had been absorbed into the varnish, turning it uniformly gray to the naked eye.

The black cow at center in the lower register of *Cattle* was varnished with carnauba wax (Parker 2004a, b). This treatment is also undocumented. At the time of the examination the paint on the body remained in excellent condition, but on the head and neck it was so fragmented and curled that separation from the *intonaco* was virtually complete. The flakes were fragile and easily disturbed, and a number of them appeared to have no point of anchorage (Fig. 6). If there had

been a preexisting condition of separation at the time of treatment, some displacement of paint would have occurred. However, displacement was entirely absent here, and the paint layer remained complete, despite the damage. It would appear therefore that the carnauba wax was solely responsible for loosening the paint, and so the rationale for its application is not at all clear.

Areas of a black-and-white photographic print of *Dancers* located in the departmental archive are annotated with "X" and accompanied by a note, dated November 1956, to the effect that loose paint was readhered (i.e., coated) with soluble nylon in alcohol in those areas. Soluble nylon has also been applied over most of the perimeter zone of *Cattle*—that is, over the earlier application of cellulose acetate. It is still transparent, but the layer has not weathered uniformly. Where shrinkage of the nylon has occurred, it has either pulled paint away from the substrate or has pulled itself away from the paint. On rough or uneven surfaces it has tended to contract and remain adhered to the prominences. Where it was thinly applied, it has turned milkily opaque, but most of it is thick, glutinous, and highly disfiguring.

Many of the lacunae and fissures created by the fragmentation of the *intonaco* during the detachment in 1820 have been filled with plaster. Impact damages were also filled, even though this frequently concealed crushed paint and traces of *intonaco* still clinging to the mud plaster.

FIGURE 5 *Census of Geese* (EA37978): 1.75x magnification of rabbit skin glue treatment layer fragmented by shrinkage cracks and partial loss. Photo: Jennifer Dinsmore.

FIGURE 6 *Census of Cattle* (EA37976): 1.75x magnification of paint lifted by carnauba wax. Photo: Eric Miller.

Conservation

Meticulous microscopic examination has provided a deeper understanding of the problems afflicting the paintings and has informed our conservation strategy. The principal concern is the readhesion of loose paint. The removal of past treatments is generally a separate issue, but in practice much of the lifted paint cannot be relaxed unless the adhesive holding it is removed. These adhesive layers are also locking in displaced flakes, and must be removed so the flakes can be freed and returned to their original locations, where identified.

The stabilization of Egyptian blue and green paints presents a different problem. The issues here are consolidating the paint and strengthening its adhesion to the substrate. Powdery background paint, by contrast, is a minor problem calling for consolidation with a low-concentration adhesive.

Readhering Loose Paint

In this situation, resecuring paint flakes has been found to be most efficiently performed using acrylic or polyvinyl acetate resins in aqueous emulsion in conjunction with white spirit or industrial methylated spirit as a prewetting agent. The system works by liberally prewetting the area of loosened paint using a pipette and then allowing adhesive to be drawn underneath with a loaded oo-grade sable-hair brush placed in contact with the raised edge of the paint layer. By occupying the pores of the paint and *intonaco*, the wetting agent allows the adhesive to flow freely and at the same time prevents the adhesive from soaking away. Primal (Rhoplex) B60A,[5] diluted 1:3 or 1:7 with deionized water, is used to readhere flaking paint. Vinamul 3252[6] was used on *Owner* because it is not dissolved by acetone, which was used here to remove an overlying coating (see below).

Consolidating Egyptian Blue and Green

A 2 percent (w/v) solution of Mowital B30H[7] (polyvinyl-butyral in 1:1 acetone/industrial methylated spirit), introduced in sufficiently large quantity to find its way into the *intonaco*, is calculated to bond to a subsequent application of a 5 percent solution that is required to consolidate the paint.

Consolidating Powdery Background Paint

Primal (Rhoplex) B60A, diluted 1:7 with deionized water, is used to consolidate the background paint. Impregnation is assisted by wetting with white spirits.

Grouting the *Intonaco*

Readhesion of the separated layers of plaster is an unresolved issue. A grout (an adhesive with a bulking aggregate) will fill the gaps and readhere the two layers, but the danger in using incompatible materials is that the hardened filling can shrink away from one or both of the layers. A detailed investigation into the use of earthen grouts in wall-painting conservation has been carried out (Griffin 1999), but the principal concern here is the gypsum layer, not the mud plaster (which is stable, provided it remains enclosed and protected from vibration). In other words, while the weakness of the gypsum is not the primary cause of the loss of adhesion, in devising a treatment system, it should be the starting point.

Removal of Earlier Treatment Layers

The cellulose acetate used on *Owner* and *Cattle* remains soluble in acetone, but the only mechanical action the paint could withstand was brushing with sable-hair brushes. The adhesive and dirt can be picked up by this action and discharged from the brush onto absorbent tissue. On the other hand, soluble nylon is virtually insoluble (Hanna and Lee 1988), but films formed by this material are permeable to water. Therefore, where it had been applied over cellulose acetate, water could be introduced through it to assist in the separation of the two layers. Once separated, the soluble nylon layer could be lifted with a sable-hair brush (Fig. 7). Soluble nylon applied directly on paint, however, is impossible to

FIGURE 7 *Census of Cattle* (EA37976): 1.75x magnification of soluble nylon layer during removal. Photo: Eric Miller.

remove without also removing paint. Since the nylon is not harming the paint, leaving it alone is the least-damaging option, and its glossy effect must be accepted.

The carnauba wax applied to the head and neck of the black cow had inexplicably become soluble in water, but attempts to remove it after the paint flakes had been readhered were frustrated. The black paint is fugitive when subjected to a brushing action with water, hence the wax will be left in place.

Remounting

The nineteenth-century mounters troweled gypsum plaster right up to the paint layer, hiding the mud plaster, which generally extends beyond the *intonaco* profiles. Nowadays, evidence of the ancient technologies and working practices does not distract us from the object as artifact. In fact, allowing the mud plaster *arriccio* to be seen is mandatory for modern display. The modern mounting material best suited to replace the old gypsum plaster is epoxy foam. Epoxy polymers have a high strength-to-weight ratio, and they possess other essential properties, including long-term stability and reversibility. To date, five fragments have been remounted using this technique: *Musicians* (Fig. 8), *Bringing Produce, Geese, Owner,* and *Garden Pool* (Miller, Lee, and Ellam 1987: 289–95)—although the last of these still retains its gypsum backing. *Musicians* and *Dancers* were recently found to be adjoining pieces, and these are to be remounted together. Owing to a limitation on time for the project, however, work on the remaining fragments will be limited to cutting away plaster to reveal the *arriccio*.

Conclusion

Completion of the conservation project will lead directly into the final part of the program: exhibition in a new gallery location. The plan involves displaying the Nebamun paintings all together for the first time in a spectacular setting designed to re-create the atmosphere of the tomb. However, this close encounter with these fragile treasures has demonstrated that simply leaving them alone is not enough to preserve them. Fluctuations in atmospheric conditions act on the materials comprising their fabric in different ways, causing minute but chaotic movement. The atmosphere of London is widely erratic, and in the long term these minute movements cause damage, including the loosening of paint. In the future they will occupy a sealed environment, and active controls will maintain a stable, protective microclimate. In addition, they will lean back at an angle designed to arrest any fragments of paint that become detached despite the protective measures taken.

Conservation is a continuing process, and to ensure that future decisions can be based on factual information, digital imaging of the surfaces under incident and raking light, at 5× magnification, is planned for the end of the project. This will prepare the way for a close monitoring regime by providing the data to reveal paint losses and alterations in surface topography, including those undetectable to the naked eye.

FIGURE 8 *Banqueting Scene with Musicians* (EA37981): This painting was remounted in 1987; the surface of the mount is recessed to allow the mud plaster to be seen. Photo: Trevor Springett.

Acknowledgments

The author thanks his colleagues on the conservation team, Karen Birkhölzer, Karin Hignett, and Ruth Scott, for their work on the project, and on behalf of the team, he also thanks curators and scientists at the British Museum for their help and advice.

Notes

1 For visual reference, go to http://www.thebritishmuseum.ac.uk/compass and search for "Nebamun."

2 R. B. Parkinson, personal communication.

3 Ibid.

4 In this paper, *arriccio* is the coarse mud plaster layer applied to the stone walls of the tomb, and *intonaco* is the fine gypsum-based plaster applied over the mud plaster on which the painting is executed.

5 Primal B60A (acrylic emulsion) is the preferred adhesive mainly because of its handling properties and its high tack, enabling small-quantity efficacy. Primal B60A is the successor to AC33 and is essentially the same product without an added thickener. AC33 was found to turn acidic under artificial light and heat (Down et al. 1996), but samples held at the British Museum were assessed at pH 6.2 after eleven years. In a test at the British Museum, a newly cast film of Primal B60A was assessed at pH 5.86 and judged suitable for use for the Nebamun paintings (Parker 2003).

6 Vinamul 3252 (PVA emulsion) possesses good handling and aging properties (Down et al. 1996) but poor reversibility (Parker 2003).

7 Mowital B30H (polyvinylbutyral) was selected because it is a stable adhesive and, under tests, showed no perceptible darkening of the paint.

Materials and Suppliers

Primal B60A, Vinamul 3252, and Mowital B30H: Conservation Resources (UK) Ltd., Unit 2, Ashville Way, Off Watlington Road, Cowley, Oxford OX4 TU, UK

Epoxy foam components (Rencast CW2215, Hardener HY5161, Foaming Agent DY5054): John Burn & Co (Birmingham) Ltd., 74 Albert Road, Stechford, Birmingham B33 9AJ, UK

References

Bryan, B. M. 2001. Painting techniques and artisan organization in the Tomb of Suemniwet, Theban Tomb 92. In *Color and Painting in Ancient Egypt* (proceedings of British Museum Department of Egyptian Antiquities' colloquium, July 11–12, 1996), ed. W. V. Davies, 63–72. London: British Museum Press.

Dinsmore, J., and H. Howard. 1988. The treatment of an Eighteenth Dynasty wall painting fragment at the British Museum. In *Conservation of Ancient Egyptian Materials* (preprints of Bristol conference, Dec. 15–18, 1988), ed. S. Watkins and C. Brown, 61–68. London: United Kingdom Institute for Conservation.

Down, Jane L., Maureen A. MacDonald, Jean Tétreault, and R. Scott Williams. 1996. Adhesive testing at the Canadian Conservation Institute—An evaluation of selected poly(vinyl acetate) and acrylic adhesives. *Studies in Conservation* 41:19–44.

Griffin, I. 1999. Earthen grouts in wall painting conservation: An investigation of their working properties and performance characteristics. Master's thesis, Conservation of Wall Paintings Department, Courtauld Institute of Art, University of London.

Hanna, S. B., and N. J. Lee. 1988. The consequences of previous adhesives and consolidants used for stone conservation at the British Museum. In *Early Advances in Conservation* (proceedings of the British Museum's 4th conservation symposium), ed. V. Daniels, 89–102. London: British Museum Publications.

James, T. G. H. 1985. *Egyptian Painting.* London: British Museum Press.

Manniche, L. 1988. *Lost Tombs—A Study of Certain 18th Dynasty Monuments in the Theban Necropolis.* London: Kegan Paul International.

Miller, E. G., N. J. Lee, and D. R. Ellam. 1987. Remounting and conservation of archaeological wall paintings at the British Museum. In *Recent Advances in the Conservation and Analysis of Artifacts: Jubilee Conservation Conference, London 6–10 July, 1987,* ed. James Black, 289–95. London: Summer Schools Press.

Miller, E. G., and R. B. Parkinson. 2001. Reflections on a gilded eye in *Fowling in the Marshes* (British Museum, EA37977). In *Color and Painting in Ancient Egypt*, ed. W. V. Davies, 49–52. London: British Museum Press.

Parker, J. 2003. *The testing of three adhesive emulsions for use in the British Museum.* Internal report 2003/13, Department of Conservation, Documentation and Science, British Museum.

———. 2004a. *Analysis of a coating on the Nebamun wall painting "Census of Cattle" (EA 37976).* Internal report AR2004/28, Department of Conservation, Documentation, and Science, British Museum.

————. 2004b. *Analysis of surface coating on the Nebamun wall painting "Cattle Brought for Inspection" (EA 37976).* Internal report AR2004/7, Department of Conservation, Documentation, and Science, British Museum.

Parkinson, R. B. 2004. The painted tomb-chapel of Nebamun. Unpublished manuscript.

Robinet, L. 2002. *Analysis of a modern coating on the Nebamun wall painting EA 37979.* Internal report CA2002/21, Department of Conservation, Documentation, and Science, British Museum.

Thickett, D. 2002. *Analysis of Soluble Salt Concentrations in Wall Painting EA37982.* Internal report CA2002/50, Department of Conservation, Documentation, and Science, British Museum.

PART THREE

Historic Buildings

Introduction

Anthony Crosby

The papers in this section, on the conservation of decorated surfaces on historic buildings, cover a wide range of conservation issues and associated challenges, including selection and use of appropriate materials and preservation of traditions that evolve as materials change and skills are lost.

Lisa Shekede and Stephen Rickerby discuss the challenges of designing conservation treatments using local materials that are compatible with the original decorative surface materials and are appropriate for their continued preservation. In their paper they show that identification of the material characteristics of the original and conservation materials is critical and can often be accomplished using simple and effective methods conducted on-site.

Jun Zheng, through several case studies, emphasizes the importance of a methodological approach that includes a thorough understanding of the characteristics of the original materials, techniques, and causes of deterioration. This rigorous approach can be compromised by the lack of availability of appropriate conservation materials. Zheng emphasizes that

it is the conservator's responsibility to adhere to this rigorous approach and select the best conservation materials for treatment, even in challenging conditions.

Ishanlosen Odiaua presents an overview of the regional architecture and decorative traditions of the Hausa people of northern Nigeria who are reviving their tradition of exterior surface decoration on houses that have undergone change because of the passing of the older generation and the lack of readily available traditional materials. While this renewed interest by the local community, administrators, and universities is encouraging, Odiaua questions whether the attention focused on traditional materials and design will result in the loss of the spirit embodied in the traditional design by local people.

The common theme in these papers is the emphasis on a sound methodological approach, beginning with the identification of local values and resources. This approach also includes an understanding of the materials being treated and the causes of deterioration. Moreover, it demands recognition of the consequences of any treatment or decision not to treat.

Theory into Practice: Establishing Compatibility in Earth-Based Repair Materials

Lisa Shekede and Stephen Rickerby

It is a well-established conservation principle that to function well together, original and repair materials should have the same or similar performance characteristics, including porosity, density, compressive strength, hygroscopic potential, and coefficient of thermal expansion. In the case of earthen construction and support materials for paintings, adherence to this principle is particularly crucial. This paper presents case studies taken from historic buildings containing wall paintings on earthen supports, where the analytical techniques described were used to develop appropriate conservation treatments.

Earth is an extremely heterogeneous material, its physical and chemical composition uniquely determined by localized geological, topographical, and climatic conditions. Particle size, particle morphology, and mineral composition play a pivotal role in determining many aspects of soil behavior, including shear strength, permeability, volume change, and resistance to deformation and loss of cohesion in the presence of water.[1] The clay fraction is a particularly influential factor in soil behavior. Typically, soils contain a number of different clays, whose structure and chemical composition cause them to react differently on hydration (Bell 1993). For example, some high-swelling clays are capable of absorbing 700 percent water (w/w) before losing cohesion, while some low-swelling clays can absorb less than 40 percent (Clifton and Robbins 1978: 25; Fig. 1). The geotechnical data presented in Figures 1–3, which were identified by Atterberg in 1911 and refined by Casagrande in 1932, are known as the *plastic* and *liquid limits* (Head 1980: 50). The plastic limit can be defined as the percentage of water the tested material can absorb before it becomes malleable and deformable. The liquid limit is the percentage of water the tested material can absorb before it passes from a deformable into a liquid state. The difference between these two measures is known as the *plasticity index*. Establishing these limits through analysis provides crucial information on the performance characteristics of not only pure clays but also soils.

Soils used in painting supports are rarely dominated by clay, although they often contain a range of different clay minerals and clay-sized particles. Their behavior is not usually as extreme as that of pure clays, but they can nevertheless have very varied properties. To illustrate this, the plastic and liquid limit data of three geographically dispersed earth-based painting supports—a daub from England, a mortar from Cyprus, and a render from China—and of their parent soils, are shown in Figures 2 and 3. These demonstrate a significant diversity of response to moisture, diverging in both parameters by around 20 percent.

The data also demonstrate some radical differences in performance between the support materials and the soils from which they were derived. The pattern—which has also been observed in other studies—is one in which the earthen supports consistently demonstrate lower plasticity indices and lower activity than the parent soil (Shekede 1997). Why should this be the case? In almost every situation, the performance of selected soils is intentionally enhanced by the addition of physical and chemical stabilizers (plant oils, dung, ashes, chalk, etc.), with the ultimate intention of rendering the soils more stable in the presence of water, their worst enemy. Occasionally, these additions can alter the properties of the earthen support materials to such a degree that links with the parent soil may be difficult to establish.

FIGURE 1 Liquid limits of some clays. (Sources: Plastic and liquid limits data published by Clifton and Robbins 1978, and compiled from Yong and Warrenton 1975, and Seed et al. 1962.)

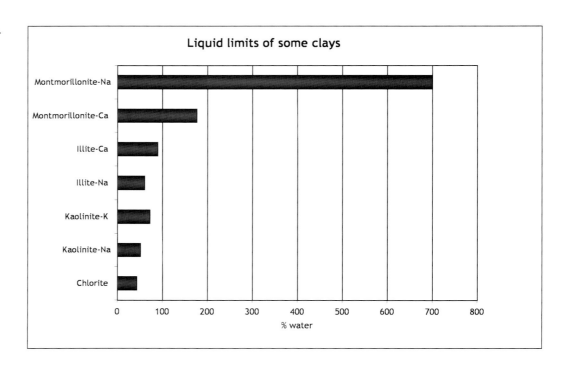

FIGURE 2 Plastic limits of some soils and earthen painting supports. (Sources: Alvechurch and Galata data obtained from unpublished reports by Shekede and Rickerby, 2004. Mogao data obtained from unpublished data produced for the Getty Conservation Institute by G. S. Austin, New Mexico Bureau of Mines and Mineral Resources, 2000.)

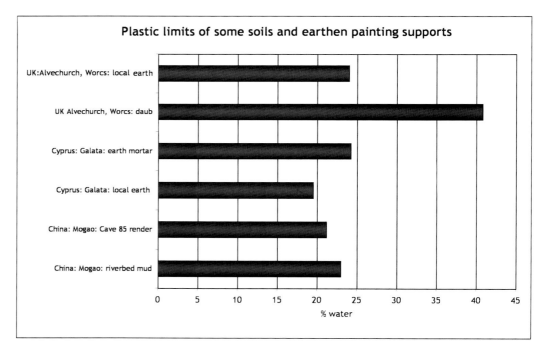

Because earthen support materials are so heterogeneous in composition and behavior, one of the conservator's most important preliminary tasks in making an earthen repair is to establish its compatible source, the parent soil. This is not always easy since, as already mentioned, the parent soil is likely to have been adapted by the addition of stabilizers, and support materials may not always resemble the soil from which they are derived, either in physical appearance or in performance. Nor can it be assumed that soil in the immediate vicinity would be automatically selected for use. Even in

FIGURE 3 Liquid limits of some soils and earthen painting supports. (Sources: Alvechurch and Galata data obtained from unpublished reports by Shekede and Rickerby, 2002. Mogao data obtained from unpublished data produced for the Getty Conservation Institute by G. S. Austin, New Mexico Bureau of Mines and Mineral Resources, 2000.)

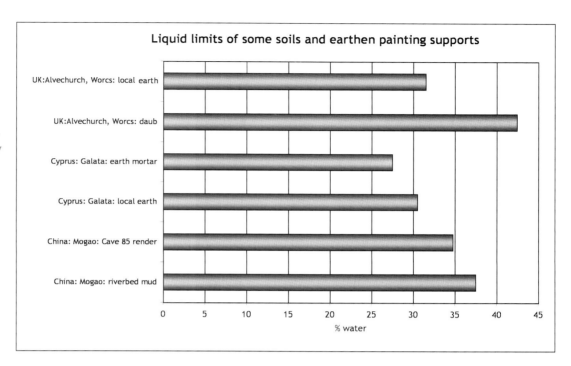

cases where a local provenance is expected, the frequent presence in close geographic proximity of deposits with very different origins and behavior is a further complication.

The implications for the conservator of paintings on earthen supports are obvious: we cannot hope to achieve compatible repair materials without examining and testing both the original support materials and local soils. Two paths of investigation can help in the search for appropriate earth-based repair materials: qualitative and quantitative analysis of individual components (for example, particle-size distribution, identification of clay type, and identification of organic additives), and performance characterization through testing (such as plasticity and shrinkage). These can be performed on collected samples of original earthen support materials, on potentially compatible soils, and on soils modified as repair materials, to assess their suitability. Many of the simplest and most useful tests can be undertaken by the conservator in the field or off-site, as demonstrated in the following case studies.

Case Study 1: Agios Sozomenos, Galata, Cyprus

The sixteenth-century church of Agios Sozomenos, Galata, Cyprus, is located in a region with a long and complex geological history. The Troodos massif is a plutonic igneous complex, the bulk of which consists of granophyre and gabbro. Galata is located at the northern edge of this formation, at a point where it adjoins a sheeted dolerite complex (Bear 1963: 12). Dolerite weathering yields mainly reddish brown clay soils dominated by montmorillonite, deposits of which occur at Galata and adjoining villages, where they are used for making fired bricks (Bear 1963: 143; Gass et al. 1994: 198). Other soils in the area are greenish brown in color and are probably weathered pillow lavas, their coloration due to the presence of chlorite and celadonite (Gass et al. 1994: 20).

Church Structure

The church is a composite structure of earth, timber, and stone, whose vernacular features include a high stone plinth and the steep-pitched, wide-eaved, double roofing system typical of churches in the Troodos mountains (Myrianthefs 2002: 75; Fig. 4). This architectural form is uniquely adapted to the seasonal heavy rain and snowfalls of the region—the double roof providing an effective barrier against infiltration, and the wide eaves and stone plinth offering protection against basal erosion. The church is built on a steep hillside, however, with its south wall partly buried by the incline, and is therefore vulnerable both to dispersed groundwater and to snow banking in the winter.

The structure and paintings are coeval, an exact completion date of September 3, 1513, being provided—unusually and fortuitously—by an inscription incorporated into the painting scheme over the west door, which also provides the

FIGURE 4 The church of Agios Sozomenos, Galata, Cyprus, view from the east end. Photo courtesy of the Courtauld Institute of Art, Conservation of Wall Painting Department, 2002.

name of the artist, Symeon Axenti, and the circumstances of the painting commission. Almost every surface of the interior was originally painted, most of which survives in remarkably pristine condition. The scheme also incorporates an unusually extensive series of paintings on the exterior north wall, two scenes of which are iconographically rare and extremely significant: *The Seven Councils of the Church* and *The Triumph of Orthodoxy* (Stylianou and Stylianou 1985).

Earth is a major construction material at Agios Sozomenos, and it has been used in a variety of ways. The deep plinth constituting the wall bases is constructed of large, rounded boulders, of a type traditionally obtained from riverbeds. These are interspersed and stabilized with fired brick and tile pieces, and bedded in a thick, reddish earth mortar containing a large quantity of vegetable fibers. Wooden beams running the length of each wall and tied at each corner form a stable support structure above the high plinth. These also provide lintels for each of the three door openings and a level surface for the mud-brick construction of parts of the upper walls and the gable ends. These mud bricks are made from the local greenish brown soil, which is still frequently used in their manufacture today. Particularly uneven surfaces of the primary support—typically within doorjambs and cupboards and around the walls of the apse—were leveled using a plaster constituted from the same reddish

earthen material as the mortar. Finally, a plaster of lime and fermented chaff and straw—a method of plaster preparation commonly used in the Greek Byzantine tradition—was applied as a support for the painting, which was executed mainly in fresco technique (Dionysius of Fourna 1981: 14).

Painting Conservation

Although the paintings survived in generally good condition prior to conservation, they were heavily obscured by smoke-blackening (the effects of an internal fire, as well as the residue of centuries of candle and incense burning) and had also suffered from a number of different forms of physical damage. The latter included abrasion and loss due to general building use and the application of fixtures, and selective, intentional damage of various types.[2] In addition, stress cracking and decohesion of original materials were occurring behind and in the vicinity of a large number of crudely applied cement plasters and repairs.

Conservation work was undertaken in four campaigns from 2001 to 2003 by the Courtauld Institute of Art, Conservation of Wall Painting Department (London), in collaboration with the Antiquities Department of Cyprus and the Bishopric of Morphou. As earthen repairs were to form an important treatment component, the role of earthen analysis in finding a compatible source material was given priority in the initial, investigative stage of the conservation program, and a temporary earthen-materials laboratory was established in the narthex of the church (Fig. 5). Relatively simple but extremely useful analytical techniques were chosen (Shekede 2000; Table 1). These included particle-size analysis, involving wet sieving to grade the larger particles and separate them from the clay and silt-sized particles. This was followed by measuring of the finer particles using the hydrometer method, liquid limits testing using the Casagrande device, plastic limits using the rolling method, and linear shrinkage, using purpose-made molds to measure shrinkage of the material at around liquid limit (Head 1980; Teutonico 1988). In addition, pH testing and aqueous anion analysis were undertaken using indicator strips to provide information on soluble salts.

Table 1 Tests recommended for in situ analysis

Test name	BS	ASTM	References
Particle-size analysis: sieving procedure	BS 1377 test 7(B)	D422-63	Head 1980: 143–82; Teutonico 1988: 73–82
Particle-size analysis: sedimentation procedure (hydrometer method)	BS 1377 test 7(D)	D422-63	Head 1980: 182–216; Teutonico 1988: 82–95
Linear shrinkage test	BS 1377: 1995 test 5		Head 1980: 93–94
Plastic limit	BS 1377: 1995 test 3		Head 1980: 66–85; Teutonico 1988: 96-101
Liquid limit	BS 1377: 1995 test 2(B)		Head 1980: 66–85; Teutonico 1988: 102–107

FIGURE 5 Temporary earthen-materials analysis laboratory set up in the narthex of the church. Photo courtesy of the Courtauld Institute of Art, Conservation of Wall Painting Department, 2002.

The initial focus of analysis was to identify the parent soil of the red mortar and selective plaster used at Agios Sozomenos. The most abundantly available local earth—and that used for the majority of extant local mud-brick structures—was a greenish brown color. However, due to the difference in color between this and the red mortar, local reddish earths were initially sought out, and two different types were obtained for testing. Particle-size analysis was conducted on these and the red earth mortar, using the sieving method to separate out the larger fraction materials. The results were initially puzzling, as the particle-size distribution curves generated were dissimilar, and visual comparison of the larger aggregates demonstrated discrepancies in mineral content. Closer examination of the particles derived from the mortar showed that the reddish color was imparted solely by a large quantity of added brick dust, constituting approximately 5 percent of the fraction greater than 75 μm, and 13 percent of the fraction less than 75 μm. Following further particle-size analysis, the mineral content of the larger fraction was found to match that of the local greenish brown earth. Comparison of results following plastic and liquid limits, and linear shrinkage testing of the local greenish brown earth and the mortar, revealed that the addition of the brick dust had greatly influenced the plasticity of the parent soil, resulting in a material far less prone to volume change (Shekede 2002).[3]

The next step was to use these analytical results to modify the local soil with 20 percent brick dust and to subject the resulting material to plastic and liquid limits and linear shrinkage testing to check that its properties were compatible with the original mortar. This proved to be the case, the main difference being its slightly lighter color, probably owing to the lack of decayed organic matter in the new mixture. For preparation on a large scale, the repair mortar was made using four parts local earth, one part pulverized brick (two-thirds of which passed through a 75 μm sieve), and—based both on visual examination of the fibers contained in the original mortar and on primary sources—two parts chaff and chopped straw sieved to remove both fine dust and larger fibers (Dionysius of Fourna 1981: 14). Water was added, and the components combined thoroughly by hand. The mixture was then allowed to settle for up to two days before a final, thorough mixing prior to application.

One of the uses of the repair mortar was to repoint and stabilize large sections of the internal and external faces of the wall plinth, which had been inappropriately repaired with cement. On removal of the cement, much of the original earthen pointing and interstitial tiling between the river stones was found to be loosened and damaged, destabilizing the wall structure. In particular, water-related deterioration had led to severe decohesion of the earth mortar along the base of the vulnerable south wall, partly due to the rotting of its vegetable fiber content.

All the newly exposed areas of the wall plinth were repointed, and destabilized or missing interstitial tiling was reset or replaced (Fig. 6). A replacement underpinning was carried out at the base of the south wall using flat tiles and earth mortar. Losses of the earthen painting support were also repaired using the earth mortar. After application, the earth mortar was left to dry, but reworked and pressed back while still plastic to reduce cracking and the risk of delamination. Finally, the interior walls were replastered at dado level using a traditional lime-and-fermented-straw plaster, similar to the original lime plaster used elsewhere in the church. On the exterior walls, the earthen renders and pointing were left exposed, as is the traditional practice. On drying, the renders and pointing were brushed down with a stiff brush to remove all loose material.

The importance of the on-site earthen materials analysis in this case study was twofold. In determining the composition of the original earth mortar, the relationship between the local greenish brown earth and the addition of brick dust would probably not have been established had in situ analysis not been undertaken. Nor would it have been possible to refine the repair mortar by retesting, had analytical facilities not been available on-site.

Drawbacks to setting up a testing facility in the field were minimal, but the advantages were significant. Although some of the equipment was delicate and breakable, none of the items was sufficiently bulky or heavy that it presented major transportation problems. All the equipment could be used on-site without recourse to specialist laboratory facilities or professional operatives, and none was prohibitively expensive. In summary, the major advantage of in situ analysis was that it facilitated incremental and iterative testing through a range of processes, beginning with analysis and testing of the original material, through to the development, refinement, and eventual application of the selected repair material.

Case Study 2: Knightstone Manor, Ottery St. Mary, Devon, England

The second case study is of a painting from Devon, England, a region renowned for its earthen building tradition. The solid geological formation of the area consists of Triassic (New Red

FIGURE 6 Repointing of the stone plinth using the tested repair mortar. Photo courtesy of the Courtauld Institute of Art, Conservation of Wall Painting Department, 2002.

Sandstone) mudstone "marl," yielding dark red sandy soils containing oxidized iron. The predominant clay present is illite, which may occur alone or in combination with kaolinite or chlorite. No highly active clays are present, which, together with the stabilizing properties of its high iron content, makes these soils very suitable for construction (Durrance and Lamming 1982).

Knightstone Manor, near Ottery St. Mary, is a substantial Devon manor house, dating back to the late medieval period. Its façade and load-bearing interior walls are of stone, but non-load-bearing walls are of timber and earth, a composite construction style typical of the region (Beacham 2001: 14). Within the timber framing, the infill paneling consists of a sandy red earthen daub applied to an armature of riven oak staves and unbarked oak wattles. This timber-and-earth structure also forms the primary painting support, the secondary support being a lime-sand-hair plaster.

The painting is located within the roof space above the great hall, where it had been hidden for years, first by layers of limewash and subsequently behind a partition wall. Originally, it probably decorated the wall behind a gallery at the service end of the great hall, being visible from the dais end. It dates to the late sixteenth century and depicts the temptation of Adam and Eve, and the expulsion from the garden of Eden, executed in a crude and primitive, but undeniably vigorous style (Figs. 7–8).

The painting was rediscovered—and inadvertently severely damaged—during major building work in 1996, which included the insertion of piping and a water tank (Shekede and Rickerby 1998). During subsequent conservation treatment—which involved revealing the painting by removing the limewash covering—the earthen support was repaired and stabilized based on the investigation and analysis of original construction materials.

FIGURE 7 Knightstone Manor, Ottery St. Mary, Devon, England: detail of *The Expulsion from the Garden of Eden* during uncovering and conservation. (Source: Shekede and Rickerby 1998.)

FIGURE 8 Detail of Eve from *The Temptation in the Garden of Eden*, after conservation. (Source: Shekede and Rickerby 1998.)

Following particle-size analysis both of the sandy red daub support and earth gathered from a stream bank a few yards from the house, the plotted graphs displayed a virtual confluence.[4] Plotted on a soil-texture triangle, the collected data demonstrated that both materials were loams. Activity graphs based on clay content and plasticity indices showed that both were also stable, displaying low activity. X-ray diffraction (XRD) identification of the clay minerals determined that each material shared the same broad illite-dominated clay mineral range.[5] It was therefore concluded that the local soil had desirable properties for use as a construction and support material, with little further stabilization needed. Evidently, the organic fibers present in the original daub functioned more to enhance tensile strength than to minimize shrinkage.

The organic fibers separated out during particle-size analysis were found to include quantities of animal hair, burnt chaff, and both whole and macerated vegetable fibers, the latter suggesting the possible addition of a small quantity of dung. Quantitative ion analysis by aqueous extraction found concentrations of nitrate and ammonium, which although small (respectively 13.0 and 29.9 µmol/g), were significantly greater than the majority in a test sample of fourteen English daubs of a similar age (Shekede 1997: 80).[6] In view of these analytical results and investigations, the local soil was used as a repair material, with no changes or additions besides a little chopped straw and dung, both obtained from farm buildings adjoining the house.

This case study was a rare instance where the original earthen construction material had been used in an essentially unmodified state. Typically in conservation practice, however, earthen repair materials are automatically modified with fillers and other additives to counter perceived drawbacks, such as shrinkage. Without this analytical information, therefore, it would have been all too easy to adapt the parent soil unnecessarily, and possibly adversely. While a greater range of instrumental analysis was available than at Agios Sozomenos in Cyprus, the data that enabled this decision making was derived from the same basic set of analytical procedures that can be readily undertaken by the conservator.

Case Study 3: 8 Red Lion Street, Alvechurch, Worcestershire, England

The final case study is of an early seventeenth-century painting discovered in July 2004 at 8 Red Lion Street, Alvechurch, Worcestershire, England. The painting is located in what had been the great hall of an early timber-framed hall house,

which was subsequently divided into three cottages. Prior to this, painting probably extended over all the original wall surfaces, carried over plaster panels and timber framing alike. Unfortunately, no painting now survives on the lower walls, and much of the painting on the timbers was destroyed during refurbishment between the time of discovery and the conservation inspection. The remaining painting consists of a frieze of foliate scrollwork with grotesque masks and texts.

The painting support of daub and wattles has been severely disrupted by the insertion of a brick wall behind the painting, and in several places the painting is almost completely separated from its support. Grouting and earthen repairs are urgently required if the painting is to survive.

Samples of the daub and of the original beaten earth flooring were obtained for analysis, to assess the possibility of using the latter as a source for the repair material. Particle-size analysis indicated that there were strong mineralogical similarities between the two. Their particle-size distribution curves are close, characterized in particular by a sharp shoulder at 425 µm indicating large quantities of fine sand (45 percent in the daub and 50 percent in the floor earth). The soil texture of the daub is sandy loam, while the floor earth lies between sandy loam and sandy clay loam.[7] Visual examination of the coarser particles indicated that the two contained large quantities of red sand, indicating a similar mineral composition. Both also contained quantities of broken brick, coal, and charcoal in the higher fraction, suggesting a common source contaminated by building use, perhaps the site itself.

However, despite these similarities (including almost identical appearance), the behavior of the two materials was found to be significantly at variance. Plastic and liquid limits and linear shrinkage testing demonstrated that less water was required to activate the floor earth, and that its greater plasticity made it vulnerable to greater volume change in the presence of moisture, probably owing to the slightly larger clay content of the floor earth.[8] In order to use the earth floor as a repair material, it must be adapted to reduce its plasticity index. By adding 5–10 percent fine sand, the soil texture of the floor earth will approach that of the daub.[9] The next step will be to test the adapted floor earth to check its compatibility with the daub before use and to then make further changes as necessary. In preparation for the forthcoming conservation of this painting, earth from the floor has been collected and will be adapted for grouting and repairs.

As with the previous case studies, basic earthen materials analysis proved to be a crucial yet practicable tool for determining appropriate conservation repair materials. Since injection grouting with an earth-based grout is required at this site—a difficult intervention that can be disastrously undermined by adverse shrinkage of the introduced material—it is clearly critical to know the plastic and liquid limits of the potential source material and to modify it accordingly.

Conclusions

Even this small selection of case studies provides an insight into the variety and complexity of earthen supports and highlights the considerable effort taken by the craftsmen responsible to produce resilient and stable materials for construction, despite the sometimes considerable drawbacks of the source materials available. This information, in turn, emphasizes the need for conservators to evaluate and design their repair materials with equal diligence. While the conservation profession has adopted the principles of reversibility and/or retreatability to allow for treatment failure, it is generally recognized that most interventions cannot fully meet these criteria. In their place, compatibility has assumed greater importance. At present, there is no substitute for the basic analytical procedures outlined in this paper for determining the compatibility of earthen repair materials for conservators in the field.

The importance of these procedures as diagnostic tools therefore goes hand in hand with their versatility. Most of the information presented in these case studies was obtained using simple analytical techniques that can be performed relatively easily in the field. This is a distinct advantage when the work site may be in a different country than the laboratory, particularly as this enables the sample range to be broadened if the initial sample of local earths does not provide a good match with the earthen support material. It also facilitates an iterative approach to problem solving, particularly with regard to refining and retesting potential repair materials to ensure compatibility with the original.

Whether conducted in the field or in the laboratory, earthen-materials analysis should therefore be a standard tool for the conservator of paintings on earth supports. Indeed, it is surprising that so few conservators have, to date, adopted these simple procedures. It is hoped that this situation will soon change, and that as a result the conservation of paintings on earthen supports will be improved.

Finally, it is also hoped that greater practical emphasis on earthen-materials analysis will provide a much-needed spur to this area of research, for example, in examining the significance of soil pore size and structure and the nature of clay-organic interactions. Such research is long overdue and would benefit conservation practice in the longer term.

Notes

1   For the purposes of this paper, the term *earth* is used generically to encompass both the modified materials constituting earthen buildings and supports and the naturally occurring (i.e., unadapted) earthen materials of which they are made. *Soil* is used more specifically to describe variants in naturally occurring earths.

2   The intentional damage includes iconoclastic activity carried out during the Ottoman period. Other defacement of a different intent—the gouging of eyes from representations of saints—is probably an early local superstitious practice relating to the perceived talismanic properties of the eyes. There is also a great deal of recent incised graffiti on the exterior walls and in the apse.

3   The plasticity indices of the Galata local earth and the mortar were respectively 11.01 and 3.29; percentages of linear shrinkage were 12.85 and 4.64, respectively.

4   The Knightstone local earth consisted of 47.3 percent sand, 41.8 percent silt, and 10.9 percent clay. The daub consisted of 47.9 percent sand, 41.3 percent silt, and 10.8 percent clay.

5   XRD analysis was performed by Dr. Jennifer Huggett of Petroclays Ltd.

6   The Merck reflectoquant method was used for nitrate, nitrite, ammonia, and phosphate analysis. Chloride testing was undertaken using a Merck chloride titration kit. All the ion analysis was undertaken by Dr. Christine Bläuer Bohm, Director, Expert-Center für Denkmalpflege, Zürich.

7   The Alvechurch daub consists of 66 percent sand, 23.4 percent silt, and 10.6 percent clay The floor earth consists of 62.6 percent sand, 21.9 percent silt, and 15.5 percent clay.

8   The plasticity index of the Alvechurch daub is 1.64; that of the floor earth is 7.51.

9   Adapted by the addition of 5 percent sand, the Alvechurch repair daub would consist of 67.6 percent sand, 19 percent silt, and 13.4 percent clay. With an addition of 10 percent sand, the ratios would be 72.6 percent sand, 16 percent silt, and 11.4 percent clay.

References

Beacham, P., ed. 2001. *Devon Building: An Introduction to Local Traditions.* Tiverton: Devon County Council.

Bear, L. M. 1963. *The Mineral Resources and Mining Industry of Cyprus* (Bulletin no. 1). Nicosia: Ministry of Commerce and Industry, Geological Survey Department.

Bell, F. G. 1993. *Engineering Geology.* Oxford: Blackwell.

Clifton, J. R., and C. R. Robbins. 1978. *Methods for Characterizing Adobe Building Materials* (NBS Technical Note 977). Washington, DC: U.S. Department of Commerce/National Bureau of Standards.

Dionysius of Fourna. 1981. *The Painter's Manual of Dionysius of Fourna* (an English translation, with commentary, of Cod. Gr. 708 in the Saltykov-Shchedrin State Public Library, Leningrad). Trans. Paul Hetherington. London: Sagittarius Press.

Durrance, E. M., and D. J. C. Lamming, eds. 1982. *The Geology of Devon.* Exeter: University of Exeter.

Gass, I. G., et al. 1994. *The Geology of the Southern Troodos Transform Fault Zone* (Cyprus Geological Survey Department Memoir no. 9). Nicosia: Geological Survey Department.

Head, K. H. 1980. *Manual of Soil Laboratory Testing: Vol. 1: Soil Classification and Compaction Tests.* London: Pentech.

Myrianthefs, D. 2002. Church Architecture (13th–20th Century). In *Holy Bishopric Morphou: 2,000 Years of Art and Holiness.* Nicosia: Bank of Cyprus Cultural Foundation/Holy Bishopric of Morphou: 71–96.

Schilling, M. 2000. Analysis of plaster from Cave 85. Unpublished memorandum on analysis carried out by G. S. Austin, New Mexico Bureau of Mines and Mineral Resources. Los Angeles: Getty Conservation Institute.

Seed, H. B., et al. 1962. Prediction of swelling potential for compacted clays. *Journal of the Soil Mechanics and Foundations Division, ASCE* 80:53–87.

Shekede, L. 1997. English domestic wall paintings on earthen supports: Materials and deterioration. Master's thesis, Conservation of Wall Paintings Department, Courtauld Institute of Art, London.

———. 2000. Wall paintings on earthen supports: Evaluating analytical methods for conservation. In *Terra 2000: 8th International Conference on the Study and Conservation of Earthen Architecture, Torquay, Devon, UK, May 2000: Preprints,* ed. English Heritage, ICOMOS-UK, and University of Plymouth Centre for Earthen Architecture, 169–75. London: James & James.

———. 2002. Agios Sozomenos, Galata, Cyprus: Earthen analysis report. Unpublished report.

Shekede, L., and S. Rickerby. 1998. Knightstone Manor, Ottery St. Mary: Report on the conservation of the wall painting. Unpublished report.

———. 2005. 8 Red Lion Street, Alvechurch, Worcs.: Conservation of the wall painting. Unpublished report.

Stylianou, A., and Stylianou, J. 1985. *The Painted Churches of Cyprus: Treasures of Byzantine Art.* London: Trigraph.

Teutonico, J. M. 1988. *A Laboratory Manual for Architectural Conservators.* Rome: ICCROM.

Yong, R. N., and B. P. Warrenton. 1975. *Soil Properties and Behavior.* New York: Elsevier.

Choice of Materials for the Conservation of Wall Paintings on Earthen Supports in China

Jun Zheng

The great majority of historic sites in China are of earthen architecture, including such famous early examples as the ruins of Gao Chang City in Xinjiang Uigur Autonomous Region, dating from the first century BCE, and part of the Han Dynasty section of the Great Wall near the Jade Gate in Gansu Province. Even the majority of standing buildings are at least partly of earthen construction, such as the Tang Dynasty Nan Chan Monastery (Steinhardt 2002: 114–15) in Shanxi Province, where the columns are of wood and the exterior of the walls is protected by a layer of fired brick, but the interior wall paintings are executed on earthen plaster over adobe. Many thousands of earthen houses—some round and some square or rectangular, dating from the Yuan Dynasty to the present—are still in use in Fujian Province;[1] while caves excavated from the earth are still popular dwellings in Shanxi Province (Golany 1992).

Wall paintings are the main type of decorative surface of these earthen structures. But with the passage of time, deterioration inevitably occurs, and therefore conservation interventions—preventive, passive, and remedial—may become necessary. Damage may be natural or man-made; for instance, natural deterioration of the binding media in the paint layer of the Ming Dynasty wall paintings of the Pilu Temple (Hebei Province) has caused powdering of the paint layer, and as Garland and Rogers illustrate in this volume, detachment of the early fourteenth-century wall paintings from the Guangsheng Monastery (Shanxi Province) in the 1930s brought extensive damage.

Past Practice

The history of conservation interventions in China is relatively short, and the last half century does not demonstrate the same intensive exploration of new conservation materials as has occurred in the West. This is partly the result of the government system of controlling new materials that are applied to cultural property in China, which was formulated in the 1950s and has been enforced since the 1980s. By governmental regulation, a new material can only be recommended for application to a cultural property if it has passed a review by a board of experts. This cautious approach aims to use collective wisdom to overcome personal bias or ignorance in the selection of materials. As a result, the arbitrary use of materials on cultural properties has been much reduced. Under the same principle, associated with the designation of historic sites which began in 1961, annual review of conservation projects by an expert panel has been enforced since the 1980s. The panel evaluates the conservation proposals for a site, which may include the materials to be employed. *Principles for the Conservation of Heritage Sites in China* also provides guidelines for the selection of conservation materials (Agnew and Demas 2002: 7, 27). All this now forms the framework for the choice of conservation materials in China.

In the 1950s, only traditional materials were used in conservation interventions, since these were all that were available. For example, when the Yongle Palace (Shanxi Province) had to be relocated in 1958 because of the construction of a dam, all the wall paintings had to be detached. After extensive tests it was decided to use alum-glue solution as a temporary consolidation agent (Qi 1960: 84).[2] Because there were only a few previous cases in China to refer to, and little foreign experience was available, the range of materials for selection was extremely limited. In the early 1950s, the Central Academy of Fine Art conducted an investigation into how folk artists made wall paintings. Many such artists still using the traditional methods and materials were consulted, and the results were published in several articles (Lu 1956: 15; Liu 1958: 52–56, 1984: 30–34). According to these articles, alum-glue solution was applied prior to the underdrawing to improve the surface properties for executing wall paintings.

Yu Feian, a famous painter, described the binding media commonly used in Chinese paintings, which are mainly animal glues derived from hides, sinews, bones, and horns. He also described the function of alum in fixing and consolidating colors when multiple paint layers are applied (Yu 1955: 14–16, 1988: 17–18). At Yongle Palace, it seemed appropriate to select an alum-glue solution as the consolidant. Because the methods employed in detaching and reattaching the wall paintings were widely regarded as successful, the Yongle project was considered to be a model in wall painting conservation at that time, and the same materials have been widely used in many parts of China, especially in Shanxi Province.[3]

From the 1960s, foreign conservation influences resulted in an increasing use of synthetic materials. As published by Li Yunhe, the chief conservator of the wall paintings in the caves at Dunhuang, a set of criteria was drawn up for selection of consolidants and adhesives to reattach flaking paint on these paintings (Table 1), and a comparative test of traditional and synthetic materials was carried out in 1961 (Table 2). In the end, only water-based synthetic materials were selected (Table 3). The decision was based on the following assumptions:

- Traditional materials are less durable than synthetic ones.
- Solvent-based synthetic materials contaminate the air inside the badly ventilated caves, which was assumed to damage the wall paintings as well as the conservators' health.
- The original materials are all water-based, therefore solvent-based materials were considered to be incompatible (Li 1985).

Although the tests were undertaken carefully in one of the caves, they clearly favored synthetic materials without objectively assessing the merits of each material against the criteria. Presumed durability was the basis of the selection. This trial had a profound influence, since the selected materials were then used on many other paintings at Dunhuang as well as at many other sites in northwest China.[4]

These two examples illustrate typical reasons for the choice of materials in the past, which can be summarized as follows: Locally available materials have often been preferred

Table 1 Criteria for the selection of consolidants and adhesives

- Non-toxic
- Odorless
- Colorless
- Transparent
- Good adhesion
- Durable
- No harm to the wall paintings after aging
- No change to the color of the wall paintings
- No gloss after application

Table 2 Comparative tests

Traditional materials	Synthetic materials
5% Animal glue	Polyvinyl acetate
8–12% Deer skin glue	Polyvinyl alcohol
5–10% Asparagus paste	Polyvinyl butyl
2–8% Isinglass	Ethyl cellulose
3–6% Peach gum	Polymethyl methacrylate

Table 3 Test results

Materials selected as consolidants and adhesives for the wall paintings at Dunhuang Grottoes

3% PVAL
1–1.5% PVAC
PVAL (5% in H_2O) : PVAC (1% in H_2O) = 4:1
PVAL (2.5% in H_2O): PVAC (1% in H_2O) = 4:1

for economic reasons and were also often chosen for their presumed compatibility. Synthetic materials have often been selected for their presumed durability and because of their widespread use in other countries. Such selection has been affected by an absence of scientific facilities to perform necessary investigation and analysis as well as a lack of understanding of the scientific methodology for selection of conservation materials.

From the 1980s onward, conservation interventions in China became much more widespread, and both traditional and synthetic materials were used. In addition to the materials described above, polyvinyl butyl ethanol solution was applied on wall paintings in Hebei, Henan, and Shanxi provinces and in Tibetan Autonomous Region.[5] Paraloid B-72,[6] a new material in China, was applied on the Tang Dynasty wall paintings from the Tomb of Feng Hui in Shaanxi Province when they were detached in 1993 (Bai et al. 1994: 18) and on the nineteenth-century wall paintings in Er Yi Lou in

Fujian Province in 2000. *San jia shu zhi*[7] was employed as the consolidant for the wall paintings in Koguryo Tomb in Jilin Province in 1978 (Conservation of the Wall Paintings of Tomb No. 4, 1978) and for the Liao Dynasty tombs at Lianhuashan, Liaoning Province in 1983 (Li 1988: 656), whereas animal glue was used for the consolidation of the sixth-century wall paintings in the Tomb of General Xu Xianxiu. These varied approaches reflect the efforts that Chinese conservators have made in selecting appropriate materials for conservation, echoing to some extent international practice.

The great majority of materials selected for filling plaster losses were compatible with the original materials, except that cement was occasionally used by nonprofessionals, as for the seventeenth-century wall paintings in Yong'an Temple in Shanxi Province.

Current Methodology

The current methodology for choosing conservation materials can be summarized as follows: learning from the past; following the well-established general principles for selecting conservation materials—which include compatibility, durability/stability, reversibility/retreatability, no harmful content, and health and safety; and analyzing the original and added materials of wall paintings. These are essential in informing the selection of materials and understanding the causes of deterioration. Based on these principles and using such information, a set of criteria for the performance and working properties of the materials can be set forth. The potential materials, singly or in combination, should then be assessed on their own merits, without bias in favor of either traditional or synthetic materials. Laboratory tests of selected materials should be carried out, using a careful assessment strategy to evaluate the materials' impact. Field tests should then follow to determine the best materials.

This methodology has been well demonstrated in the Cave 85 Project at Dunhuang (Agnew 1997; Whitfield et al. 2000: 104–19).[8] Extensive analysis of the original and added materials of these Tang Dynasty wall paintings, and thorough investigations of the causes of deterioration, were conducted to establish criteria for selecting the conservation materials. Both laboratory and field tests of the potential materials were undertaken to assess their properties against these criteria, and monitoring of the impact of the selected materials was also performed. The grout developed in this project (Rickerby et al. 2004: 35) passed the review process and has been officially approved for use on wall paintings at Dunhuang.

Implementation of such a methodology to a full extent requires considerable resources. The Cave 85 Project at Dunhuang is exceptional in terms of the expertise, funding, and time that have been committed. Between the number of wall paintings in China (with new discoveries constantly being made) and the limited resources and number of conservators, this methodology is seldom achieved. How can conservators follow the methodology given these constraints?

Conservators must have a thorough understanding of the methodology in order to adapt it to individual situations accordingly. A conservator's knowledge of and experience with original materials, of the causes of deterioration, and of conservation materials and their effects play an important part in compensating for the absence of scientific analytical facilities. His or her in situ judgments are crucial in formulating the selection criteria. Simple tests and investigation of local materials and techniques can provide very useful information. Materials developed in similar cases can be adapted according to the criteria, with tests undertaken both in the laboratory and in situ. Also, of course, consultation with other experts in the field can be invaluable.

Case Studies

Three examples in which the author has been involved are given here to demonstrate how this methodology has been applied within strict resource constraints.

The Tomb of General Xu Xianxiu, Taiyuan, Shanxi Province

The first case is the emergency treatment of the painting of the tomb, dating from 571 CE, of General Xu Xianxiu of the Northern Qi Kingdom. The tomb is located on the outskirts of Taiyuan, the capital city of Shanxi Province. In summer 1999, local farmers noticed that some thieves were trying to rob the tomb and alerted the local government, which then sent an archaeological team to conduct a proper excavation as a "rescue archaeology" exercise. When they started excavating, they found that the entrance was painted with a marching scene demonstrating the official rank of the general. Extensive growth of roots, water infiltration, and natural deterioration of the binding media made it extremely difficult to uncover these wall paintings. Having failed in several attempts, they contacted me for help. I went to the site and helped and trained them to uncover and stabilize the wall paintings.

Regarding the original technique, the support was prepared by leveling of the raw earth, and applying a layer of white skim as a ground, with a typical thickness of about 1 mm. In situ tests have proved the ground is lime skim.⁹ The preliminary drawing was then undertaken, and the colors were filled in (Fig. 1). An unusual discovery made at the entrance of the tomb was two original containers still containing remains of pigments (Fig. 2).

Three interventions were necessary to ensure the safety of the paintings during excavation: readhesion of the ground to the support, securing the exposed edges, and consolidation of the powdered paint layer. Due to the urgency of this case, proper scientific analysis was not possible, and in general no analytical work has been done on the original materials and techniques of wall paintings of this period in China. However, my previous experience in conserving both Han and Tang Dynasty wall paintings, and publications on tomb paintings from this period and the Tang Dynasty that are similar to this one, all proved useful.¹⁰ The causes of deterioration were determined, and these were partially eliminated by the excavation process (for example, roots were removed), but some remain unsolved, such as salts accumulating on and in the paint layer.

When selecting materials for small-scale grouting, a list of criteria was produced based on existing information and in situ judgments. Preliminary selection was based on compatibility, and only earth- and lime-based grouts met this criterion. But further considerations eliminated the lime-based grout, since its high alkalinity might cause degradation of the

FIGURE 2 Tomb of General Xu Xianxiu. Remains of pigment container found in the entranceway. Photo: Jun Zheng, 2001.

already-deteriorated organic binder, among other problems. Following the criteria of the working properties of the grout, earth slurry was selected and tested in situ, and proved to perform well. Local earth was selected, washed with distilled water to reduce soluble salt content, and a thin slurry was grouted into the gaps with syringes. The edges were fixed with thicker earth slurries.

When the tomb itself was opened, more stunning wall paintings were found showing General Xu Xianxiu and his wife sitting in a tent, with servants and musicians entertaining them (Fig. 3); an oxcart and horse ready for them to depart; and lotus flowers and a divine tomb guard under the galaxy depicted on the dome. Because of the significance of the wall paintings, the tomb was listed as one of the ten most important archaeological discoveries in China in 2000. Edge repair was conducted as an emergency stabilization of these wall paintings, environmental monitoring of both surface and ambient temperatures and relative humidity have been carried out to provide information for future conservation, and the local government is considering developing a conservation plan for the tomb's long-term preservation.

Yong'an Temple, Hunyuan, Shanxi Province

The second example shows how simple in situ tests can inform decisions for selecting conservation materials. I was called upon in the middle of the conservation project of the Yong'an Temple in 2000. Located in Hunyuan Town in the north of Shanxi Province, the Chuan Fa Zheng Zong Temple

FIGURE 1 Tomb of General Xu Xianxiu, Taiyuan (Shanxi Province), 571 CE. Detail of the paintings in the entryway showing the original marks for leveling the surface. Photo: Jun Zheng, 2001.

FIGURE 3 Tomb of General Xu Xianxiu. Detail of paintings inside the tomb, showing the general and his wife being entertained by musicians. Photo: Jun Zheng, 2001.

Hall preserves 275 square meters of seventeenth-century Taoist wall painting, including over four hundred figures from heaven, earth, and hell shown approaching the sculpted figures of gods for blessing (Fig. 4). It is one of the most important examples of this subject in China (Chai 1997: 114).

The support is an adobe wall with the exterior protected by a layer of fired gray bricks. The interior is finished with two earthen-based plasters on which a ground was applied. The drawing was then made, and the colors filled in.

The original painting technique may be contributing to the deterioration. Flaking and selective loss of certain pigments may be caused by the use of too much binding media. Lack of maintenance has resulted in infiltration, which brought dirt onto the surface, and in some areas the paint layer has partially washed away. The cracks had been filled with cement (Fig. 5). Graffiti and soot deposition were also evident.

Among other interventions, the cement fills in the cracks were removed, and the gaps and other losses filled to

FIGURE 4 Yong'an Temple, Hunyuan (Shanxi Province), seventeenth century. Detail of the wall paintings in the Chuan Fa Zheng Zong Temple Hall. A group of Taoist figures are depicted, with their names on the banner and the donor's name at bottom left. Photo: Jun Zheng, 2000.

prevent further deterioration. Again, in the absence of analytical facilities, simple in situ tests were performed on two small fragments of the plaster from each layer. The proportions of clay, sand, and fibers were determined, and the type of fibers identified; they included straw fibers and a type of coarse hemp paper. These tests informed the criteria for compatibility. In searching for earth to use for the filling, some broken adobe from the old walls was saved and compared with samples from six locations where local people still commonly acquire earth for construction. Particle-size analysis confirmed that the adobe matched the earth of the plaster.

A search for fibers was also conducted by checking locally available fibers against those found in the plaster. A type of coarse hemp paper was found that matched the paper in the plaster. A mixture of these materials was tested in situ (Fig. 6), with different proportions and surface textures, to achieve the best match to the original. No retouching was performed on the fills. Although sophisticated technical analysis is always desirable for selecting conservation materials, in the absence of such resources sometimes simple tests can be of considerable value.

Er Yi Lou, Zhangzhou, Fujian Province

The final case study shows that an investigation of traditional techniques can inform the choice of materials. Also, since the site is inhabited, it is an example of how local people can be involved in conservation and, indeed, how necessary it can be to have their participation.

Er Yi Lou is located in a mountainous area in Fujian Province where bandit attacks often occurred in the past. The local people developed a unique type of defensive dwelling,

FIGURE 5 Yong'an Temple. Cement fills added by nonprofessionals in the 1970s have caused deterioration of the wall paintings. Photo: Jun Zheng, 2000.

FIGURE 6 Yong'an Temple. A conservator is chopping the hemp paper into the fill mixture. Photo: Jun Zheng, 2000.

FIGURE 7 Er Yi Lou, Zhangzhou (Fujian Province). Built between 1770 and 1806, this is an outstanding example of the earthen houses in China of that period. Photo: Jun Zheng, 2001.

and Er Yi Lou is one of the best examples (Fig. 7). Begun in 1770, it took the Jiang family thirty-six years to build. It comprises two concentric circles of rammed-earth construction—the outer circle is 74 meters in diameter. In addition to its perfect feng shui, its outstanding architectural features, sophisticated carvings, and nineteenth-century paintings are of great artistic and historic value, although this was not recognized by either residents or experts until the first investigation was conducted in 1999.

Over 600 square meters of wall paintings comprise the largest amount in any single dwelling in China. Many of them are dated and signed by the painters, which is very rare. They are a combination of painting and calligraphy, with a wide iconographic range—from the intellectually appreciated lifestyle to Taoist and Buddhist subjects, and from trompe l'oeil depicting traditional Chinese scroll paintings to what the residents call the *Foreign Beauty* (Fig. 8). *New York Times* newspapers from 1938 were also found as wallpaper in some rooms. Two to eleven layers of earthen plaster were applied to the rough surface of the rammed-earth structure, covered with a lime finish plaster on which the paintings were executed.

Thirty-eight families descended from the same ancestors currently live in the house. Over two hundred years of continuous use have resulted in much man-made damage, such as soot deposition, mechanical damage, and surface contamination with materials in daily use, such as lipstick.

Natural deterioration at the ground-floor level has been caused by the capillary rise of moisture.

In searching for materials to fill losses, an investigation into the original materials of these paintings was conducted. It indicated that the same techniques have been employed since the nineteenth century: original patterns found in Er Yi Lou are currently being painted on a new building only a hundred meters away. This investigation has provided valuable information on selecting the conservation materials. For example, examination of the original plaster found a type of hairline fiber that is not commonly seen elsewhere. The local painter told us that these fibers were derived from retting rice stems. A sample was compared with the fiber from the original plaster, and they were found to be of the same type, so fibers prepared with this technique were selected as a component of the fill materials.

Before the conservation campaign was undertaken in 2000, the residents had already made an agreement among themselves concerning the protection of their shared property. A copy of the agreement is displayed on the entrance wall next to a copy of the "Law of the People's Republic of China on the Protection of Cultural Relics," and the local authorities were invited to help enforce this agreement. When the investigation of the painting was being conducted, residents were involved in the documentation. They were surprised by the results and feel proud of their ancestors' achievements. They

FIGURE 8 Er Yi Lou. Unusual foreign influence is shown in this nineteenth-century wall painting. Photo: Jun Zheng, 2001.

are all willing to preserve these paintings. To safeguard them in the long term following the conservation campaign, a resident was involved and trained in the whole process to ensure that she is competent in maintaining the paintings. Recommendations were also made to the resident committee and local authority, with an emphasis on changing their cooking fuel from wood to gas to reduce soot deposition.

Conclusions

The choice of materials for use in the conservation of wall paintings on earthen supports in China has developed significantly within the governmental framework. In the 1950s, only traditional materials were available, and their selection was based on limited knowledge and experience. From the 1960s onward, synthetic materials were introduced under foreign influence and increasingly used.

Many past failures in selecting appropriate conservation materials were due partly to the lack of scientific facilities needed to perform necessary investigations and partly to lack of knowledge, but largely to the lack of understanding of the scientific methodology.

The methodology for selecting conservation materials that derived from past failures and currently prevailing international practice is one of the most crucial factors in design-ing conservation interventions. Although its implementation requires scientific rigor and significant resources, in the long term, the decisions are beneficial to both the wall paintings and those providing the resources. The Cave 85 Project at Dunhuang has set an impressive example, and although most conservation programs will suffer from far more constraints, their conservators have a duty to follow such a methodology to the limit of their ability and resources.

Acknowledgments

The author wishes to thank David Park and Sharon Cather of the Courtauld Institute's Conservation of Wall Painting Department for their valuable comments and suggestions.

Notes

1   Q. Wang 2000. Figures 54–59 (p. 126), and illustrations on pp. 148–49 provide details of this type of earthen architecture.

2   Alum-glue solution is an aqueous solution of $KAl(SO_4)_2$ and animal glue.

3 For instance, the alum-glue solution was applied on the wall paintings of the Guanyin Temple in Sichuan Province in 1984 (personal interview with Mr. Ma, the chief conservator of the campaign, in September 2003); the No. 1 Sui Dynasty tomb in Jiaxiang, Shandong Province in 1980 (Meng 1981); and the Qianfo Hall in Shaolin Temple in Henan Province in 1980 (Chen and Cai 1987). Many other wall paintings in Liaoning, Qinghai, Shanxi, and Yunnan provinces and in Tibetan Autonomous Region have received consolidation with alum-glue solution, but these projects have not been published.

4 Polyvinyl acetate and polyvinyl alcohol were continually used at the Dunhuang Grottoes after this trial and were also applied to a number of grotto sites in Gansu Province, as well as at Qutan Temple in Qinghai Province in 1986 (Wang et al. 1993: 266) and 1989 (Li et al. 1993: 280).

5 These projects have not been published, but the author has been involved in many of them.

6 Paraloid B72 is manufactured by Rohm & Haas. In this case it was supplied by RH China Inc., Beijing Office, Suite 819–825, Beijing Golden Land Building, No. 32 Liang Ma Qiao Road, Chaoyang District, Beijing 100016; tel. 86-10-6464-3450, fax 86-10-6464-3466.

7 The literal translation is "tri-methyl resin," a noncommercial copolymer of three types of acrylic monomers, all with a methyl group. The polymerization is processed by the conservators themselves.

8 Also see the forthcoming proceedings of the Second International Conference on the Conservation of Grotto Sites held at Dunhuang in June–July 2004, organized by the Dunhuang Academy and the Getty Conservation Institute. The proceedings will be published by the J. Paul Getty Trust.

9 A drop of 0.1 mol HCl on a small fragment of the white skim collected from the base of the wall showed gas production. This gas was guided into a clear solution of $Ca(OH)_2$, which resulted in clouding of the solution. This simple chemical analysis, indicating the presence of carbonate (CO_3), suggests the white skim is $CaCO_3$.

10 Among the tomb paintings of the Northern Qi Kingdom, important examples are the Tomb of Gao Run (Cultural Center of Ci County 1979; Tang 1979), the Tomb of Lou Rui (Shanxi Provincial 1983), the Tomb of Yao Jun (Cultural Center of Ci County 1984), the Tombs at Ma Jia Zhuang (Jinan Museum 1985), the tombs at Jiangwu City (Hebei Provincial 1959), and the tomb at Wanzhang, Ci County of the Hebei Province (Institute of Archaeology 1990). During the 1960s and 1970s, several important Tang Dynasty tombs were discovered in the Xi'an area of Shaanxi Province, among which the tombs of Princess Yongtai (Shaanxi Provincial 1964), Prince Zhang Huai (Shaanxi Provincial 1972a), Prince Yi De (Shaanxi Provincial 1972b), Li Shou (Shaanxi Provincial 1974a, b), and Zheng Rentai (Shaanxi Provincial 1972) are very important in terms of wall paintings. Wang Renbo (1989) provides a comprehensive introduction to the tomb paintings of Sui and Tang dynasties with a bibliography.

References

Agnew, Neville, ed. 1997. *Conservation of Ancient Sites on the Silk Road*. Los Angeles: Getty Conservation Institute.

Agnew, Neville, and Martha Demas, eds. 2002. *Principles for the Conservation of Heritage Sites in China* (two-part PDF file). Los Angeles: Getty Conservation Institute.

Anon. 1978. 四号墓壁画维修简结 (*Conservation of the Wall Paintings of Tomb No. 4, a Summary*). Unpublished report.

白崇斌, 樊娟, 张孝绒, 杨军昌 (Bai, C. B., J. Fan, X. R. Zhang, and J. C. Yang). 1994. 彬县五代冯晖墓壁画加固技术小结 (Summary of the consolidation technique applied to the Five Dynasty wall paintings from the Tomb of Feng Hui in Bin County, Shaanxi Province). 考古与文物 (*Kao Gu Yu Wen Wu*), 6:16–19.

柴泽俊 (Chai Zejun). 1997. 山西寺观壁画 (*Temple Murals in Shanxi Province*). Beijing: Cultural Relic Publishing House.

陈进良, 蔡全法 (Chen Jinliang and Quanfa Cai). 1987. 少林寺千佛殿壁画的临摹、揭取、复原 (The copying, detachment, and reattachment of the wall paintings of the Qianfo Hall in Shaolin Temple). 中原文物 (*Zhong Yuan Wen Wu*), 4:29–36.

磁县文化馆 (Cultural Center of Ci County). 1979. 河北磁县北齐高润墓 (Tomb of Gao Run in Ci County, Hebei Province). 考古 (*Kao Gu*), 3:235–43.

磁县文化馆 (Cultural Center of Ci County). 1984. 河北磁县北齐高润墓 (The Tomb of Yao Jun of the Northern Qi Kingdom in Dongchen Village, Ci County, Hebei Province). 文物 (*Wen Wu*) 4:16–22.

Golany, Gideon S. 1992. *Chinese Earth-sheltered Dwellings, Indigenous Lessons for Modern Urban Design*. Honolulu: University of Hawaii Press.

河北省文物管理委员会 (Hebei Provincial Management Committee of Cultural Relics). 1959. 河北磁县讲武城古墓清理简报 (Preliminary report on the excavation of the ancient tombs at Jiangwu City, Ci County, Hebei Province). 考古 (*Kao Gu*), 1:24–26.

中国社会科学院考古研究所, 河北省文物研究所, 邺城考古工作队 (Institute of Archaeology of the China Academy of Social Science, Hebei Provincial Institute of Cultural Relics, Archaeological Team of Ye city). 1990. 河北磁县湾漳北朝墓 (The Northern Dynasty tomb at Wanzhang, Ci County, Hebei Province). 考古 (*Kao Gu*), 7:601–7.

济南市博物馆 (Ji'nan Museum). 1985. 济南市马家庄北齐墓 (The Northern Qi Tombs at Majia Zhuang, Ji'nan, Shandong Province). 文物 (*Wen Wu*), 10:42–48.

李宏伟 (Li Hongwei). 1988. 辽宁北票莲花山辽墓壁画的揭取 (Detachment of the wall paintings of the Liao Dynasty tombs at Lianhuashan, Liaoning Province). 考古 (*Kao Gu*), 7:655–57.

李云鹤 (Li Yunhe). 1985. 莫高窟壁画修复初探 (A preliminary study of the restoration of the wall paintings at Mogao Grottoes). 敦煌研究 (*Dun Huang Yan Jiu*), 2:174–83.

李云鹤, 侯兴, 孙洪才 (Li, Y., X. Hou, and H. Sun). 1993. 瞿昙寺壁画修复 (Report on the restoration of the Qutan Temple wall paintings, Qinghai Province). In 敦煌研究文集, 石窟保护篇, 下, (*Dunhuang Research: Collected Articles on Grotto Conservation*) vol. 2, 279–87. Dunhuang: Dunhuang Academy.

刘凌沧 (Liu Lingcang). 1958. 民间壁画的制作法 (Folk techniques for executing wall paintings). 美术研究 (*Mei Shu Yan Jiu*), 2:52–56.

———. 1984. 传统壁画的制作和技法 (The method and technique for executing traditional wall paintings). 美术研究 (*Mei Shu Yan Jiu*), 3:30–34.

陆鸿年 (Lu Hongnian). 1956. 陆鸿年 (Brief introduction to the techniques for executing wall paintings). 文物参考资料 (*Wen Wu Can Kao Zi Liao*), 8:15.

孟振亚 (Meng Zhenya). 1981. 山东嘉祥英山一号隋墓壁画的揭取 (Detachment of the wall paintings from Yingshan No. 1 Sui Dynasty tomb at Jiaxiang, Shandong Province). 文物 (*Wen Wu*), 4:36–38.

齐英涛 (Qi Yingtao). 1960. 永乐宫壁画的揭取方法 (Method for detaching the wall paintings from Yongle Palace). 文物 (*Wen Wu*), 8–9:82–86.

Rickerby, S., L. Shekede, Z. Fan, W. Tang, H. Qiao, J. Yang, J. Zheng, F. Piqué. 2004. Development and testing of the principal remedial treatment of Cave 85: Injection grouting and soluble-salt reduction. In *Conservation of Ancient Sites on the Silk Road, Second International Conference on the Conservation of Grotto Sites, June 28–July 5, 2004*, Mogao Grottoes, Dunhuang, Gansu Province, The People's Republic of China, Abstracts, 35. Los Angeles: J. Paul Getty Trust.

陕西省文物管理委员会 (Shaanxi Provincial Committee on Management of Cultural Relics). 1964. 唐永泰公主墓发掘简报 (Preliminary report on the excavation of the Tomb of Princess Yongtai). 文物 (*Wen Wu*), 1:7–33.

陕西省博物馆, 乾县文教局唐墓发掘组 (Shaanxi Provincial Museum and Tang Tomb Excavation Team of the Bureau of Culture and Education of the Liquan County). 1972. (Preliminary report on the excavation of the Tomb of Zheng Rentai). 文物 (*Wen Wu*), 7:33–43.

陕西省博物馆, 礼泉县文教局唐墓发掘组 (Shaanxi Provincial Museum and Tang Tomb Excavation Team of the Bureau of Culture and Education of Qian County). 1972a. 唐郑仁泰墓发掘简报 (Preliminary report on the excavation of the Tomb of Prince Zhang Huai). 文物 (*Wen Wu*), 7:13–25.

———. 1972b. 怀太子墓发掘简报 (Preliminary report on the excavation of the Tomb of Prince Yi De). 文物 (*Wen Wu*), 7:26–32.

陕西省博物馆, 陕西省文物管理委员会 (Shaanxi Provincial Museum and Shaanxi Provincial Committee on the Management of Cultural Relics). 1974a. 唐李寿墓壁画初探 (Preliminary study of the wall paintings of the Tomb of Li Shou). 文物 (*Wen Wu*), 9:89–94.

———. 1974b. (Preliminary report on the excavation of the Tomb of Li Shou). 文物 (*Wen Wu*), 9:71–88.

山西省考古研究所, 太原市文物管理委员会 (Shanxi Provincial Institute of Archaeology, Taiyuan Management Committee of Cultural Relics). 1983. 太原市北齐娄睿墓发掘简报 (Preliminary report on the excavation of the Tomb of Lou Rui of the Northern Qi Kingdom in Taiyuan). 文物 (*Wen Wu*), 10:1–23.

Steinhardt, Nancy S. 2002. *Chinese Architecture*. New Haven: Yale University Press.

汤池 (Tang Chi). 1979. 北齐高润墓壁画简介 (Brief introduction to the wall paintings of the Tomb of Gao Run of the Northern Qi Kingdom). 考古 (*Kao Gu*), 3:244.

王进玉, 段修业, 樊再轩, 李树若 (Wang, J., X. Duan, Z. Fan, and S. Li). 1993. 青海瞿昙寺大面积脱落壁画的修复 (Report on the restoration of the Qutan Temple wall paintings, Qinghai Province). In 敦煌研究文集, 石窟保护篇, 下, (*Dunhuang Research: Collected Articles on Grotto Conservation*), vol. 2, 264–71. Dunhuang: Dunhuang Academy.

Wang, Qijun. 2000. *Vernacular Dwellings, Ancient Chinese Architecture*. New York: Springer-Verlag Wein.

王仁波 (Wang Renbo). 1989. 隋唐时期的墓室壁画 (The tomb paintings of the Sui and Tang dynasties). In 中国美术全集绘画编 (*Zhong Guo Mei Shu Quan Ji Hui Hua Bian*), vol. 12, 宿白，汤池，王仁波 (B. Su, C. Tang, and R. Wang, eds.), 21–34. Beijing: Cultural Relic Publishing House.

Whitfield, Roderick, S. Whitfield, and N. Agnew. 2000. *Cave Temples of Mogao: Art and History on the Silk Road*. Los Angeles: Getty Conservation Institute and J. Paul Getty Museum.

于非闇 (Yu Feian). 1955. 中国画颜色的研究 (*Chinese Painting Colors*). Beijing: 朝花美术出版社 (Zhao Hua Mei Shu Chu Ban She).

———. 1988. *Chinese Painting Colors: Studies of Their Preparation and Application in Traditional and Modern Times*. Hong Kong: Hong Kong University Press.

The Preservation of Earth Wall Surface Finishes in Historic Buildings of Northern Nigeria: A Case Study of *Babban Gwani*, Bauchi, Nigeria

Ishanlosen Odiaua

Traditional Hausa architecture is a developed urban style, the Sudanese style, which is known for its architectural and structural systems as well as for its intricate wall designs, which are highly stylized and avoid the representation of living forms, in keeping with Islamic traditions. The art of earth wall designs is currently undergoing an evolution as a result of changes occasioned by industrialization in the area. The traditional systems are experiencing a radical change, and there is a real danger that the traditional decorative art may be gradually dying out along with the master craftsmen who practiced it.

In spite of the challenges of change, death, and modernity, there are remarkable efforts across Hausaland to preserve the rich architectural and decorative motifs of the earth buildings across the area. These conservation efforts are brought to bear through the perpetuation of the annual traditional practice of maintenance, thus, it is hoped, ensuring the continuity of the cultural expression of earth wall decorations.

Background

The Hausa occupy the northern reaches of West Africa and are predominantly found in Nigeria, Chad, Niger, and Cameroon. The Sudanese style of architecture extends across the western Sudan, within the Niger and Chad basins of West Africa, and coincides closely with the areas where people have embraced Islam (Elleh 1997: 297–99). The central characteristics of this style are a courtyard plan, a flat or vaulted roof, and parapets pierced with gutter pipes or channels. The walls are constructed of unfired earth bricks. The bricks are set in earth mortar, and the roofs are supported by palm frond joists. A principal feature of the style is the courtyard plan,

which gives privacy, especially for women. This feature is also seen in Muslim domestic architecture in the Mediterranean area and elsewhere.

Despite a marked similarity over the entire area as a whole, the Sudanese-style buildings show significant variations both in technique and style. In Oualata (Mauritania), some houses are built of stone set in mud mortar, whereas in the upper Niger area, rectangular earth bricks are more frequently used. Traditionally, cone-shaped bricks, called *tubali*, were used in Hausa towns, whereas in Borno, burnt bricks were used up to the eighteenth century (Denyer 1978: 159–63).

This paper resulted from an inventory of immovable cultural heritage of Bauchi state, and examines the existing traditional practice of conserving an historic building, the *Babban Gwani*, Bauchi. Bauchi is located in the northeastern part of the Federal Republic of Nigeria. Its climate is characterized by long, hot dry seasons (from November to April) with temperatures ranging between 27°C and 40°C. The wet season occurs from the months of May to September, when temperatures range from 20°C to 35°C.

The *Babban Gwani*, Bauchi, is an example of the rich architectural style of the Hausa. It is the living room of the emir of Bauchi. This building type is called a *soro*; however, where the construction of a *soro* is recognized as an exceptional feat, it is called *Babban Gwani* (master builder) as a tribute to its builder. There are several *Babban Gwani*s across northern Nigeria.

According to the *Ajiyan Bauchi*, Alhaji Adamu Tafawa Balewa,[1] one of the five kingmakers of the Bauchi Emirate, the *Babban Gwani* of Bauchi was built when the Bauchi emirate was established, and may be as much as 150 years old.[2] Its use has also changed. It is presently used to receive small delega-

110

tions of up to twenty persons and dignitaries who come to pay homage to the emir during traditional religious festivals and at times of appointments, as well as for the meetings of the small general purpose committee and other small meetings of the emirate council (Fig. 1). For larger gatherings, a modern council building was built within the palace walls in the 1970s. The general council meetings of the emirate council have been relocated into this new building, which also serves as a reception room for receiving sizable delegations.

The entrance of the *Babban Gwani* is characterized by three wide, oblong earth wall panels, set against each other in relief. The middle panel is richly decorated with the incised bas reliefs that are a distinguishing feature of Hausa architecture. The flanking walls are left bare, thus bringing the richness of the middle panel into sharp contrast.

The interior of the building is covered with a wide range of incised lines in molded relief that are cast upon the surface of the columns and arches supporting the roof structure. The wall decorations that remain on the wall today are different from those commonly found in the larger Hausa towns of Kano and Zaria, which are more profuse in their expression. However, the predominant factor is the use of geometric designs and depictions of inanimate objects, in keeping with the requirements of Islamic religion.

Construction Techniques and Finish

In traditional Hausa architecture, plaster types are characterized by their composition, as follows (Dmochowski 1990: 1.7–1.9):

- *Makuba* plaster takes its name from the fluid derived from the pods of the locust bean tree (*Parkia filicoidea*), which is locally known as *dorowa*. A gelatinous, viscous liquid is obtained from the pods by either boiling or soaking them in water. The liquid is poured onto the building earth and carefully mixed in. *Makuba* improves the waterproofing properties of the plaster and protects it from attack by termites. It has good plastic properties, and lends itself to the making of molded decorations on wall surfaces.
- *Laso* plaster is reputed to have properties similar to that of cement. It is produced from the following:
  — *Katsi,* a by-product of indigo dyeing, improves the strength of the *laso* plaster

  — *Gashin jima,* goat hair mixed with the grease of previously soaked skins, gives the plaster waterproofing qualities.
  — *Dafara,* a gumlike material obtained from the root of a wild vine (*Cissus populnea*) also called *dafara,* serves as a binder. The roots are pounded into a soft pulp onto which water is poured. It can also be dried and reconstituted by being pounded and then soaked overnight in water. The viscous solution obtained is mixed with the *katsi* and *gashin jima* and thoroughly mixed. The mixing is repeated twice a day for ten days.

  Laso plaster was most often used in those parts of the building that required the greatest degree of waterproofing: surfaces of the flat or domed roofs, wall parapets, and the like.
- *Chafe* plaster is made from black earth to which a glutinous fluid is added. This fluid is obtained either from the locust bean pod (*makuba*) or from the acacia tree (*Acacia senegal*), locally known as *gabaruwa*. The wall surface is then covered with the mixture, and sieved gravel is gently pressed into the partly dried plaster with a flat tool. Before the plaster completely hardens, the surface is incised with geometric patterns. Finally, two coats of *gabaruwa* and two of *makuba* are applied to the surface.

FIGURE 1 Interior of the *Babban Gwani*. The emir (seated left) receiving visitors in August 2003. Photo: Ishanlosen Odiaua.

The traditional plant-based additives, especially *dafara* and *makuba*, are no longer in use; they have been abandoned in favor of cement. This can be attributed to several factors: increased growth of human settlements, depletion of the plants in the wild, and lack of interest by the younger generation, which makes it difficult to pass on the knowledge of how to identify and process these plant extracts.

The work of decorating walls was and still is carried out by men, in the dry season, after the harvest. The work is directed by a master builder, *Sarkin Magina*, who is aided by assistants (*magina*) in the final realization of the work. The evolution of the earth wall decoration is usually spontaneous in origin, depending on the inspiration of the *Sarkin Magina*. The earth is usually applied in thick layers and shaped and molded by hand.

The *Babban Gwani*, Bauchi palace complex, was originally built of unfired conical earth bricks (*tubali*) laid in earth mortar, and the walls were covered in earth plaster. Shortly before the independence of Nigeria, cement became a widely used material. Photographic records (Denyer 1978: 178) from 1960, the year of independence, show the use of cement-based plaster on the surface of the walls of the *Babban Gwani*, Bauchi. These early photos (Fig. 2) show the central, decorated panel finished in cement plaster while the flanking panels are left bare and have plain earth plaster.

The use of cement plaster on earth walls is becoming increasingly common across the world, and this is true of the *Babban Gwani*. Today, cement-based plaster is used throughout the entire building. However, there is the issue of compatibility between two materials of differing strengths and characteristics. Earth walls need to "breathe"—to have a humidity exchange with the surrounding atmosphere in order to lose water absorbed from the surface or through capillary action from the ground. For this reason, any plaster surface covering should have properties similar to the underlying wall. The application of cement-sand plasters on earth walls makes this moisture exchange difficult, as the cement plaster is waterproof. This leads to the buildup of moisture between the wall and the plaster, and eventually adherence fails and the plaster cracks and begins to fall off in large bits, leaving the earth wall exposed (Fig. 3). The cement plaster on the entrance façade of the *Babban Gwani* exhibits cracks.

Previous Conservation Work

Each time the *Babban Gwani* undergoes conservation work, the detailing of the decorations on the central panel changes,

but certain features remain constant (Fig. 4). Where the surface decorations are still intact, repair work is carried out on the wall support to ensure the stability of the ensemble. Traditionally, when repair work was due to be carried out, the palace authorities would send for and assemble the traditional builders (*magina*), who are organized into guilds and led by the *Sarkin Magina*. In addition to repairs, the work to be done could be mere renewal of the existing decorative works or complete replacement of the decorative plaster. This remains the practice today. The extent of work is determined by the extent of damage observed on inspection.

FIGURE 2 The *Babban Gwani* in 1960. The decorations on the central panel are more intricate than the present day's. The decorated lintel shown is no longer in existence. Photo courtesy of Nigeria Ministries of Education (Source: Susan Denyer, *African Traditional Architecture*, 1978. London: Heinemann).

The most recent conservation effort was carried out in 2003 and entailed complete replacement of the decorative panel. The process described below was carried out on the building. It was related by the craftsman who handled the work, Alhaji Musa, a 71-year-old builder and farmer who bears the traditional title of *Mabuddin Hardo*.

According to Alhaji Musa, the *Babban Gwani* has had very few structural repairs in his lifetime and has outlived all the other *soros* in the emir's palace. The major repairs that have been carried out were on the roof, when the earth dome was covered with asbestos sheets to reduce the problems of leakage. The internal wall surfaces have also been covered with paint, and they remain in very good condition.

To carry out the repair work on the external decorative panel, the old moldings were removed and the wall cleaned. The wall support was then prepared by smoothing it with an earth-cement mortar. The earth used is obtained from the ruins of the other *soros* within the palace grounds. This is done because the quality of the earth is assured, as it had previously undergone all the necessary treatment for it to be used in construction. The earth is mixed with water and then left to mellow for a few days to obtain the required consistency. It is then mixed with cement at a proportion of approximately one wheelbarrow of earth to half of a 50 kg bag of cement. This gives a proportion of roughly 1:3—cement to earth. The only other traditional additive that is still consistently used is horse manure, obtained from the stables of the emir.

There is no preconceived plan for the decoration, and the craftsman works from his own memory and initiative. In his lifetime, this was the first time that the *Mabuddin Hardo* carried out this work. Prior to this time, he had been an assistant to the master craftsman, the *Sarkin Magina*, who died before the conservation work was due to be carried out. According to him, there are only seven craftsmen left alive within the Bauchi

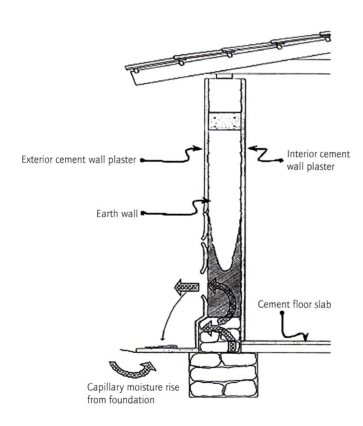
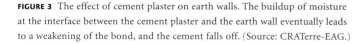

FIGURE 3 The effect of cement plaster on earth walls. The buildup of moisture at the interface between the cement plaster and the earth wall eventually leads to a weakening of the bond, and the cement falls off. (Source: CRATerre-EAG.)

FIGURE 4 External view of central panel in 2004. The decorative motifs have been changed from those of 1960 and the decorated lintel has disappeared, but the general concept remains the same. Photo: Ishanlosen Odiaua.

area, although more can be found in the outlying villages in the emirate council. The present decorations on the wall surface are a result of Alhaji Musa's initiative and recollections of the previous works of the late *Sarkin Magina*.

The work of decorating can take up to a week, as it is highly dependent on the creative inspiration of the builder at any given time. There is no set work plan. The decoration of the panel starts from the top and is gradually extended to the bottom. All the work, including the molding of the most intricate portions, is carefully fashioned by hand, without instruments. The wall decorations are raised in relief to thicknesses varying between 1 and 2 cm. When the decoration has been completed, it is left to dry. Once dry, it is painted with commercial water- or oil-based paints.

The *Babban Gwani* of Bauchi is maintained entirely by the Bauchi Emirate Council, although it is on the tentative list of national monuments. This listing assures that it is protected and that funds are made available for its conservation. The emirate council is provided with a certain percentage of funds from the eight local government councils within its domain. The council draws on its diminishing pool of traditional builders to carry out the necessary work on the building.

The Challenges of Conserving the *Babban Gwani*, Bauchi

Current conservation work on the *Babban Gwani* is carried out within the reality of current practice in the Bauchi area, a practice that has lasted from the time of the founding of the emirate. This practice entails annual building maintenance carried out after every harvest, during the dry season. Its practitioners are skilled artisans and craftsmen who bring an incredible intuitive feel to their work. Although the maintenance work on this building is carried out by a group of people with little or no background in the science of conservation, their empirical knowledge serves them well to meet the challenges of conserving the *Babban Gwani*.

A close look at the existing traditional conservation methods described above reveals impressive logic and consideration for the changes taking place within the society. The approach to the conservation work can be itemized as follows:

1 Inspection of the wall surface to determine the extent of deterioration and assess the work to be carried out
2 Mobilization of the necessary manpower and materials needed to effect the work

3 Repairs made where damage to the wall support is identified
4 Application of the decorative wall plaster

The *Mabuddin Hardo* related that one of the challenges he faces in conserving the *Babban Gwani* is the change in repair materials, occasioned by the fact that it is increasingly difficult to find young men who are willing to tread, or "puddle," the earth with their feet for the required length of time. This process of puddling is absolutely necessary to get the soil to the right consistency for work. Economic factors, as well as the fact that very few people practice traditional earth construction anymore, makes it very difficult to get younger men interested in it. Even where an attempt is made to pass on these skills, the younger generation is not interested in acquiring these skills, as they do not offer much in the way of earning a livelihood. However, within the confines of the emirate, a gradual change in this attitude is being seen; the progeny of traditional builders are gradually beginning to show an interest in acquiring these skills.

In evaluating the work of the decorative earth wall plaster of the *Babban Gwani*, one thing comes across clearly: the interest of the traditional leadership in preserving both the technological know-how and the building itself as testimony to the technological feats realized by this culture. However, this political will has yet to be translated into practical action. Perpetuation of the know-how by training and transfer of knowledge to the younger generation will require that their participation be made sufficiently attractive.

The Way Forward

In the words of Jokilehto and King,

One of the major challenges for modern conservation policies is the demand to conciliate two extremes, maintaining a status quo and allowing change. In fact, it may sometimes be taken as arrogance to insist on conservation of traditional ways of life if the population does not appreciate this or does not have the necessary conditions to make it feasible. It also means that the present community should be given every opportunity to appreciate and respect what is being inherited from previous generations. This is a learning process, which may require incentives and examples, and which is especially founded in a close collaboration between the population and authorities. (Jokilehto and King 2001: ref. 6, p. 38)

The fact that there is a conscious effort by the traditional authorities in the Bauchi Emirate to preserve this architectural masterpiece, the *Babban Gwani*, shows a positive attitude to acknowledging and preserving traditional building technology skills.

There is a need to document the traditional building and conservation process for future use and for reference purposes. The general building process has been well documented by Dmochowski in his three volumes on traditional Nigerian architecture; however, little has been recorded on the aspect of decorative work on earth walls as specific to the Bauchi area.

The existing practice, by traditional builders, of conserving and carrying out repair works on the *Babban Gwani* suggests a methodology for the preservation of the living tradition of decorating earth walls in the area, as outlined here:

- The adaptive reuse of materials from buildings that have fallen into disuse
- The identification of materials that are compatible with earth and meet its necessary requirement of moisture exchange with the atmosphere
- The introduction of new materials, compatible with earth, which would ensure the long life and durability of applied plasters. (The ready and widespread acceptance of another "new" material, cement, lends credence to the idea that new materials are acceptable, provided they can be locally sourced and are physically and chemically compatible with the earthen walls.)

Within the Bauchi Emirate Council, there lies a zone of heritage sites that includes the *Babban Gwani* of Bauchi, the *Babban Gwani* of Kafin Madaki (the seat of the third-in-command in the emirate), the old Bauchi Mosque, and the Bauchi wall, an earth wall that encompasses the old town settlement of Bauchi. With the exception of the Bauchi wall, which is in an advanced state of degradation due to natural and human factors, all the other earth structures have undergone surface treatment with cement-based plaster.

A proposal for a multidisciplinary, interorganizational, community-based approach to recovering and documenting these lost practices has been made. The approach being considered would be a joint effort of the Bauchi Emirate Council; the Abubakar Tafawa Balewa University (ATBU),[3] Bauchi; the National Commission for Museums and Monuments (NCMM); and the local communities in the areas concerned.

Within the framework of this proposed cooperation are interesting possibilities for research into earth wall plasters. One of these is to carry out material analyses of original earth plasters on traditional buildings to identify the composition of the mixtures and the properties provided by the plaster additives—especially those of plant extraction, which give the final plasters their cementlike properties. There is also the possibility of carrying out research on the suitability of mineral stabilizers, such as gypsum, which have desirable properties of porosity and allow earth walls to "breathe." The climatic conditions of Bauchi make this consideration possible, particularly when viewed in the light of other regions of the world (e.g., Iran, Peru) where traditional practices have involved the use of gypsum plasters on earth walls. Gypsum offers exciting possibilities, as there are rich deposits in the Bauchi-Gombe area, the processing of the material requires little energy, and the technology of the transformation is simple enough to be adapted to local conditions.

The NCMM is the statutory body charged with the conservation of heritage in Nigeria. The earth structures mentioned earlier are under the charge of the NCMM, and it is hoped that the commission will give its approval to create a conservation program to revive the traditional practices of decorating earth walls as well as maintaining them. The local community will be involved through training provided by the university to students from the School of Environmental Technology of the ATBU and to younger members of the traditional guilds in the art of wall decoration. The result of this will be to ensure the availability of skills for the execution of conservation plan–based actions. This will no doubt prove a big challenge, but there is a glimmer of hope in the willingness shown by the *magina* to pass on these skills to a younger generation.

With regard to the introduction of new materials, the question that readily comes to mind is, Whither the authenticity in this? Does it mean guaranteeing faithfulness to material, or rather to the spirit of the designs? It must be borne in mind that the use of cement-based plaster to carry out these designs on the *Babban Gwani*, Bauchi, dates back over forty years, and a mind-set has been established in the intervening period. Cement is considered to be a "modern" material, and more durable than earth. However, the durability of cement becomes questionable in the context of earth buildings. Increasingly, these buildings are covered in cement plaster to avoid the "fuss" of the annual maintenance required for earth plaster. However, examples abound in the area of buildings that, like the *Babban Gwani*, require regular care to repair or replace the cement plaster that peels off the underlying earth structure.

Conclusion

If living traditions are related to the preservation of materials and traditions, should the use of cement plaster be considered as a living tradition? Or is this applicable only to the traditional practices of conservation? Should the additives that were traditionally used be recalled? If not, what suitable substitutes can be found to guarantee the durability of the surface? It must also be remembered that the very nature of earth plaster and mortars lends them a flexibility that is not obtainable with cement, as a result of its inherent setting and hardening properties. Observations of the sand-cement plaster on the earth walls of the *Babban Gwani*, as compared with cement plasters on cement-based walls, show a difference in behavior (Figs. 5 and 6) that necessitates its constant renewal.

The living tradition of conserving the *Babban Gwani*, Bauchi, is a commendable practice, but its long-term perpetuation depends on the willing involvement of younger members of the community. Their involvement can only be secured if they are assured that it will result in economic benefits. In Nigerian society, as in many other places, traditional values are being neglected in favor of "modern" values. This syndrome cuts across all sectors of the Nigerian economy, and there is a need to educate the populace on the importance and value of the traditional society's technological accomplishments with a view to enhancing and improving on them.

Notes

1   Personal communication with the *Ajiyan Bauchi*, August 30, 2004. (Alhaji Adamu Tafawa Balewa passed on in December 2004, after this paper had been presented.)

2   The first monumental building in Bauchi was the Friday mosque, which was commissioned in 1817, in keeping with the practice of establishing a place of worship first whenever a new town was founded.

FIGURE 5 *Babban Gwani* in 2002. Note the detached cement plaster at the base of the left pillar. Photo: Ishanlosen Odiaua.

FIGURE 6 View of the *Babban Gwani* in 2003. Note the cracked plaster to the right of the decorated panel. Photo: Ishanlosen Odiaua.

3 The School of Environmental Technology of the ATBU has an existing memorandum of understanding with CRATerre-EAG, France, to develop a curriculum for the teaching of earth construction and the promotion of activities in the area of conservation and earth construction.

References

Denyer, Susan. 1978. *African Traditional Architecture*. London: Heinemann Educational Books.

Dmochowski, Zbiegniew R. 1990. *An Introduction to Nigerian Traditional Architecture*, vol. 1. London: Ethnographica.

Elleh, Nnamdi. 1997. *African Architecture: Evolution and Transformation*. New York: McGraw-Hill.

Jokilehto, J., and J. King. 2001. Authenticity and conservation: Reflections on the current state of understanding. In *Authenticity and Integrity in an African Context*, ed. Galia Saouma-Forero, 33–39. Paris: UNESCO.

PART FOUR

Living Traditions

Introduction

George Abungu

This section of the proceedings comprises four papers, by Karel Bakker and Chris van Vuuren, Pamela Jerome, Sébastien Moriset, and Gisèle Taxil and Ann Bourgès. The papers focus on the living tradition of decorating surfaces as practiced in South Africa in the Ndebele KwaMsiza wall decorations, in Yemen in the multistory mudbrick and lime-plastered buildings of Wadi Hadhramaut, in central Ghana in the threatened Asante shrines, and in northern Ghana in the painted and bas-relief traditions of the Nankani women.

A common element found throughout these papers is that the valuable human inventions and practices employed to create and conserve magnificent decorated surfaces occur in the context of modern societies that are not static but dynamic. These societies are rapidly changing and are in different states of transition and transformation. This raises issues of long-term sustainable maintenance, preservation, and the continuation of the various traditions in such fast-changing societies.

The papers also stress that the involvement of the local people in the preservation of this heritage is crucial. The community is the source of living traditions, and as such, it should be involved in and benefit from the conservation efforts taking place. The living traditions as practiced must therefore be taken into consideration in the conservation process—both as part of human values and as a way to humanize conservation and bring it to the community.

The papers by Jerome, Moriset, and Taxil and Bourgès emphasize the importance of promoting training and continuity of traditions, as well as creating honor in the artistic profession. By tapping the knowledge of the masters and elders as teachers, a vital link is made between old and young—most significantly, providing the young with a link to their culture. The papers by Moriset and by Taxil and Bourgès further demonstrate the importance of research on materials and forms of decoration. Bakker and Van Vuuren's paper effectively uses an example of a fluid tradition in a society under pressure. They reiterate the importance of the role of intangible knowledge, meanings, and symbols in the conservation of the Ndebele heritage.

While Moriset's paper focuses on a successful attempt to reintroduce the threatened but unique Asante wall decorations, the papers by Bakker and Van Vuuren, Taxil and Bourgès, and Jerome demonstrate the resilience of this art of architectural decoration in, respectively, southern and western Africa and in Yemen. All these examples actively involve their societies. Jerome's paper on the Yemeni case clearly demonstrates how political, economic, and social developments can positively or negatively affect the survival and appreciation of the heritage.

The papers presented here demonstrate the need for community recognition and involvement in the conservation of decorated surfaces. While the projects described recognize the threats to the heritage posed by changing attitudes and socioeconomic order, they also propose and implement vital solutions. Based on the authors' experiences, the solutions encompass sustained promotion of the heritage not only through laboratory research and documentation but also through training and financial benefit to individuals and communities.

Change and Continuity in Ndebele Earthen Architecture: Toward a Model for Conservation of Meaning in Architectural Decoration

Karel A. Bakker and Chris J. van Vuuren

Ndebele decorated earthen architecture in South Africa is part of a living tradition at risk. Ndebele art in its various forms constitutes highly visible, globally known icons—from historic propaganda images and the "postcard Ndebele" constructed by the South African tourism agencies during Apartheid (see Fig. 1) to recent glossy interior style publications and the globalizing reach of the work by Esther Mahlangu. Yet extant Ndebele living in earthen dwellings with mural decorations are diminishing fast, and knowledge of the tradition of mural decoration is at risk and in need of conservation. Due to these works' fluidity, they also demand renewed interpretation. This paper attempts to add to the currently stagnant state of conservation and practice of Ndebele mural decoration. This is partly done through a review of the historic interpretation, but more especially we point toward the necessity of a richer conservation-management approach—one that acknowledges the intertwined nature of the tangible and intangible components of heritage and relies on a model that includes a process of archaeologizing cultural layers and the use of personal histories within a co-constructed cultural ecology of a target community. Toward that end, we relate the eventful stories and current settlement of the Msiza family of KwaMsiza at Klipgat 249JQ. The academically conserved remains and history of their demolished settlement at Hartebeestfontein where they lived from 1903 to 1953, as well as newly recorded memories, are together identified as an important wellspring for the study and interpretation of Ndebele architectural decoration per se. They also provide an important laboratory for the much-needed conservation, for a fuller understanding of Ndebele architectural decoration, and for sustaining a living tradition.

FIGURE 1 The anonymity of the "postcard"' Ndebele: Natshabangu (wife of Soni Msiza of Hartebeestfontein) and her daughters Marama and Kholekile, depicted on a South Africa Tourism Corporation photograph. The photograph also appeared in *SA Panorama* with the description "Ndebele woman painting her hut (near Pretoria)" (1963: 17); without description in the brochure of the 1953 reconstruction of their village at the Pretoria Fair (Meiring 1953a); and in Meiring's 1955 architectural study, with the caption "a mother supervising work carried out by her daughter"(p. 33). Photo from Meiring 1955.

An Existing Knowledge Base

The Ndebele ethnographic discourse originated from an interest in their architecture and mural art on the one hand, and Ndebele beadwork and ritual clothing on the other. Only a few early researchers explored nonartistic issues such as history, religion, and ritual. While these nonartistic issues are addressed in more-recent research on Ndebele culture, the overriding impression gained from the majority of research on Ndebele art and architecture remains the facelessness of the people who are studied and the lack of integration of nonartistic issues into the interpretation of material culture. These negative aspects are identified as obstacles for a fuller understanding of Ndebele mural decoration.

Literature on Ndebele material culture with a focus on architecture and art mainly started to appear in the later 1940s and followed two streams: popular or tourist, and academic. The former was embedded at the one pole in the "tribal-primitive" paradigm, which became popular in the case of the Ndebele during the 1940s and 1950s but dates back far beyond. It was also supported and informed by the local colonial-Apartheid paradigm of the time, together with the global perceptions of the "other," with its specific reference to "primitive" Africa.[1] A spate of academic discourse from the disciplines of architectural and art history emerged from fieldwork in the 1940s and afterwards,[2] and the architectural and art research was later taken further by other researchers, including the authors.[3] The work of Courtney-Clarke and of Frescura and Van Vuuren started to break the mold of facelessness and anonymity that characterizes this field of study.

Analysis of both streams of literature mentioned above shows that, (1) thus far, architects, art historians, anthropologists, and museum scientists have operated more or less independently; (2) even though the research foci of the works by the earlier scholars were often reductionist or isolated, their work remains valuable in terms of the academic content (and often also in terms of the ethnographic reportage and the researchers' modes of interaction with the Msiza villagers); and (3) extraordinarily, most of the populist and the academic literature referred to the Msiza family's two settlements focused on in this paper. The latter gives us the unique situation of having a well-documented history of a hundred-year period of settlement of one Ndebele family group. There is a written record of the family's particular history and genealogy, the arranged encounters with tourists that started early in the twentieth century, and the support and intervention on a political level by the family's benefactor, the head of the School of Architecture of the University of Pretoria, Professor A. L. Meiring, at the start of the time of forced removal of Blacks in the 1940s–1950s, as well as his orchestration of the replication of the village at the Pretoria Showgrounds in 1953. These events, in addition to the Msiza family's interaction with museums in conservation work, the continuing exposure to tourism and use of the village for television shoots (Fig. 2), funding by international corporations, and misplaced physical additions by state departments, have all played their part to elevate the importance of, and establish the settlement as a visible representative of wider Ndebele culture.

A Research Approach

Having surveyed the status quo of research, the approach we chose for the continuing research was to construct an "ecology of knowledge" through gaining a synthetic view of existing research and understanding the relationships and overlaps between the various research strategies. The memories of elderly members of the Msiza family were explored in order to discover life histories and construct a family genealogy.

Our approach is not a de novo exercise in which the contributions of early scholars are negated. We rather believe this to be a process of verification of data emanating from the early period of research, as well as a way to construct a matrix or framework whereby an interdisciplinary approach to the

FIGURE 2   Television shoot at Klipgat: The filming of a childrens' program on Ndebele culture. Photo: K. A. Bakker, 2004.

conservation of Ndebele earthen decoration, earth building technology, and indigenous knowledge (as part of indigenous knowledge systems) can be formulated.

As mentioned, the existing discourse on Ndebele architecture and art was remarkable because it was mainly inspired (and researched) from a single source—the two settlements of the Msiza family. Their three-generational homestead (called an *umuzi*) was first built on the farm Hartebeestfontein, against the slopes of the Magaliesburg range, on the northern side of Pretoria ca. 1903. Its inhabitants were forcefully resettled in 1953 to their present location, Klipgat (249JQ),[4] some 30 kilometers (18 miles) north of Pretoria (Fig. 3). The residents of the present village refer to it as KwaMsiza ("place of Msiza"), which refers to the clan name of the ruling family (although some refer to it as KoKlipgat, "at Klipgat"). The earthen architecture of the KwaMsiza village, together with many of its original founders and its succession of mural decorations, have now survived for fifty-one years at the current

location, and the products of fifty years of habitation in the preceding village were well recorded during its last decade of existence. In addition, images of the intense tourist "gaze" (after Urry 1990) on the family and their villages, stretching from the 1940s until the present, have been recorded.

This rich research base served as the foundation for further fieldwork during intermittent periods of involvement in the settlement architecture of the Msiza family. The works by the architects Meiring and Frescura are particularly important. Their respective 1945 and 1983 plans of the two Msiza homesteads at Hartebeestfontein and Klipgat stand out as key documents for linking decorations to family members and for further research.

Research focus areas varied over the period of involvement. Bakker and his architecture students surveyed and documented the settlement pattern and individual homesteads in KwaMsiza at Klipgat from 1998 to 2001. Due to the intended multidisciplinary nature of future research, documentation of

FIGURE 3 The Msiza villages: (a) indentured settlement on the farm at Hartebeestfontein in 1953, (b) at Klipgat in 1981. Photos: (a) Dotman Pretorius, from Bowen 1957, courtesy of Van Schaik Publishers, (b) from Frescura 1984, courtesy of the South African Institute of Architects.

FIGURE 4 Additional ethno-autobiography being collected by Van Vuuren; the family patriarch, Maselwane Msiza, and his wife, NoKesikile, from Klipgat, identify family members from historic photographs of their first village. Photo: K. A. Bakker, 2004.

the material aspects of the settlement were prepared for use in various levels of interpretation, but it was also desirable to be able to easily add future variations in the settlement to the documentation. The settlement plan contains various levels of data pertaining to building walls, small outside structures, low walls and fences, paths and vegetation as they were in 1998 (and updated in 2001).[5] A detailed photographic survey of wall decoration on the homestead walls, as well as of house walls as they existed in 1998, was made, and sections were drawn for constructing a three-dimensional drawing of the totality, within which patterns of space use will in the future be recorded and documented.

In 2004, we conducted brief fieldwork to compile a full and comprehensive genealogy of the village residents and to record the narratives and testimonies of village elders in preparation for the Decorated Surfaces colloquium. We added what some anthropologists refer to as the ethno-autobiography of villagers, for example, that of the patriarchal head of the village, Maselwane Johannes Msiza—at the time, more than ninety years old.[6] His memory was markedly vivid, as proved by the seven-generation genealogy that we were able to compile (with assistance from younger family members, who will keep future records). By using the earliest recorded photographs of individuals from the Msiza family village members (Fig. 4), as well as watercolor drawings of homesteads made in the 1940s (Fig. 5), the surviving elders of the village were able to identify these previously "faceless"

individuals and their homesteads, from which we could trace their stories and position them in the genealogical structure. The site plan of the settlement as it was in 2001 was used by the research team to document the current spatial genealogical pattern and to link that to the spatial genealogy of the first village (Fig. 6). The comprehensive genealogy enabled us to integrate differing names of inhabitants used earlier by authors such as Meiring (1955) and Frescura (1981a).

The data collated for this paper is the culmination of these initial efforts at synthesis and research. We hope to augment both the biographical and social histories related to the already identified decorated surfaces and to trace the more recent trends in motif, pattern, base layer, and paint material. An awareness of continuity and fuller understanding of a possible conservation model is also needed—not only for KwaMsiza but for Ndebele mural decorations overall.

Toward a Relevant Conservation Model

Intangible Aspects with a Significance for the Conservation of Ndebele Architectural Decoration

The inclusion of intangible aspects of heritage has until recently been much neglected in conservation projects. However, the research has already indicated various intangible aspects of heritage that will have a strong bearing in the manner of conservation of meaning in Ndebele architectural decoration.

FIGURE 5 Watercolor rendition of the homestead of Musimunye Msiza of the Hartebeestfontein village, drawn by Professor A. L. Meiring (1953b) in the 1940s and used in the genealogical verification process. Photo from Meiring 1953b.

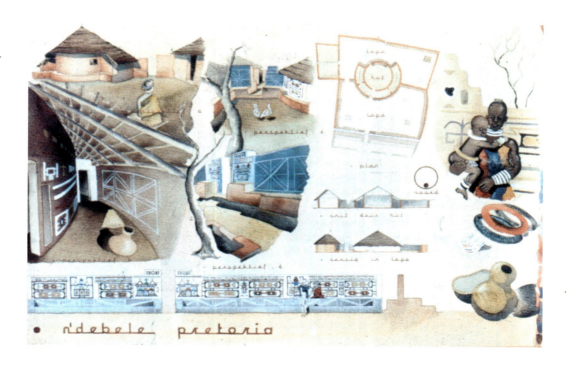

FIGURE 6 Reconciliation of verified names: (a) inhabitants of the Msiza village at Hartebeestfontein (new names overlaid by Bakker on plan by Frescura [1983]), (b) the group of transplanted homesteads at Klipgat (new names overlaid by Bakker on portion of plan by Frescura [1983]). Both illustrations from Frescura 1983.

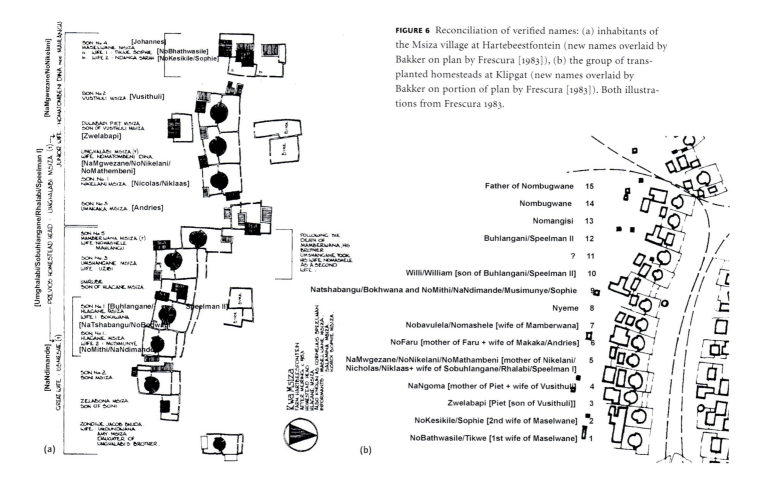

Father of Nombugwane — 15
Nombugwane — 14
Nomangisi — 13
Buhlangani/Speelman II — 12
? — 11
Willi/William [son of Buhlangani/Speelman II] — 10
Natshabangu/Bokhwana and NoMithi/NaNdimande/Musimunye/Sophie — 9
Nyeme — 8
Nobavulela/Nomashele [wife of Mamberwana] — 7
NoFaru [mother of Faru + wife of Makaka/Andries] — 6
NaMwgezane/NoNikelani/NoMathambeni [mother of Nikelani/Nicholas/Niklaas+ wife of Sobuhlangane/Rhalabi/Speelman I] — 5
NaNgoma [mother of Piet + wife of Vusithuli] — 4
Zwelabapi [Piet [son of Vusithuli]] — 3
NoKesikile/Sophie [2nd wife of Maselwane] — 2
NoBathwasile/Tikwe [1st wife of Maselwane] — 1

(a)

(b)

Political-Historical Context

The iconographic value of Ndebele beads in combination with surface art is unsurpassed elsewhere in South Africa and probably in Africa. The architecture and dress of the Msiza family created much of the tourist "gaze" identity that the post-1950s Ndebele became famous for. This identity exists, but it is different from that held within Ndebele society (see Van Vuuren 2003).

KwaMsiza as a tourism encounter has over the years amplified the ideologies of "us" and "them" (compare Bruner 2001, Tilley 1991, Kasfir 1999, Van Vuuren 2003). The two successive villages of the Msiza family, and their conservation, became an inspiration for some architects from the Apartheid era, partly because they admired the villages' beauty and partly because they represented the type of "trapped" and timeless primitive tribal identity that these protagonists hoped for. Visual images from the conserved villages were also manipulated for propaganda and tourism purposes. The tribal image of primitive people mirrored the rationale for the creation of ethnic Bantustans. The memory of these images must be included in conservation processes.

A specific brand of village tourism, in which tourists interact with "natives," has a peculiar and tainted history in South Africa, although the phenomenon is not unique to South Africa, as Bruner (2001) and Tilley (1991) explained. Cultural villages in South Africa have been masked and marketed in various types of ventures. The first type is a private enterprise—cultural authenticity is sacrificed for an intensified African experience, often one that is highly choreographed. The second type is the "open-air museum." This ethnic type of village (or open-air museum), which historically was to be created for each of the ethnic groups in the former Transvaal, was based on an ideology embedded in Apartheid dogma (see Frescura 1983). These are not lived-in villages, but static, reified entities. These enterprises depended heavily on the state budget, and most of them are now either struggling for survival or dwindling.

This brings us to the third type, namely villages like KwaMsiza at Klipgat, of which there are few left in South Africa. It is possible that KwaMsiza is the oldest surviving living cultural village in South Africa. As a Ndebele settlement, KwaMsiza is probably the only remaining cultural village where authentic remnants of historical settlement practice are extant and where cultural traditions live on in the daily life experience of its dwellers, rather than being "performed." As such, the settlement is a highly significant cultural resource, and offers an insight into living, evolving indigenous knowl-

edge systems beyond that which the privatized cultural village or open-air museum can offer or achieve.

The destiny of the Msiza family became intertwined with the vision of their historic benefactor, the academic and architect Meiring. One should ask whether he was a protector or a creator of heritage. Conservation politics in South Africa in the 1950s were always going to be one-sided and weighted against conserving an African village—however ironic or contradictory this may appear. The Apartheid dogma that entrenched the tribal did not imply that its conservation would be funded. Testimonials to the author from architects who knew Meiring provide a picture of a selfless person who admired Ndebele architecture, who in the 1940s and 1950s was aware of the tenuous nature of Black settlements close to White cities (even in the fledgling days of Apartheid South Africa), and who did not force his own vision of conservation onto the Msiza family, contrary to the view expressed by Pienaar (1991). Nevertheless, he had a strong idea of what was "pure" or real Ndebele architecture and wall painting heritage. What Meiring achieved was isolated and in some ways naïve, seen in today's conservation environment. In later conservation efforts, Naude (2000), of the South African National Cultural History Museum, pointed to a noninterventionist, facilitating role for conservators in a participative conservation process for KwaMsiza. Current and future conservation efforts must be both aware and critical of the role and agendas of the "experts," relative to those of the living community.

Displacement and diaspora are major aspects of the cultural significance of KwaMsiza, as they are of most Ndebele. The South African Ndebele have been singled out like no other tribe for subjection, indenture, and regional displacement since their encounter with the forces of the Zuid Afrikaansche Republiek (ZAR) of the later 1800s to the early 1900s, and further oppressed by those forces' successors in the Nationalist Apartheid regime. Ever since the end of the Mapoch War of 1883, the Ndebele have petitioned their landless dilemma and requested the restitution of the KoNomtjharhelo (Mapochsgronden [500JS]) homeland. The Msiza family, in their turn, is a case study among this larger whole. They were indentured on the farm Hartebeestfontein, which in the 1940s belonged to a farmer called Oubaas (subservient name for the senior landowner) or "Vet" ("Fat") Wolmarans. Importantly, they were closely related to the imprisoned King Nyabela through marriage, and their settlement was physically near the locality of the homestead and eventual grave of their persecuted king.

The advent of the 1953 removal of the Msiza family from the Hartebeestfontein farm was sparked by anti-Ndebele sentiments harking back to the original Ndebele wars. This time, it did not seem to have been based on a fear of their regrouping against the Boers, but was rather born out of a "sick" blend of racism and jealousy directed towards the settlement. Vet Wolmarans, the owner of Hartebeestfontein, was on a good footing and friendly with his farm tenants (interview with William Msiza). Most importantly, he allowed foreign tourists to visit the Msiza family, photograph the murals, and purchase beadwork, and he had the Msizas dance and sing for the visitors and ply them with sorghum beer (Van Vuuren interview with Maselwane Msiza). Historical data suggests that the mainly Afrikaner residents of the Waverley suburb, close to which the Msiza family resided, protested against the presence of the village so close to a White suburb. Their lobby saw the eventual removal of the Msiza family and the torching of their village. In an interview, Maselwane Johannes Msiza explained that the Waverley Whites were suspicious about the kind of racial interaction that took place at the Msiza village between tourists and the villagers. It appears that tourists who "enjoyed themselves" were accused of threatening the separateness charter devised and upheld by White society, and it was feared that they would influence the "kafirs" or "natives" (both historically used derogatory terms for Africans) with "liberal ideas."

The role that the isolated position of Ndebele, within the Bantustan or homeland policy of the Nationalist regime, played in the expression of an identity—and therefore also in terms of settlement and decoration—is an important part of heritage conservation. When the Apartheid architects designed the ethnic Bantustan dispensation and gazetted its implementation through various statutes in 1951, 1956, 1970, and 1971, the only "ethnic" category that was continuously excluded was that of the Ndebele. Independence was only to be offered within the parameters of the Transkei-Bophuthatswana-Venda-Ciskei Bantustan group (called TBVC). This offer was made to the Ndebele in 1985. The Msiza family, however, chose to remain at KwaMsiza even though the area became a Tswana Bantustan.

Naming Traditions

An understanding of name giving in Ndebele culture is important in the process of recording and tracing architectural settlement patterns and the evolution of mural styles. A single Ndebele woman is known by at least four names. Let us offer Dina Msiza as an example: (1) her clan (*isibongo*) name is NaMahlangu (here referring to the royal Ndzundza clan); (2) her subclan name (*isinanazelo*) is NaMgwezane (the royal subclan); (3) she is named after her firstborn child as well, NoNikelani (mother of Nikelani); followed by her (4) European name, Dina. Often other names are added. The name giving is often confusing in the research process. Previous researchers (e.g., Meiring and Frescura) often only recorded the European name and transcribed these in either Afrikaans or English spelling: Nicholas or Niklaas for Nikelani, Seun (son) for Soni, and the like. Even corrupted versions of Ndebele names are problematic. The challenge in this case was to recognize names of residents in the recorded documentation, to integrate these names with a single individual, and to verify this process through consultation with the community.

Dating of historic built material culture can be facilitated by identifying birth dates of inhabitants. Establishing the age of Ndebele individuals is made possible by using their regimental name (the *indanga*) and date of initiation (the *ingoma*), and from that to calculate dates such as birth and settlement occupation. The system has been used successfully on Ndebele archaeological sites (Van Vuuren 1993).

Social Structure

The conservation process must acknowledge the range of fluidity and change in social structure. Interpretation of layout patterns in a Ndebele settlement must rely on intimate knowledge of family genealogies, social rank, and gender issues surrounding social structure and space appropriation.

Indigenous Practice vs. Outside Influences

Conservation process must recognize the indigenous. Studies by Coplan (1987) and James (1990) on women migrants in southern Africa led to informative discussions around the concept of *sesotho* (tradition), as contrasted with *segoa* (the ways of Whites). Among the Ndebele, women contrast "ways of doing" or *isikhethu* (ours), with "foreign ideas" or *isikhuwa* (those of Whites). Elaborating on this concept, *isikhethu* became synonymous with *isiNdebele* (as culture) and *isindru* (that of a human nature, meaning Ndebele) in daily usage.

Observations by the author Van Vuuren during the late 1970s were that *isikhethu* in its inclusive/exclusive capacity appeared to belong to female vocabulary. Ndebele women classified early mural paintings and beadwork (e.g., those sewn onto goatskin of an *umaphotho*) as "real Ndebele" or *isikhethu*, as opposed to modern influences where plastic (see Levy 1989: 30) and canvas were introduced—the latter being *isikhuwa*. In the same way, earlier bead types are *isikhethu* and recent types, colors, and even motifs are *isikhuwa*. Ndebele women today still talk about whether certain items are suitable for buyers who prefer *isikhethu* (for the gallery market) as opposed to *isikhuwa* (items for the informal market).

The differentiation is similarly extended to mural art in terms of the past and the present, the rural and the "urban" (KwaNdebele), generational differences, and so forth. Conservation process must acknowledge the concept of *isikethu* and the amount of fluidity and change that is tolerated or practiced within it. The preservation or reconstruction of ritual spaces and homesteads, or of historical settlement form and order, fall within this domain. In the domain of traditional architecture there are methods, skills, and material that the Ndebele recognize as either *isikhethu* (indigenous) or Western. Material might include binding rope (*indambo*) for securing rafters and beams, and rope for the thatching of grass. Most of these are natural materials that are difficult to obtain in present times due to depletion of natural resources or other causes of scarcity. At KwaMsiza, since the 1970s the residents have used modern sisal rope and nails in roof construction. They still however recognize the feeling of working with *isifunzi* rope (made from the *Velozia* species).

Technologies like modern building practice, electricity, motor vehicles, and telecommunication have a significant effect on conservation practice. Research on the KwaMsiza village over a period of fifty years has shown the rapid change in homestead configuration and form due to family growth, but also due to the acceptance of foreign building process, forms, and technologies. A process of continuous documentation is required to keep track of this evolution and change, and to study it further.

Some Tangible Aspects with a Significance for the Conservation of Ndebele Architectural Decoration

Ndebele mural decoration and its interpretation partly hinge on a stylistic or typological taxonomy. Scholars have divided Ndebele decorated surfaces in two broad categories or types: painting on a flat surface, and relief work on door and window frames, pillars, and façades. House walls as well as courtyard walls, which may be single, double, or triple, are always painted. Two broad types of paint material are used: one natural (cow dung and mixtures with colored pigments) and the other synthetic (commercially available paints).

Ndebele patterns are mostly linear in design. The faces of *isirhodlo* (courtyard walls) are usually more elaborate and "attractive" in appearance than the inner vertical surfaces.[7] As

to the paintings' further classification, various methods rely on formal aesthetic principles, such as types of symmetry, hierarchy, pattern, color (multicolor or monochromatic); the type of material used (natural or synthetic pigments); and the regional traits or motifs used. Guidelines follow from Walton (1965), Weiss (1963: 84), Matthews (1971: 71, 83), Schneider (1985: 64), and Van Vuuren (1986).

The wall painting work of the Msiza family can be synchronized with all known chronological and style developments, even those from Hartebeestfontein (before 1953). One could indeed postulate that KwaMsiza was the driving force and trendsetter for some of the post-1950s multicolor designs, since Ndebele women were arguably responsive to the tourist encounter at KwaMsiza, which at that stage was the only such venture. The more the "postcard" Ndebele were reproduced to the outside world, the more they responded by exploring new patterns and color variety. In the words of Maselwane Msiza, "The Whites (tourists) liked what they saw, so they came back." In addition, the villagers' close proximity to the urban domain and its architectural forms, relative to other Ndebele, inspired changes in motifs. Ndebele women from far outlying rural areas traded (e.g., in beads, blankets, paint) more frequently in urban Pretoria after the 1950s. Such rural Ndebele women knew about the Msiza village—those few individuals who visited the site obviously introduced changes in mural art and beadwork in previously isolated rural areas.

The strong relationship between mural decoration and beadwork must again be acknowledged in the interpretation of both. The similarities in patterns are most striking in the earliest mural decoration and bead designs (Matthews 1971: 71). Cow dung floor patterns, on the other hand, are similar to those inspired by the *isithebe* mat of the Ndebele (Van Vuuren 1986: 105; Levy 1989: 29).

The recognition and strengthening of a living tradition with accompanying local knowledge of building is pivotal in any conservation initiative. The walls of historic Ndebele cone-on-cylinder dwellings were constructed of columns made from tree trunks or branches, filled in with wattle and daub, and plastered with mud which was decorated seasonally. The conical roofs were constructed of beams made from branches, had twig purlins tied to the beams with thongs or rope, and were thatched with long grass.

The artisans, over decades, devised their own methods of restoration, conservation, and structural maintenance. They knew exactly when and at what stage to rethatch roofs and to apply bundles of grass for short-term restoration, such as after a severe storm. They also knew how to deal with the problem of collapsing roof beams and how to insert a short *ikapa* (support beam) to strengthen the structure. Women knew when to resurface horizontal and vertical surfaces. Cracking hut and courtyard walls were always repaired before it was too late. Although most resurfacing and painting was conducted during the dry winter season, villagers were on constant alert for signs of decay. Floor surfaces were frequently smeared with cow dung, in particular before important ritual occasions such as girls' and boys' initiations. The problem of *umuhlwa* (termites) was solved by spreading the ash of the aloe on the perimeter of inner and outer walls of the hut.

These methods or sets of indigenous knowledge, already referred to as the *isikhethu* way, are disappearing with the use of foreign building methods and materials. At KwaMsiza, cement additives have been added to all the old mud plaster on the earthen walls, with unforeseen and disastrous effects: flaking and structural failures are endemic (Fig. 7). Current decorations are all of commercial acrylic paint (see Fig. 8)[8]. Yet, the decision that mud plaster must make way for cement, which decorated surfaces should change in design and color, and which wall structures should be demolished and/or rebuilt, have remained with the Ndebele women at KwaMsiza themselves. Any conservation model should be cognizant of these factors.

The research has indicated the fast pace of change and fluidity of architectural form and detail over time. It is known that many of the second and third outer *isirhodlo* of KwaMsiza homesteads have disappeared, that decorations on the outer walls of homesteads were altered between 1983 and 2001, and that there is no precise continuation in pattern making on any one single wall (Fig. 9). Regular documentation of successive changes is a requisite tool for the conservation-management process.

KwaMsiza at Klipgat: Public Spectacle or Real-Life Village?

It could be argued that, after a century of public exposure as a result of the tourism encounter, KwaMsiza and its residents have been robbed of their private lives, and sociocultural life has been eroded to the extent that the village has been rendered artificial. However, this has most certainly not been the case. Apart from offering tourists what they wanted, or what the villagers perceived the tourist demand to be, the sociocultural fabric seems to have sustained itself on a daily basis. One such indicator, one could argue, is the continuation of ritual life. The current research has indicated that two such ritual institutions have managed to keep the Msizas in touch with the

FIGURE 7 Damage resulting from the use of cement additives. Here typical delamination and structural failures can be seen where the cement plaster layer has become detached from the original mud plasterwork of a Klipgat home. Photo: K. A. Bakker, 2004.

FIGURE 8 Leah Msiza demonstrating the application of commercial acrylic paint with a toothbrush on the wall surface of a house. Photo: K. A. Bakker, 2004.

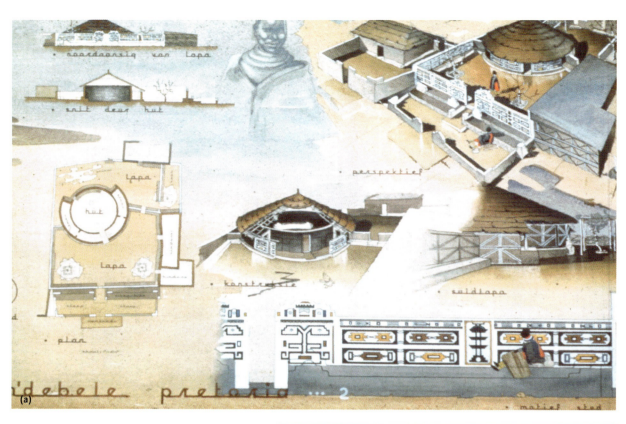

FIGURE 9 Change and fluidity captured in the evolution of the *isirhodlo* of one woman from the Msiza family: (a) 'NaTshabangu Msiza's *isirhodlo* at Hartebeestfontein in 1953 before its destruction and (b) the open space at Klipgat in 2001, after her death, when the wall was left to decay. (Sources: [a] Meiring 1953b, courtesy of the Department of Architecture at the University of Pretoria; [b] K. A. Bakker, 2001.)

Ndebele ritual corpus, namely *iqhude* (female initiation) and the *ingoma* or *ukuwela* (male initiation rites, which include circumcision). Both institutions have been uninterrupted since 1953. Initiation rites reaffirm KwaMsiza as a center of regional importance, with considerable numbers of Ndebele guests attending from neighboring Ndebele villages and afar.

Sobuhlangane Speelman Msiza was granted permission to act as an *induna* (regional headman) in 1955, when the first male initiation was installed at KwaMsiza at Klipgat.[9] Since that time, he has officiated at thirteen initiations in the village.

The next installation will be in 2005. The village still houses, at the main entrance, an enclosure where the boys' initiation is concluded.

The patriarchal line of authority of the Msiza family of Sobungane extends beyond the ritual domain. Ever since the death of King Nyabela, the Ndzunza royal house has bestowed special authority on the Msizas—after 1903 the Msizas seem to have been entrusted with the guardianship of the royal grave at Wonderboom, close to their original home at Hartebeestfontein.

A Way Forward

A model for the conservation of decoration on Ndebele earthen architecture is needed, within which the intangible dimensions of both academically conserved and extant heritage fabric can be included, in order to enhance definitions of cultural significance that are required as foundation for heritage interpretation, conservation, and management decisions.

In working toward a model, one must recognize that the KwaMsiza villagers, like the Ndebele community at large, have been bombarded by interventionist strategies disguised as "development." Even before the Bantustan period, institutions and individuals endeavored to promote Ndebele culture and heritage, mainly cloth and beadwork and the decorated mural. Yet the only successful ventures seem to have been those where the women plotted their own course and resisted institutional intervention.

In view of this, any drive to preserve the remaining murals or to restore the architecture at KwaMsiza or any other Ndebele site, should be approached with considerable caution. How the residents value the future conservation of the village is of the utmost importance. The notions of continuity and change are once more at issue here. If independent conservation counsel or assistance had been available, the villagers might not have given consent to the (in our opinion) gross type of developmentally oriented interventions imposed upon them, such as the conference center and guesthouse built in the village by the Northwest Province government.

The authors are engaged with the community of Klipgat in an ongoing manner in the formulation of a conservation process in which community members are the decision makers and the consulting conservators act in a supportive or facilitating role only. During the colloquium and after our return to the village, we put up for critical debate a model for the conservation of the settlement that is inclusive of the aspects identified in this paper.

In discussions with the village elders, we have come to the conclusion that a possibly relevant conservation model would include a verified, detailed biographical and social history of the family and clan, the compilation and synthesis of existing research data, regular future site documentation, a complete family genealogy, and a settlement chronology, all of which would be linked to a matrix that includes the multidisciplinary description, analysis, and interpretation of the relevant abstract and concrete contexts within which settlement and related mural decorations occur and within which critical relationships may be discerned.

A definition of cultural significance will be co-constructed with various stakeholders. The first discussion meeting towards devising a conservation policy and action plan—within which future conservation management will occur—has taken place. The authors chose to act as brokers in relationships with donors or state agencies. Due to the fact that the village is representative of a wider Ndebele identity, and due to the integrity and authenticity of the heritage resources, we envisage for the near future that the villagers agree to allow their settlement to become a laboratory for the collective study of ways of conserving aspects of a wider Ndebele culture.

A two-pronged conservation action strategy has been put forward. Firstly, the authors and community have formulated a proposal to initiate an ethnographic salvage action project, in the vein of the Africa 2009 *projet situé* concept. This concept, which has been co-authored and endorsed by the community, includes that a homestead unit, together with its movable material culture content, be restored to the 1953 founding period, based on early photographs and memory. Representatives of various generations will take part in this, and annual maintenance and embellishing work will continue as in the traditional earth building. The action also concerns salvaging of indigenous knowledge skills and reintroducing early indigenous technologies, such as step thatching, use of organic paints, earthen plaster, and earth building technology. Movable objects could be recovered from museum stores or reconstructed in the community from references available in archival records. This action is to be documented for future dissemination of indigenous knowledge into the Ndebele community and to a broader public.

Secondly, the community has also welcomed the idea of positioning the village as a center of learning regarding a wider Ndebele culture, which can function for the family as well as for the broader Ndebele community, despite and regardless of the tourist industry. This involves setting up and consolidating the extensive existing and future database of site documentation and multidisciplinary research on aspects of the Msiza history—inclusive of the evolution and change in settlement pattern, built form, and decoration of architecture—into an in situ archive that is run and owned by the Msiza family but that is linked to archiving systems outside the village. The current conference hall, which is empty for most of the year, can be rehabilitated as a depository and interpretation center.

These proposals may ideally be directed toward an integrated understanding of the settlement as a social construct and of its importance in a wider ecology. The inhabitants would provide the bulk of that understanding, and any development aid and professional engagement would be in the manner of a partnership, controlled by the inhabitants. This partnership should have as an aim various means of support for the inhabitants in their quest to sustain a living cultural heritage site, as well as acknowledgment of their control of the development and conservation policy and procedure (within the ambit of national or regional conservation legislation), rather than its being subject to detailed government or specialist intervention and control.

Acknowledgments

The authors are indebted to the Msiza family, in particular Maselwane Msiza, Bricks Bhuda, and the countless family members who have spent time on the project so far. We also thank Professor Franco Frescura for the use of his and his students' drawings of KwaMsiza at Klipgat, and for the time spent discussing his experiences and research.

Glossary of Ndebele Terms

ikapa roof beam, rafter

indambo rope

indanga regimental name

induna headman

ingoma male initiation

iqhude female initiation

isibongo clan name, also surname

isifunzi plant species used in the manufacture of rope

isikhethu our tradition

isikhuwa White, European tradition

isinanazelo subclan name

isiNdebele Ndebele language, tradition, culture

isindru human, own culture, tradition

isirhodlo courtyard (frontal) wall

isithebe grass mat

sesotho Sotho tradition, culture, South Sotho language

umaphotho beaded apron

umuhlwa termites

umuzi homestead, village

Notes

1 Examples include those from popular Afrikaner magazines (Potgieter 1949; Meiring 1949, 1951, 1956; Brinckner 1961; and *BaNtu* 1960; *SA Panorama* 1963; *Vuka* 1998), and also the excellent photo essay publication of Bowen (1957), which has become an important source of visual reference material for the authors.

2 The discourse includes that of Spence and Bierman (1954), Meiring (1951, 1953a, b, c, 1954, 1955), Moss (1955), Walton (1965), Tyrrel (1968), and Elliot (1989).

3 For example, Frescura (1981a, b, 1983, 1984), Rich (1977) Courtney-Clarke (1986), Schneider (1986), Naude (2000), Van Vuuren (1986, 1988, 1993) and Bakker (2002).

4 Since many farms in the Republic of South Africa can bear the same name, a number is assigned to each farm on the Land Surveyor maps, and both name and number are used to differentiate individual farms.

5 The plan was manipulated to account for the distortions present in the aerial photograph. A greater level of accuracy may be obtained through computer manipulation of the aerial photograph, but this is a time-consuming, specialized, and costly process, and the accuracy of the present site plan is deemed appropriate for the task at hand.

6 Chief Maselwane died in early March 2005.

7 The interior of a woman's house is sometimes also painted, but this is more the exception than the rule as it is costly for most people. See also Berman 1970: 207.

8 Cement additives and acrylic paint are used for their perceived longevity, convenience, and aesthetic appeal. Due to the disappearance of the cyclical agrarian lifestyle, people spend most of their time away from the village, looking for work. Previously, time was available in winter for maintenance and decoration, including the time-consuming process of sourcing some of the pigments that were customarily used. In addition, acrylic paint offers a range of bright colors that are currently preferred for a variety of reasons.

9 A description of the initiation system is provided in Van Vuuren 1995.

References

Bakker, K. A. 2002. Crossing the future. In *Southern Crossings: Sixth Bi-Annual Australasian Urban History/Urban Planning Conference, University of Auckland,* ed. E. Haarhoff. Auckland: University of Auckland.

BaNtu. 1960. Homeland of the Ndebele. *BaNtu,* June: 367–76.

Berman, E. 1970. *Ndebele Painting: Art and Artists of South Africa.* Cape Town: A. A. Balkema.

Bowen, C. 1957. *15 Essays in Half-Tone.* Pretoria: Van Schaick.

Brinckner, V. H. 1961. Kleurrykste Bantoestam in Transvaal. *Huisgenoot* 3 (11).

Bruner, E. M. 2001. The Masaai and the Lion King: Authenticity, nationalism, and globalization in African tourism. *American Ethnologist* 28 (4): 881–908.

Coplan, D. 1987. Eloquent knowledge: Lesotho migrant songs and the anthropology of experience. In *Readings in African Popular Culture,* ed. B. Barber, 29–40. Bloomington: Indiana University Press.

Courtney-Clarke, M. 1986. *Ndebele: The Art of an African Tribe.* Cape Town: Struik.

Elliot, A. 1989. *The Ndebele: Art and Culture.* Cape Town: Struik.

Frescura, F. 1981a. *Kwa-Mapoch: A Ndebele village.* Memorandum on behalf of the Heritage Committee, Transvaal Chapter, Institute of South African Architects. Drawings by first-year students, Department of Architecture, University of the Witwatersrand, Sept. 1981. Johannesburg: Institute of South African Architects.

———. 1981b. *Rural Shelter in Southern Africa.* Pretoria: Sigma Press.

———. 1983. Indigenous architecture: Revising some old misconceptions. *Transvaal Provincial Institute of Architects (TPIA) Newsletter* no. 6:8–23.

———. 1984. *Kwa Matabeleng: A Survey of an Amandebele Village.* Report to the Institute for the Study of Man (ISMA).

James, D. 1990. A question of ethnicity: Ndzundza Ndebele in a Lebowa village. *Journal of Southern African Studies,* pp. 41–54.

Kasfir, S. L. 1999. Samburu souvenirs: Representations of a land in amber. In *Unpacking Culture: Art and Commodity in Colonial and Post Colonial Worlds,* ed. C. Steiner and R. B. Phillips, 67–83. Berkeley: University of California Press.

Levy, D. 1989. Ndebele beadwork. In *Catalogue: Ten Years of Collecting (1979–1989),* ed. W. D. Hammond-Tooke and A. Nettleton. Johannesburg: Wits University Press.

Matthews, T. H. 1971. Tribal painting in South Africa with particular reference to Xhosa painting (vols. 1–2). PhD diss., University of South Africa.

Meiring, A. L. 1949. Kultuur van die Bantoe: Blanke S A moet die Kuns van die Tradisionele Mapoggers help bewaar (Mapoggerwonings). *Die Huisgenoot* no. 34.

———. 1951. Iets oor die Amandebele. *Lantern,* June: 219–21.

———. 1953a. *Amandebele van Pretoria.* Brochure of the Pretoria Agricultural Show.

———. 1953b. Slides of a series of watercolor posters, nos. 1–4 of KwaMsiza. Archive collection of the Department of Architecture, University of Pretoria.

———. 1953c. So bou die Ndebele hul hutte. *Lantern,* pp. 160, 224.

———. 1954. Die Amandebele van Pretoria. *Helicon* 4 (16): 79–86.

———. 1955. The Amandebele of Pretoria. *SA Architectural Record,* April, 26–35.

———. 1956. Modes onder die Amandebele. *SA Panorama,* no. 3, back page.

Moss, J. L. 1955. The master craftswomen of the Ndebele. *The Outspan,* March 11, 35–37.

Naude, M. 2000. From conservation to sustainable use: The Mapoch Ndebele village at Klipgat. *The Urban Green File,* Feb., 26–27.

Pienaar, H. 1991. *Die Derde oorlog teen Mapoch.* Cape Town: Institute for a Democratic Alternative for South Africa.

Potgieter, E. F. 1949. Dit moet mos so wees. *Die Brandwag,* July 22: 23, 30.

Rich, P. 1997. Pride of the Ndebele. *Architectural Review* 197: 73–77.

SA Panorama. 1963. Vakansieland. *SA Panorama,* January: 17.

Schneider, E. A. 1985. Ndebele mural art. *African Arts* 18 (3): 60–67.

———. 1986. Paint, pride and politics: Aesthetic and meaning in Transvaal Ndebele wall art. PhD diss, University of the Witwatersrand.

Spence, B., and B. Bierman. 1954. M'pogga. *Architectural Review,* February: 35–40.

Tilley, C. 1991. *Metaphor in Material Culture.* Oxford: Blackwell.

Tyrrel, B. 1968. *Tribal Peoples of Southern Africa.* Cape Town: Books of Africa.

Urry, J. 1990. *The Tourist Gaze.* London: Sage.

Van Vuuren, C. J. 1986. Mural art of the Ndebele. *South African Journal for Ethnology* 9 (3): 101–11.

———. 1988. The KwaNdebele monuments committee: Ethnological contributions. *SAMAB* 8 (1): 89.

———. 1993. Let's go visit the ruins: Oral tradition and settlement reconstruction: Two Ndebele case studies. *SA Journal of Art History* 11: 43–57.

———. 1995. Royals and real men: Male initiation and ethnicity in Ndebele society. IUAES Inter-Congress, Cortona, Italy, April.

———. 2003. Authenticity, hyperreal experiences and heritage and South African cultural villages. Anthropology SA Conference, University of Cape Town, September.

Vuka. 1998. Brave old world. *Vuka* 3 (4): 30–31.

Walton, J. 1965. Muurskilderinge van die Bantoe. *SA Panorama,* April: 30–37.

Weiss, O. 1963. Funksionele Kunsuitinge by die Ndzundza. Master's thesis, University of Stellenbosch.

Asante Shrines, Ghana: Revival of the Bas-Relief Decoration Techniques

Sébastien Moriset

This article illustrates through a case study how a recently vanished living tradition can be revitalized. It describes the various activities developed between 1999 and 2002 by the Ghana Museums and Monuments Board, in collaboration with CRATerre-EAG, to revive the lost Asante decoration technique and restart the traditional maintenance system that continually replaces the damaged wall decorations.

The philosophy of the project was to restore and maintain the living tradition, rather than to conserve the remaining elements of decorated wall, as the Western approach would generally recommend. The methodology adopted integrated the implementation of a management strategy, the training of a competent person at the local level, the restoration of most of the damaged wall surfaces with this person, and the launching of support activities to raise funds.

The traditional Asante architecture in Ghana, documented by early European travelers as far back as the eighteenth century, is amongst the most famous of West African immovable cultural heritage. The remaining ten examples of this architectural style are shrine houses located around Kumasi. They were inscribed on the UNESCO World Heritage List in 1980.

Background

Traditional Asante architecture is characterized by elaborate ornamentation of the walls with intricate interlacing geometric designs, depictions of animals, and Adinkra symbols— popular symbols that are specific to the Asante culture. Each Adinkra sign has a symbolic meaning derived from various sources, including, among others, historical events, proverbs, human attitudes, and animal behavior. Those symbols are widely used in Ghana, but also internationally, on clothes, wallpaper, pottery, logos, and the like.

This architectural ornamentation can be divided into two main categories: the white designs on the upper walls and the red ones on the lower sections of the walls (Fig. 1). The lower sections of the walls and columns show a variety of decorations modeled in bas-relief. Shapes commonly found on these red plinth walls include spiral and arabesque designs, as well as representations of animals and plants having symbolic meanings. The lower walls are only modeled with earth and are regularly painted with a red clay slurry.

The upper sections of the walls, beams, and columns are also made of earth, but reinforced with palm sticks and protected with a limewash. Technically more elaborate and difficult to produce, they show complex interlacing geometric designs, also modeled in bas-relief.

Erosion of the exposed wall surfaces is continuous (Fig. 2). The decorations are rather fragile and can vanish quite quickly if the roof leaks or when heavy rainstorms occur (Fig. 3). Most of the Asante bas-reliefs have survived thanks to past traditions of monitoring and regular daily maintenance, but many of them have also been lost forever.

Threats

The religious and spiritual decline of the Asante culture has gradually altered the physical integrity of the shrines. Most of the buildings are no longer in use, and are therefore not maintained. The deceased fetish priests, who played a key role in the maintenance process, have not been replaced, and the craftsmen who mastered the decoration techniques have also

FIGURE 1 Various decoration categories (Abirim shrine): (a) red decorations on the lower section of a wall (Besease shrine); (b) white decoration (Besease shrine); (c) screen wall (Adarko Jachi shrine). Drawing by Arnaud Misse, CRATerre-EAG; Photos: (a) and (b) Sébastien Moriset, CRATerre-EAG; (c) Thierry Joffroy, CRATerre-EAG.

FIGURE 2 Eroded decoration (Saaman shrine). Photo: Sébastien Moriset, CRATerre-EAG.

FIGURE 3 Decorated beam, damaged after the displacement of a roofing sheet during a rainstorm (Patakro shrine). Photo: Sébastien Moriset, CRATerre-EAG.

passed away. The know-how, therefore, totally vanished in the 1980s, leaving the decorations exposed to various decay factors. Regular visits to the shrines over the past six years prove that mentalities are changing fast and that the human environment remains the major threat to the sites. The shrines are no longer protected by their fear-driven spiritual values, and acts of vandalism have become common. Human mistakes or ignorance, such as the dumping of materials against a shrine, road repair, or the construction of new houses near the sites, are all threatening elements that can be more destructive than storms or termite attacks.

Previous Conservation Practices

Past efforts to conserve the decorated walls have also produced bad results. In the 1990s, some experimentation using cement plasters to patch the broken spots increased the rate of deterioration of these unique decorations (Fig. 4). The cementitious waterproof coating accelerated the decay process of the decorated remains by trapping humidity and attracting termites. This cement patching was also done using trowels, resulting in a hard, smooth surface that looked completely different from the original decoration.

Objectives and Activities

Between 1999 and 2002, the Ghana Museums and Monuments Board (GMMB) developed a training program with CRATerre-

EAG, to save the decorated shrines and revive the lost traditional knowledge. This program was financially supported by the UNESCO World Heritage Fund and by the French Embassy in Ghana. The aim was not to restore all the shrines with their specific decorations; rather, it was to revive the traditional maintenance system and develop new activities to fund this maintenance.

To achieve these objectives, a set of activities was developed over four years:

- setting up of a management committee
- implementation of a regular monitoring system
- implementation of preventive conservation on all the shrines
- promotion of the sites to tourists
- production and selling of promotional/educational materials
- training of a decoration specialist

Table 1 gives the time line for these activities.

Preventive Conservation

A preliminary step, taken in 1998, consisted of stabilizing the structures, for example, by addressing the roof and drainage problems. For each shrine, the most critical problems were addressed to reduce the deterioration rate and prevent major problems. This was done by providing on-site training

FIGURE 4 White decoration patched with cement (Asawase shrine). Photo: Sébastien Moriset, CRATerre-EAG.

Table 1 Summary of Activities 1998–2004

	1998	1999	2000	2001	2002	2003	2004
Structures	Emergency conservation of the shrines	Restoration of Besease shrine	Preventive conservation of all the shrines				Replacement of the thatch at Besease
Decorated walls		Production of sample decorations	On-site training of a GMMB staff member				
			Restoration of most of the decorated walls				
Other	Gathering archive materials		Work on the sites, management and monitoring		Installation of road signs		
	Preparation of an exhibition						
	Production of promotional materials						
			Management committee set up in Besease				

sessions for all the technical staff of the GMMB office in Kumasi and members of the various communities. The idea was to demonstrate all the modest but fundamental preventive actions that can be implemented, even with limited financial means. Changing a roofing sheet, increasing the eaves over a decorated wall, or simply creating a gentle slope with rammed earth along a wall can significantly increase the durability of the structures. During this preventive conservation phase, none of the decorations were conserved, but first experiments were carried out on sample walls to study the decoration technique.

Experimentation on the Decorations

Once problems with the buildings were repaired, facsimiles of the decorations were produced on separate panels to test the proper materials and tools and to get the feel of the technique. This was based on discussions with elders who, although they had not mastered the technique, could remember how the decorations were produced. Once the technique was understood, initial restoration attempts were made at the Besease shrine. The first restoration samples gave encouraging, but not satisfactory results. This was because we first tried to replace the missing elements by adding soil only, without replacing the missing palm sticks. We were afraid to damage the surfaces even more if we had to pull out what remained of the decayed sticks.

We discovered the following year that the palm sticks played a key role in the technique, and that nothing could be done without replacing them. The "minimal intervention" approach was almost impossible on the very damaged surface. We had to redo the work the way it had been done in the past.

The Palm Sticks

The secret of the shape of the Asante decoration lies in the positioning of the palm sticks. These sticks (red-brown in color) are cut out from the central part of the leaves of the palm nut tree. Bending these sticks gives the precise shape of the motifs and the sharpness of the edges. In the long term, they also provide additional resistance at the edges. When inserting the ends of a new stick in the original holes, which are generally easy to locate, one is immediately able to read the motif that has been eroded. All missing or broken palm sticks must therefore be replaced before applying soil (Figs. 5 and 6). This part of the process can take up to two-thirds of the full restoration time. It means that for a 1 square meter restoration, up to four hours might be needed to position the new sticks. If the sticks are not well positioned, the bas-relief will have the wrong shape.

Another problem we faced at the beginning was in the workmanship. The first GMMB staff members involved in the conservation of the decorations were masons, and they did not feel comfortable with such meticulous restoration, although they performed very well on larger masonry work. Restoring the decorated surfaces is not simple patching work that can be handled by anybody. It requires experience, a good sense of observation, and a great deal of patience.

Finally, it was the youngest staff member, Bartholomew Komoah, who benefited most from the training and took responsibility for the conservation. It took approximately one hundred hours of practice spread over three years for him to

FIGURE 5 Screen wall during a restoration campaign (Abirim shrine). Photo: Sébastien Moriset, CRATerre-EAG.

FIGURE 6 White wall during restoration, showing the palm stick reinforcements inserted in the clay (Edwenase shrine). Photo: Sébastien Moriset, CRATerre-EAG.

master the technique and be able to perform repairs of good quality.

Other Activities

Another major activity alongside the management and conservation of the decorated buildings was the implementation of a promotional program aimed at providing funding for the regular maintenance of the ten shrines. This program included the following:

- opening the Besease shrine to the public (training of a guide, mounting exhibition panels, setting up the money collection system)
- creating a conservation fund supported by tourism activities (opening of a specific bank account, collection of entrance fees to the Besease shrine, selling of promotional products)
- design, production, and selling of promotional products (poster, bilingual booklet, flyer, T-shirts, and postcards)

- replacement of the corrugated iron sheets roof with a traditional thatched roof at the Besease shrine
- preparation of a traveling exhibition on the Asante shrines
- complete photographic survey of all the shrines

In addition to the first attempts to restore the decorated walls, in 1999 the Besease shrine was completely restored to its traditional appearance, based on archive photographs (Figs. 7–9). The objective of this restoration was to give an impression

FIGURE 7 Besease shrine before the replacement of the roof with a replica of the steep traditional roof covered with raffia thatch. Photo: Thierry Joffroy, CRATerre-EAG.

FIGURE 8 Construction of a new roof with a steep slope that restores the traditional roof shape (Besease shrine). Photo: Sébastien Moriset, CRATerre-EAG.

FIGURE 9 Besease shrine after the replacement of the corrugated iron sheet roof with a steep traditional roof, made of wood, bamboo, and raffia thatch. Photo: Thierry Joffroy, CRATerre-EAG.

of Asante architecture as it was in the early nineteenth century. A guide was trained to receive visitors, and entry fees started to be collected at this shrine. Consequently, a management committee was set up to oversee and monitor the site and provide recommendations for its continual repair, as well as that of the other traditional buildings in the Asante region.

Building Responsibility in Besease

Although the GMMB has a mandate to maintain the ten shrines, they do not always have the means to visit the sites on a regular basis. To keep the Besease shrine alive and strengthen the role of the community, a management committee was formed consisting of the chief of Besease, representatives of the local community, members of the district assembly, and GMMB representatives. This committee has the responsibility to monitor the site, manage the visitors, and report problems to the GMMB. A bank account was also opened in the name of this committee to help them manage funds gathered through visitation. From the funds collected at the Besease shrine, 20 percent are invested in community projects, while the remaining 80 percent are managed by the GMMB. These funds served, for instance, to rethatch the roof of the Besease shrine in 2004.

Conclusion

After five years of practice, the decoration skills, which were lost, have been revived. However, the skills lay in the hands of one person only, and more young people should be trained to ensure the continuity of this tradition. The Asante decorations cannot be conserved chemically or by smearing the damaged surfaces with a stabilized material; they have to be restored anew continually. The erosion processes are unpredictable, and significant damage occurs every year, rarely on the same walls. The only way to keep those decorations visible is to closely monitor the buildings and restore the decorations after each rainy season. This can be achieved by continuing the training of young people who are willing to learn the decoration technology and skills and who can assume responsibility for maintenance.

However, these young maintenance experts will only survive in the long term if they can earn their living from this know-how. At the moment, fixing the eroded decoration after the rains only represents two weeks' worth of work for two people. Yet this decoration technique is so rich that many other side activities using these skills could be envisaged. This could keep the craftsmen busy year-round and offer them a new role in the contemporary society. Adinkra symbols are still very popular, and there is definitely a market for new decorations.

At the moment, the shrines are well looked after by the GMMB, and the concept of preventive maintenance is well mastered by the Kumasi team in charge. However, the conservation of the decorations is an endless process, and this task will become more difficult as the intangible values associated with the shrines continue to deteriorate. Out of the ten shrines, only two are still "alive"—permanently controlled by a fetish priest who performs his duties and plays his traditional role in the community. The other shrines are either permanently closed or only open for certain ceremonies. The Asante culture will undoubtedly continue to survive through its language, music, clothing, and many other facets of its culture, but the few remaining examples of its traditional architecture are threatened.

During the past four years, approximately sixty artisans and villagers have been exposed to, or trained in, conservation of the sites. This is not yet sufficient, and more should be done to increase awareness. The upcoming generations should be sensitized to the importance of this heritage, and should be offered opportunities to play a more active role in its conservation.

Community Building and Continuity of Tradition: The Decoration of Mud-Brick Surfaces in the Hadhramaut Region of Yemen

Pamela Jerome

Wadi Hadhramaut, located in the former People's Democratic Republic of Yemen (commonly known as South Yemen), is the second-largest valley on the Arabian Peninsula (Pike 1940: 633). The Hadhramaut Valley runs roughly east-west, parallel to the Indian Ocean about a hundred miles inland from the coast, and is intersected by smaller tributary valleys such as Wadi Do'an. The *wadi* (dry riverbed) is characterized by its sheer limestone and sandstone cliffs that rise up to a thousand feet above the valley floor. Mud-brick tower houses cling to the escarpments; this protects them from occasional flash floods while permitting maximum agricultural use of the valley's fertile floor (Fig. 1).

The craft of building and decorating mud-brick tower houses survives throughout the valley. New mud-brick structures are designed by master masons and built one floor level per year, allowing the floors to settle. Building is done in the winter to avoid the extreme heat of the summer, which causes excessive cracking from rapid drying.

The tradition of applying mud, lime plaster, and painted decorations continues in new construction, and skilled carpenters still produce elaborately carved windows, columns, and doors. However, this unique cultural landscape is being threatened by development fueled by an influx of Yemeni emigrants returning from Gulf countries, who bring with them imported aesthetics and concrete construction. In addition, very little consideration is being given to the preservation of significant historic buildings (Jerome, Chiari, and Borelli 1999: 40–45).

Generally, once a building has lost its use, it is no longer maintained. A component of the Tarimi Mansions Preservation Project, begun in 2000, is a documentation and training program in which American graduate students and conservators are working side by side with personnel from the Yemeni General Organization of Antiquities and Museums (GOAM) using conventional and digital methods to produce scale drawings and photographs of important mud-brick mansions. This work is codirected by the author and Dr. Selma al-Radi, a research fellow at New York University's Institute of Fine Arts and codirector of al-'Amiriya Madrasa Restoration Project in Rada', Yemen. James Conlon, manager of interdisciplinary projects at Columbia University's Visual Media Center and a collaborator, is responsible for the Web site that disseminates the work (www.learn.columbia.edu/tarim). The Yemeni Social Fund for Development (SFD); the American Institute for Yemeni Studies (AIYS), through grants provided by the U.S. State Department's Bureau of Educational and Cultural Affairs; and the New York–based Samuel H. Kress Foundation have provided the funding.

Background

In 1997, the author and an independent filmmaker, Caterina Borelli, spent two months documenting the construction technology of the distinctive mud-brick tower houses in the valley (Borelli 2001). The significance of this unique form of architecture is recognized internationally. The walled city of Shibam, one of the three main cities in the valley along with Seyoun and Tarim, was designated a World Heritage Site in 1982 (Lewcock 1986). Celebrated for its remarkable ten-story unreinforced mud-brick buildings, Shibam is referred to as the Manhattan of the Desert (Shipman 1984: 155).

Since the unification of North and South Yemen in 1992, a building boom has introduced over 1,500 concrete structures

144

FIGURE 1 Villages of mud-brick tower houses cling to the valley escarpments in the Hadhramaut region of Yemen. Al-Qirn in Wadi Do'an contains an impressive collection of tower houses.

into the valley's once pristine built environment. We were interested in comparing the survival of the mud-brick tradition between Wadi Hadhramaut, where there is access to paved roads, and Wadi Do'an, where the roads were unpaved. What we discovered was that concrete construction is used for commercial and speculative purposes along the paved roads and to house "foreign" Yemenis (emigrants returning to Yemen or Yemenis from other areas of the country) because it can be erected rapidly. Much of the local population still prefers to live in mud-brick buildings despite the time-consuming, labor-intensive method of construction. Unlike concrete, mud-brick structures in this region do not require climate control. In addition, we found that traditional builders have incorporated newer technologies for both cost savings and to adapt to changing lifestyles. For instance, at 30 percent less cost, galvanized plumbing pipe is being used for joists instead of hardwood imported from Malaysia, which is less resistant to termites but more readily available than the local hardwood, 'ilb (*zizyphus spina-christi*). Where larger spans are needed, as at the Seyoun Airport, concrete framing with mud-brick infill is used.

The project (funded by the AIYS and the American Institute of Architects) produced an hour-long video documentary, *The Architecture of Mud*,[1] and a technical paper (Jerome, Chiari, and Borelli 1999). Dozens of interviews with masons, carpenters, lime craftsmen, government employees, and other professionals were filmed.

We found a surprising amount of resistance to being interviewed. Apparently, locals who gave freely of their knowledge to researchers in the past never saw the results of their efforts. Consequently, from the outset, community outreach became an important component of the project, because we wanted the participants to feel ownership of the resulting product.

In 1999, Caterina Borelli and I returned to Yemen with Giacomo Chiari, a materials scientist who had analyzed samples for the project, to premiere the film to those who had participated in its making. The documentary is not narrated; rather, the "story" is told through the words of the interviewees. In order to legitimize the project, it was important to us that we receive the approval of the participants who had responded to questions in the film about the living tradition of mud-brick construction and its social context. The enthusiasm our film was greeted with, the beaming pride of acknowledgment from the master craftsmen, and the extensive local press coverage validated this approach. In addition, we wanted the more accessible of the two products to be given back to the participants and the community at large. (Both English and Arabic versions of the film were produced; whereas the technical paper was never translated into Arabic.) Besides the Hadhramaut region, the film was also shown in Sana'a, in the auditorium of the Ministry of Culture, and in the architecture department of the University of Sana'a, as well as on national television.

Word quickly spread about the film's arrival, and as we traveled from town to town with our equipment, the crowds grew larger. This simple act turned the film into an exercise in community building that valorized the vernacular architecture of the region and the craftsmen who build it. A significant consequence was that it led to our acceptance by the local population and paved the way for the current project, the design of a preservation management plan for the historic town of Tarim (Conlon, Jerome, and Al-Radi 2003; Jerome, Conlon, and Al-Radi 2003).

Tarim is the religious center of the valley. Tarimi craftsmen had been the most difficult to capture on film. Over half of the Tarimis we asked refused to be interviewed, and the ones who agreed were working far from Tarim in Wadi Do'an. After the film was shown on the terrace of the 'Ishshah palace, to an audience of approximately a hundred Tarimis, we were approached for the first time by representatives of the Tarim branch of the Yemeni Society for History and Heritage Protection to work with them on the preservation of the historic mud-brick mansions of Tarim, many of which are abandoned. Shibam and Seyoun had both benefited from international attention and investment in historic preservation, but Tarim had been bypassed due to the introverted nature of the religious institutions that control the social aspects of the town. These institutions finally agreed to collaboration with foreigners.

We were very interested in this proposal, having already brought these structures to the attention of the Yemeni government, which agreed to let us propose them for inclusion on the World Monuments Fund 100 Most Endangered Sites list (also known as the WMF Watch List). It was clear that a major effort was going to be needed to save this collection of "white elephants." To begin with, we proposed to document the structures.

One of the purposes of the documentation is to focus awareness on the cultural significance of this unique ensemble of colonial mansions. Simultaneously, we are working with local stakeholders and the Yemeni government to identify adaptive reuse strategies that will act as an impetus for economic development by transforming Tarim into a cultural hub for the region. Preservation of the mansions will provide jobs for local craftsmen as well as training opportunities in traditional construction for young apprentices. We are also encouraging the government to adopt legal protection for these privately owned historic properties and to legislate the use and aesthetics of new concrete construction within Tarim.

Decoration of Hadhrami Buildings

Lime plaster is used to both protect and decorate mud-brick construction in the Hadhramaut region. Manufactured in mud-brick kilns on the outskirts of towns, lime (*nurah*) is produced using limestone cobbles gathered from the dry riverbed or the *jol,* the flat plateau above the canyon. The limestone is stacked within the kiln in a honeycomb fashion and fired for a minimum of twenty-four hours. It is permitted to cool for an additional twenty-four hours, then cleaned and weighed. The calcined limestone is set on a slaking bed, and water is added, producing a vigorous reaction. The resulting lime putty is tread underfoot in slaking pools. Finally, it is beaten for six to eight hours using wooden clubs (Jerome, Chiari, and Borelli 1999: 42–43). This removes the lumps and partially carbonates the lime putty; the carbonated material acts as a slightly reactive filler (Jerome 2000: 149).

Lime plaster (*tarqa*) is applied to mud-plastered mud-brick surfaces on the exterior and interior of buildings. Like mud bricks and mud mortar, mud plaster (*mahadha*) is made from soil collected in the valley after seasonal floods (Jerome, Chiari, and Borelli 1999: 41–42). The soil is sieved and mixed with finely chopped straw and water. The proportions are not an exact science; the mixer judges by experience, look, and feel. On the exterior, exposed mud plaster is used as a sacrificial coating. Beneath lime plaster, mud plaster acts as a smoothing layer.

Exterior Decorations

On the exterior, lime plaster can be applied directly as decorations to mud plaster (Fig. 2). In addition, it is often used to waterproof the most vulnerable areas of the building: the foundation, parapets, and roofs. If the owners are wealthy, the entire exterior is lime plastered. The mud-plastered surface is first wetted down and skim coated with a layer of mud; then it is lime plastered. The lime plaster mix is typically 1:2 (lime putty to sand). When sand is broadcast into the wet lime plaster, it acts as a mechanical key, thus providing an excellent substrate for limewash and oil-based painted decorations (Jerome, Chiari, and Borelli 1999: 43). These can be fanciful and of geometric design, as is typical of Wadi Do'an (Fig. 3), or subtle, like many of the historic examples in the Wadi Hadhramaut

FIGURE 2 Lime-plaster decorations are sometimes applied directly to mud-plastered surfaces, as in this example of the water tower from the al-Hawta Palace Hotel, Wadi Hadhramaut.

FIGURE 3 Lime plaster is used for waterproofing and as a substrate for oil-based decorations. In Wadi Do'an, geometric designs tend to be favored. This example is from Sif, a sizable Do'ani town.

FIGURE 4 Al-Munaysurah, one of the historic Tarimi mansions, has a subtle exterior polychrome decorative scheme.

(Fig. 4). The decorations can also be three-dimensional. However, in the ceaseless sun and periodic monsoons, exterior oil-based painted decorations are ephemeral at best, and these materials require frequent maintenance (Fig. 5).

Exterior lime-plaster decorations can be extremely elaborate, as exemplified by the eclectic collection of colonial mansions for which the town of Tarim is known. Tarim is acknowledged throughout the region as producing highly skilled lime craftsmen, as well as the finest lime. Since 2000, the Tarimi Mansions Preservation Project has been documenting these remarkable buildings. Initially, a feasibility study was conducted to identify their significance, understand the ownership context, prioritize repair needs, and review adaptive reuse potential (Jerome and Al-Radi 2001). This study was later updated at the request of UNESCO, identifying a total of fifty historic mansions in Tarim (Jerome 2004).

Interior Decorations

Interior finishes consist of limewash on mud-plastered surfaces, *malas*, and oil-based painted decorations. *Malas* is a form of burnished lime plaster reserved for sitting rooms, corridors, and bathrooms. *Malas* is made in the following manner: Lime plaster is applied to the mud-plastered surface to create a wainscot, using a metal rule to strike a dado at the appropriate height. Lime cream is then applied neat to the lime plaster. Lime cream is produced by adding water to lime putty and straining the lime putty through a muslin cloth. The resulting lime cream is hung in a sack so that all of the lime water drains out.

Layer upon layer of lime cream is applied. Because it is applied neat, it crazes, and more lime cream is used to heal the cracks. Lime wash (*rashah*) is also used; it typically consists of one part lime putty to two parts water. The *malas* is burnished with a trowel, stone, or the rim of a glass between applications of lime wash. The resulting high-gloss, ceramic tile–like finish repels both water and soiling (Jerome, Chiari, and Borelli 1999: 43). *Malas* is, in fact, sometimes scored to resemble tiles (Fig. 6). Some of the finest examples of historic *malas* are found in the 'Ishshah mansion, and many are three-dimensional (Fig. 7).

FIGURE 5 Exterior lime plaster and painted decorations require frequent renewal, as in this example of a Bugshan family palace in Khailah, in the left branch of Wadi Do'an.

FIGURE 6 *Malas,* a form of highly burnished lime plaster, is a labor-intensive interior finish. In this contemporary example from the ba-Zaraah house in Khoreiba, Wadi Do'an, the *malas* has been scored to resemble ceramic tiles.

FIGURE 7 The ʻIshshah palace of Tarim contains some of the finest examples of historic *malas*.

lack of maintenance. For this reason, from 2000 through 2003, the Tarimi mansions were listed on the WMF Watch List.

Documentation Efforts

The ʻIshshah palace, the most significant of the mansions, has exterior decorations that are three-dimensional and polychrome. The complex, a group of buildings and additions dating from the 1890s through the 1930s, was the seat of the al-Kaf family patriarch, ʻUmar bin Shaikh al-Kaf, who made his fortune in Singapore around the turn of the twentieth century (Conlon, Jerome, and Al-Radi 2003: 13). The main part of the palace and later additions were designed by ʻUmar's cousin Sayid Alawi Abu Bakr al-Kaf, a gentleman architect. Although it has suffered considerable structural damage (Fig. 8), the ʻIshshah is presented to the public as a house museum, the only one in the valley. The palace was recorded during the 2002–3 season.

Dar al-Salam is an art deco masterpiece also designed by Sayid Alawi Abu Bakr al-Kaf in the 1930s. While the team documented the Dar al-Salam mansion during the 2003–4 season, a hole in one of the roofs was repaired with funds from the SFD, and electricity and plumbing were introduced. Minor repairs were also implemented to the adjacent Hamtut mansion. The Hamtut, an abandoned Mughal-style mansion in fair-to-poor condition, was the subject of the 2004–5 season's

Lime-plastered ceilings can also be decorated. Since the ceilings are often the soffits of roofs or terrace setbacks, they are more likely to exhibit damage from water infiltration, thus reminding us that these decorated surfaces are indeed made of mud and lime plaster.

The Project

The Tarimi Mansions Preservation Project has succeeded in focusing national and international attention on the plight of these structures, some of which are abandoned or in poor condition because of their expropriation during the early 1970s by the Marxist government of that period. Two decades later, when they were returned to their rightful owners, these structures were in precarious condition resulting from the

FIGURE 8 The ʻIshshah palace exemplifies the hybrid of imported colonial styles executed in the local construction technology of mud-brick and lime plaster. A large section of the west elevation collapsed in 2000 and was reconstructed in 2003 through the efforts of the Tarimi Mansions Preservation Project.

survey, along with al-Riyad, another outstanding art deco structure designed by Sayid Alawi Abu Bakr al-Kaf.

Conservation Efforts

In the past, local stakeholders were unable to secure funding for preservation, and had to watch helplessly as various areas of the 'Ishshah palace collapsed and other significant structures, like al-Majaff, were bulldozed to make way for new construction. As a result of the Tarimi Mansions Preservation Project, the Yemeni government is considering the long-term lease of some of the more significant abandoned structures. Through our participation, grants have been secured from the U.S. State Department Ambassador's Fund for Cultural Preservation and the SFD to perform emergency stabilization repairs, which the project is administering. Thus far, several areas of the 'Ishshah mansion have been reconstructed, including a large section of the west elevation, which collapsed in 2000; the northwest kitchen wing, which collapsed in 2001; and the northeast and northwest wings of Dar Dawil, the oldest structure in the 'Ishshah complex. In addition, lime plaster has been reapplied to all of the 'Ishshah's roofs. Restoration of the 'Ishshah has given craftsmen the opportunity to replicate significant historic detailing no longer practiced in contemporary construction.

Progress has been slow and there is much yet to do, but at the end of 2003, the site was removed from the WMF Watch List and awarded a Certificate of Exceptional Achievement. An award ceremony was held in January 2004, in the restored west wing of the 'Ishshah palace, in which several of the stakeholders received certificates from the WMF representative, Dr. Gaetano Palumbo.

Also in January 2004, a ribbon-cutting ceremony at the Dar al-Salam mansion brought more media attention to Tarim. Nobel Prize–winning novelist Günter Grass donated a portion of his prize to the establishment of an Association of Mud Masons, with Dar al-Salam proposed as its headquarters. The association will assist in organizing traditional craftsmen to compete against concrete contractors for government construction projects. Training in reading of architectural plans, cost estimating, and apprenticeship are critical to the continuing survival of the vernacular construction tradition on a large scale.

Both of these ceremonies were used to foster community building and to elevate the importance of the local craftsmen who participated as the guests of honor. Foreign dignitaries and officials at the highest level of Yemeni government attended, thus emphasizing their recognition of the role of traditional craftsmen. Tours were given of the interiors of several of the abandoned mansions. The Günter Grass celebration was broadcast on television, and the *Yemen Observer* (the English-language newspaper) and local press coverage featured both of these events extensively.[2]

Conclusion

Yemen's Hadhramaut region is home not only to a remarkable vernacular architecture of mud-brick tower houses but also to a significant lime-based exterior and interior decorative craft. The production of decorative finishes for mud-brick structures is a living tradition that continues to survive despite ever-increasing incursions of concrete construction. Fortunately, many historic examples remain as well.

Foreign recognition of these construction technologies has assisted in awakening community and government respect for the traditional craftsmen as well as for this unique built environment. Renewed interest in the eclectic collection of colonial mansions in the historic town of Tarim has taken root from the local population to the highest levels of the Yemeni government, substantiating the need for skilled craftsmen capable of restoring these extraordinary structures and, in general, raising the level of the craft. International exposure of the Tarimi Mansions Preservation Project, through inclusion on the WMF Watch List and presentation at various conferences, has enlisted the interest and assistance of local, American, and international organizations such as the SFD, the Samuel H. Kress Foundation, the U.S. State Department, and UNESCO. Such support will serve to stabilize the significant abandoned mansions while an economic development study is performed and a preservation master plan evolves for the city of Tarim.

Notes

1   Produced by Anonymous Productions, New York. Distributed by Documentary Educational Resources. See http://der.org/docued/films/architecture-of-mud.html.

2   "Preserving the Mud Brick Palaces of Tarim," *Yemen Observer* 7, 02, January 10, 2004.

References

Borelli, Caterina. 2001. Filming "The Architecture of Mud." *Yemen Update: Bulletin of the American Institute for Yemeni Studies* 43:13–16.

Conlon, James, Pamela Jerome, and Selma Al-Radi. 2003. Documentation of the Tarimi Palaces, 2002–2003: Qasr al-'Ishshah. *Yemen Update: Bulletin of the American Institute for Yemeni Studies* 45:9–22.

Jerome, Pamela. 2000. The use of lime plasters for waterproofing and decoration of mudbrick buildings in Yemen. In *Terra 2000: 8th International Conference on the Study and Conservation of Earthen Architecture, Torquay, Devon, UK, May 2000: Preprints* ed. English Heritage, ICOMOS-UK, and University of Plymouth Centre for Earthen Architecture, 144–49. London: James & James.

———. 2004. Updated feasibility study: Preservation of the mudbrick mansions of Tarim, Yemen. Unpublished report submitted to UNESCO, Unit of Arab Countries, Division of Cultural Heritage, Paris, France.

Jerome, Pamela, and Selma Al-Radi. 2001. Feasibility study for the mudbrick palaces of Tarim, Yemen. Unpublished report submitted to the Samuel H. Kress Foundation, New York.

Jerome, Pamela, Giacomo Chiari, and Caterina Borelli. 1999. The architecture of mud: Construction and repair technology in the Hadhramaut region of Yemen. *APT Bulletin: The Journal of Preservation Technology* 30 (2–3): 39–48.

Jerome, Pamela, Selma Al-Radi, James Conlon, and Gina Crevello. 2003. Preservation of the mudbrick palaces of Tarim, Yemen. In *Terra 2003: Preprints of Papers, 9th International Conference on the Study and Conservation of Earthen Architecture,* Yazd, Iran, 29 November–2 December, 2003, ed. Sazman-i Maras-i Farhangi-i Kishvar (Iran), 319–28. Tehran: Iranian Cultural Heritage Organization.

Lewcock, Ronald. 1986. *Wadi Hadhramawt and the Walled City of Shibam.* Paris: UNESCO.

Pike, Ruthven W. 1940. Land and peoples of the Hadhramaut, Aden Protectorate. *Geographical Review* 30:631–33.

Shipman, J. G. T. 1984. The Hadhramaut. *Asian Affairs* 15 (June): 155.

Conservation of Our Lady of Seven Sorrows Cathedral and Safeguarding the Tradition of Decoration of the Nankani Women

Part I Preservation of the Nankani Tradition of Wall Decoration

Gisèle Taxil

Earth has always been one of the principal materials used in construction, despite the fact that it becomes fragile if exposed to conditions that can lead to its erosion. The design of earthen architecture through the centuries has taken this into consideration, and today an astonishing richness of architectural solutions and creativity of decorated surfaces can be seen on earthen buildings around the world.

Distinct building traditions in western Africa have produced visually striking vernacular architecture and decoration. In northern Ghana, before the rainy season, groups of Nankani women render the wall surfaces of their mud dwellings with colorfully painted low-relief adornments. These are unique, sophisticated, and of an extraordinary quality reflecting a high degree of technical knowledge about the use of indigenous materials (Fig. 1). Unfortunately, the impermanent nature of these plasters, as well as the recent and strong waves of modernism, have led to a rapid decline in the knowledge and practice of decorating with earth.

Our Lady of Seven Sorrows Cathedral in Navrongo is an extraordinary example of this decorative tradition. Constructed in 1920, following the arrival in 1906 of French Canadian missionaries, it is the last cathedral built of earthen materials in Ghana that is still regularly used for worship (Fig. 2). Its beauty lies in its unique interior decorations, which were created in 1972 by a group of seven Nankani women at the request of Monsignor Kizito Avereyire, who wanted to enhance the cathedral. Unfortunately, the cathedral has received little maintenance since that time. In 1992, it was finally reroofed and rerendered. One year later, the bell tower was threatened by imminent collapse. It became clear that the

cathedral needed urgent structural stabilization as well as restoration and protection of the earthen decoration.

Since Our Lady of Seven Sorrows Cathedral is recognized as an important historical and cultural property, its stabilization and conservation is essential. The restoration, carried out with the support of the Getty Foundation and the French Embassy in Ghana, addressed specific restoration and conservation issues and developed solutions that were useful not only for the cathedral in Navrongo but also for many other communities with similar architecture and cultural traditions. One of the critical issues was the preservation of the vanishing skills and know-how of this traditional art form.[1]

For the Nankani people of northern Ghana, wall decoration on earthen architecture is a form of both artistic expression and surface protection. The action of smoothing and polishing compacts the surface, which makes it more resistant to weathering. The final surface treatment using *dawa-dawa* decoction, a local plant-based varnish, helps render the decorated surfaces impermeable to moisture, thus protecting both the paintings and the structure.

As a living tradition, the Nankani decorations typically are not maintained but are replaced when necessary. The decorations are seen as "clothes for houses" that are changed from time to time. In the case of the Navrongo cathedral, however, it was important to preserve the decoration because the colors, motifs, and quality of the surface treatment were extraordinary and distinctly different from more-recent decorations. The restoration of the cathedral provided a good opportunity to preserve the style of decoration of the early 1970s for future generations. Additionally, the project introduced restoration techniques to the Nankani women, who, as mentioned,

FIGURE 1 View of the courtyard and the dwellings of a traditional compound in northern Ghana. Photo: Thierry Joffroy, CRATerre-EAG, 1997.

FIGURE 2 Our Lady of Seven Sorrows Cathedral, Navrongo, northern Ghana. Photo: Nicolas Lecorre, 2003.

usually create new motifs and decorations rather than restore existing decoration.

Immediate actions were taken in 1997 to complete the reconstruction of the bell tower. Complementary activities were also implemented between 1999 and 2003 as part of a comprehensive conservation and management plan. In addi-

tion to the restoration of the cathedral, restoration of an old classroom block was undertaken, as well as construction of a new museum, which serves a didactic purpose for demonstrating the use of traditional practices for future application on local housing. The plans to preserve the existing decorations and create some new decorations inside the cathedral also provided an opportunity to train younger women, conserve the know-how, and promote contemporary uses of decorations in private houses and public housing.

In 1999, Leslie Rainer, wall paintings conservator, conducted a condition assessment of the decoration in the Navrongo cathedral as part of the implementation phase of the conservation project. She developed guidelines for treatment and carried out pilot treatments on the decorated surfaces. Sirigu women who had mastered the decoration techniques assisted in the treatment. The conservation and creation of new decorations were carried out over several missions in Navrongo between 1999 and 2003 by Gisèle Taxil and Ann Bourgès, again closely assisted by the Sirigu women.

Description of the Decorated Surfaces of the Cathedral

The interior walls and columns of the Navrongo cathedral are adorned with a combination of traditional Nankani and Catholic motifs and symbols. Their coexistence suggests a recognition and acceptance of different beliefs. The decorated surfaces are located on two rows of columns and on a frieze running along the base of the north, east, and south walls. The frieze, which is both in relief and incised into the surface,

depicts various animals, such as cows, serpents, and crocodiles, and geometric patterns (Fig. 3). These designs are similar to those found on the traditional compounds. The overall chromatic scheme is composed of three colors: black, deep red, and white. The application of a local organic varnish, *dawa-dawa*, creates their deep, rich, shiny patina.

The altar area of the frieze has been repainted with commercial paints and shows a black-and-white scheme. Likewise, the columns, which were originally similar in treatment and color to the wall frieze, were repainted in the areas of black-and-white designs. The columns depict religious figures and objects and geometric patterns.

Three different traditional motifs can be distinguished in the cathedral decoration:

- Abstract, geometric designs painted on a flat surface. The common shapes are triangles and lozenges, and the patterns are arranged in horizontal registers.
- Incised designs that are predominantly rectilinear. Common shapes are again triangles and lozenges. These usually represent everyday utility objects such as the calabash rope net, broken calabash, and joined hands.

FIGURE 3 View of the existing decorated side walls inside the cathedral. Photo: Nicolas Lecorre, 2003.

- Traditional figures in bas-relief. These usually depict animals and human figures and stand in contrast to the rectilinear painted designs. Some of the bas-reliefs have incised figures.

Decoration Technique

The women use their hands to apply a first plaster layer composed of soft white earth (*gora*) mixed with cow dung. When the relief designs of that layer are completed, the surface is covered with a mixture of water and cow dung and evened with a flat stone. This liquid water-and-dung mixture is applied between every layer of plaster and paint to help the smoothing process. Over the wet plaster, a thin paint of red earth and cow dung is applied with a grass broom. This second layer is also smoothed with a flat stone. Nankani women usually have a set of stones of different shapes and sizes. A good stone has an egg shape with a flat side. They use the stones not only to smooth surfaces but also to model the relief and incise the surfaces.

The surface is left to dry before the painted composition is applied by the lead artists. The composition is generally arranged in horizontal registers starting at the top of the wall or design area. Designs are outlined in black, and the spaces between are filled with either black or dark red paint. White is applied last by rubbing a dry stone over the damp plaster. Also at this time, the motifs are incised into the surface using the edge of a stone (Fig. 4), and shells are inserted to represent the eyes of animal or human figures.

After the composition is completed, and when the right moisture level is reached, the whole surface is smoothed again, color by color, line by line, in each area, so as to avoid smudges. When almost dry, the flat, incised, and bas-relief decorations are finely polished with the stones until light reflects off the very soft surface.

The wall is left to dry for two or three days before the *dawa-dawa* varnish is prepared. It is spattered warm on the decorated surface, and gives the surface a shiny reddish patina and a waterproof quality (Fig. 5). It is important to let the plaster dry completely first, otherwise the thin polychrome layer cracks and then peels off.

Restoration of the Decorated Surfaces with the Nankani Women

The tradition of wall painting is a social event for the Nankani women. Since it involves a great deal of effort, they

FIGURE 4 New scene designed at the entrance of the cathedral. Designs are incised on the still-wet surface with the edge of a flat stone. Photo: Gisèle Taxil, CRATerre-EAG, 2002.

FIGURE 5 New scene at the entrance of the cathedral. This woman is using a vegetal broom to apply *dawa-dawa,* a local varnish. Photo: Gisèle Taxil, CRATerre-EAG, 2002.

work together as a team. The most talented and experienced women lead the work. Generations of women work side by side, the older women transmitting their knowledge to the younger. Not only is this an opportunity for the women to express their artistic talent, it also demonstrates that they are hard-working women capable of taking good care of a home. The young women usually prepare the materials under the supervision of the elders and participate in the decoration process. Together the women discuss the artistic composition of the wall decoration, but only the women leaders outline the designs and make the color choices for the space created.

Akanvole from Sirigu village is the only woman still living who had participated in the original decoration of the cathedral in 1972. Because she was still fluent in the decoration techniques, she was able to lead the decoration work. Akanvole, along with a group of artists under her leadership, helped carry out the restoration of the existing decorated surfaces and execute new decorations.

Due to the extent of existing decorations, and since the Sirigu women usually can be away from their family and home for only ten to eighteen days at a time, the restoration work was planned in stages. The leader selected the number of women and organized the work within the group. The campaign schedules were also based on the seasons that were best for that particular work, which were March–April and November–December. During these times, there are no strong winds and less heat than at other times (excessive heat and aridity can cause the plaster to dry too fast, and thus crack).

The restoration campaigns always started with a visit from the women leaders, who would evaluate the amount of work required. The painting materials were then collected, selected, and prepared at home in their village. The work schedule was adjusted to accommodate social events that happened to take place, such as funerals, birth celebrations, and so forth.

Although the artists understood the techniques of repairing the decoration, they initially needed a conservator to help guide them with the delicate conservation treatment. Once the level of quality needed was established, the conservators helped the women improve their technique and allowed them to take their time with the work. For example, the women had to learn how to use metal spatulas to shape the fine details they otherwise could not fashion with their hands. Soon they became comfortable with the tools and the rhythm of the operations required, and gained the experience needed to accomplish very precise repairs.

Restoration Techniques

Observed Deterioration Problems

Some of the decorations had been damaged by previous reconstruction and by corrugated iron sheets that fell during the building renovation. The two bas-reliefs flanking the entrance porch had been destroyed during the dismantling of the bell tower. Electrical outlets mounted on the columns also disrupted and damaged the decorated surfaces. In strong winds, the window shutters knocked against the walls, damaging the surrounding plaster and the interior decoration below the sills. Apart from this damage, the decorated surfaces were in fairly stable condition.

Stabilization and Repair

Stabilization of the structure and other architectural elements was carried out before treating the decorated surfaces. The windows were redesigned to prevent the shutters from banging, the electricity was rewired, and the outlets in the decorated surfaces were removed and relocated. During the intervention, the decorations were covered with fabric to protect them.

It took time to make the cathedral congregation aware of the importance, unique value, and fragility of the wall decorations. As the restoration work progressed and the decorations regained some of their beauty, the congregants began to appreciate the work and results. Consequently, an important decision was made by the cathedral committee to move the benches away from the decorated side walls. This created a new flow of movement within the church and allowed the congregation to admire the walls without obstructions.

Since the tradition of decorating walls is still alive and the technical skills were still viable in the community, the decision was made to use traditional materials and techniques in the conservation work and to match existing decoration as closely as possible. Conservation treatments (Fig. 6) included surface cleaning; removal of inappropriate fills; filling of losses, cracks, and scratches; removal of paint and water drips as well as other surface accumulation; treatment against insects; reintegration of fills and superficial losses; and application of the traditional colors and the protective varnish. These treatments were adapted to the living tradition. The Sirigu women used the same materials and techniques as in the original decorations.

The extent and type of conservation treatment was considered on a case-by-case basis in consultation with the Sirigu women and the conservators. Following is a brief

FIGURE 6 Sirigu women restoring the columns. Photo: Gisèle Taxil, CRATerre-EAG, 2003.

description of the major deterioration problems and the treatment solutions:

• The traditional decorated surface was covered with an accumulation of dust, sometimes dirt, especially inside the incised motifs. The overall surface was not shiny. *Treatment:* A damp sponge, wetted with water only, was used to carefully clean the surface and remove dust and dirt without disturbing the patina or the polychrome earth paint beneath.

• The black-and-white decorations painted with modern paint (columns and side walls of the altar platform) were visibly dirty, especially on areas of white overpaint.[2] *Treatment:* The water-based paint and the grime were removed with a vegetable soap and water. This often revealed the fine details of the incised motifs of the decorations. Damaged areas on the columns were repaired. To unify the colors, the black-and-white areas were repainted with oil paints.

• Termite holes and galleries were observed in many areas, especially near the wall base. The burrowing insects caused damage by creating voids (nests) behind the plaster and leaving small holes in the decoration. The caretaker of the Navrongo cathedral, Sister Bernadette, tried to exterminate the insects with kerosene, but this proved to be only a short-term solution, and the termites returned. *Treatment:* We used a product that is used against termites on wood with great success. In Ghana, the product is called Solograme. The insects' galleries were opened with a sharp metal spatula to remove the nests. Then the product was injected in the holes with a syringe, and the holes were filled using traditional techniques and materials.

• There were patches of detached and disaggregating original plaster at the base of the walls and below windowsills. Also, some of the uneven and incompatible cement-based repairs and fills had become detached (most of the cement repairs did not adhere to the wall). *Treatment:* The unstable plaster and the incompatible fills were removed and filled using traditional techniques.[3] If the void revealed the presence of insect galleries, they were treated before filling as described.

• Areas with traditional paint were degraded from water that had run down the walls and washed away the decorated surfaces. *Treatment:* The surface was treated by reapplying the same color used in the original decoration, polishing it, reincising the decoration, and applying the varnish coat. However, in some cases, reconstruction was considered more appropriate.

Extension of the Decorated Surfaces in the Cathedral

The plan to add new decorations to the existing scheme was welcomed by the cathedral committee as a way to train younger women in the decorative traditions and to the new practice of maintenance and repair. The new decorations were completed in stages, starting in March 1999 with the sacristy. In November 2001 designs were added inside the Navrongo Museum; in November 2002, in the cathedral entrance porch; and finally in November 2003, inside the baptistery (Fig. 7) and back altars.

Conclusion

Following the conservation and restoration work, the bas-relief decoration had a renewed unity and beauty. Thanks to the preventive approach taken to maintenance and the restoration and conservation treatments that were carried out, the polychrome earthen relief decoration in the cathedral will endure for a long time. The decoration is not only an integral element of the cathedral but is also a testimony to the unique and beautiful decorative traditions of the region.

The women involved in the restoration and the creation of new decoration take great pride in the work they accomplished. The parish staff and the cathedral committee understand the importance of conservation and restoration and are very pleased with the results. They will continue to maintain the decorations in recognition of their beauty and the way that the tradition of decoration makes their cathedral special (Fig. 8).

FIGURE 8 Interior of the cathedral following the restoration. Photo: Gisèle Taxil, CRATerre-EAG, 2003.

FIGURE 7 Sirigu woman creating new decoration at the baptistery. Photo: Nicolas Lecorre, 2003.

Acknowledgments

The author would like to thank the many people who contributed to this project:

Navrongo-Bolgatanga Diocese: Bishop Lucas Abadamloora, Father Augustine Ayaga, and Father Augustine Kazaresana.

Navrongo Catholic Mission: Father Charles Akabote, Father Paul Kapochina, Father Joe Awia, Father Clement Agamba, Father Joseph Grosskinsky, the late Reverend Father Joseph W. Apuri, Sister Bernadette Mary, Sister Mathilda, Sister Mary Theresa, Sister Francesca, and all the persons in charge of the Catholic Mission in Navrongo.

Navrongo Cathedral Committee: Lawrence Ayiwa; Awine Zigne, contractor; Alex Nyonayari, carpenter; Alfred Nabare, electrician; Joe Adunakebe, painter; and Simon Peter Ajoba, painter.

Navrongo: Patricia Sakeya; Mary Magdalen; Lucie Kwowe; Joseph Abatey; Raymond Felly, artist; and Peter Wedjong, retired teacher.

The women from Navrongo and all the workers involved in the restoration.

Sirigu: Melanie Kasisi, Sirigu Women Potters Association, and the women artists involved in the restoration.

CRATerre-EAG: Patrice Doat, Scientific Director DSA-Terre; Thierry Joffroy, Chairman; Alba Rivero, architect; Sébastien Moriset, architect; Olivier Moles; Mark Kwami, designer; and Alexandre Douline, Misereor/CRATerre-EAG.

Gaia Project: Hugo Houben and Alejandro Alva.

GMMB: Dr. I. N. Debrah, National Director Accra; Benjamin W. Kankpeyeng, head of regional office, Bolgatanga; Paul Duon Naa, Principal Inspector for Monuments; and Nicolas Ivor.

The Getty Foundation.

Finally, I address my greatest thanks to the Sirigu women who called us by the names of their daughters.

Notes

1   The project results are disseminated through the UNESCO Chair Network on Earthen Architecture and linked to important programs such as Africa 2009 (UNESCO, ICCROM, CRATerre-EAG), whose aim is to improve the conditions for the conservation of immovable cultural heritage in sub-Saharan Africa.

2   The modern paint was composed of two layers: an oil paint was applied over the original traditional decoration. Where this paint was damaged, a second coat was applied, but this time the black was oil-based and the white water-based, with a much thicker consistency.

3   The following technical requirements were followed in filling losses: (1) Fills had to match the surface of the surrounding plaster precisely. (The area to be filled was first prewet with a water–cow dung mixture.) (2) The red earth needed to be applied precisely, although the paint was allowed to overlap the original surrounding surface. This helped make a smooth, invisible transition between the existing surface and the repaired area. (3) The fills had to be polished in such a way that no cracks or gaps were apparent between the repair and the new plaster. The sheen of the polished fills had to match the surrounding area. (4) *Dawadawa* varnish was applied to the repairs to obtain a surface texture similar to the surrounding original areas.

Conservation of Our Lady of Seven Sorrows Cathedral and Safeguarding the Tradition of Decoration of the Nankani Women

Part II Analytical Research on Nankani Polychrome Decoration

Ann Bourgès

The cathedral of Navrongo, Our Lady of Seven Sorrows, is an exceptional example of earthen surface decorations made and restored through a living tradition. The recent conservation project described in Part I of this paper provided an excellent opportunity to apply analytical methods to characterize traditional decorative materials (earth and paints) and to assess the causes of their deterioration. In the past, only a few studies have been undertaken on the use of traditional decoration techniques, methods, and raw materials in Africa (Pibot 2000; Rainer 1992). This study also demonstrated how scientific investigation can rediscover ancient techniques.

The aim of this decorated surfaces study was to examine the stratigraphy and painting technology used on the interior of the cathedral, to determine the organic and inorganic components of the paint, to identify some of the deterioration patterns, and to help conservators select and use materials compatible with those originally used by the Nankani women. Laboratory analysis was conducted by Ann Bourgès through collaboration between the Laboratory of Research of Historical Monuments (LRMH, Paris), the Center for Research in Earthen Architecture (CRATerre-EAG) and the Center for Research in Physics Applied to Archeology (CRPAA, Bordeaux).

Analysis of the 1970s Painting Techniques and Material Identification

Materials and Methods
The painting materials and techniques used to decorate the interior of the cathedral in 1972 are still commonly used, which allows for comparison with analytical results. Tradi-tionally, a mud layer is applied to the wall by mixing earth with cow dung. The relief is then molded in the mud layer. After partial drying, a red paint mixed with decoction produced from the leaves of a local plant (*soro*) is applied over the entire surface. Drawings and the outlines of areas to be filled in with different colors (red and white) are made with the powder of a black earth mixed with the same decoction. The red pigment is derived from pulverized pebbles, and the white from a white stone bought at the market (Fig. 1). Reliefs and drawings are often enhanced by incising the surface. When the paints are dry, the surface is extensively polished (Fig. 2) and a varnish (*dawa-dawa*) is spread on the surface. The *dawa-dawa* is made from a decoction of leaves and bark from a local tree (*ampoa*).[1]

To identify these materials, samples of the paint layers and plaster were taken where the full stratigraphy was exposed, such as from existing cracks in the original decoration. Cross sections were made for optic and scanning electronic microscopy analysis, and sections were gold coated for the latter study.

Analytical Results
Cross-sectional analysis of the decorated surfaces revealed a succession of three different layers applied on the earth relief. Materials identification was accomplished through EDX-analysis, X-ray diffraction, and chromatographic analysis. The three layers are:

A preparatory layer of earth (2–3 mm thick) applied to the relief. It is composed of a ferruginous earth with some clay minerals (kaolinite) and organic fibers (Fig. 3). The layer includes angular grains of sand approximately 100 μm in diameter, which indicates that some of the material may have

160

FIGURE 1 Traditional materials used for the decorated surfaces. Counterclockwise from upper left: white stones called *kug peela* (white pigment), cracked pebbles to give the red color *gare*, the red pigment coming from these pebbles, black earth called *kug sabla* (black pigment), and red laterite earth called *zigi molego* in the large bowl (the preparation layer below the decoration). Photo: Leslie Rainer, 1999.

FIGURE 2 A Sirigu woman polishing the surface of a painting. Photo: CRATerre-EAG, 1999.

been intentionally crushed. The orange color of the earth was identified as hematite. The fibers serve to increase the tensile strength and reduce cracking of the material. The clays provide a sticky texture that both allows engraving of the drawings and increases the cohesion and stability of the preparatory layer.

The paint layer (1–2 mm thick) penetrates the preparation layer, which demonstrates that it was applied when the latter was still fresh. The pigments were all identified by EDX-analysis. The white is talc $[Mg_3(Si_4O_{10}(OH)_2)]$, aluminum, silicium, and magnesium (Fig. 3). The red is composed of hematite and kaolinite. The black is poorly crystallized iron oxide and kaolinite. Organic materials in the color layer were not analyzed.

The varnish (15 μm thick), is brown and transparent and made of organic material enriched in saccharides. Chromatographic analysis identified only a few components, as the organic materials were aged and altered.

Alteration Patterns

In the south corner of the cathedral, gypsum crystallization (calcium sulfate) was identified in the adobe wall and under the decorated surfaces (Fig. 4). The crystallization of this sol-

uble salt caused disintegration of the paint layer and the substrate. Generally, salts are transported from the soil to the inside of the wall by capillary action, and the water then evaporates on or beneath the surfaces. Although the soil was not analyzed for soluble salts in this case, it is assumed that the origin of the calcium sulfate is from a concrete plate (tomb plate) that abuts the inside wall of the cathedral. The concrete plate inhibits the evaporation of moisture through the ground, and instead pushes the moisture up through the adobe wall. Additional scientific investigation should be conducted to identify the source of the calcium sulfates and to prevent further decay of the decorated surfaces.

A second alteration pattern was also identified, this time in the varnish layer. Under changing temperature and relative humidity levels, the varnish expands and contracts. These movements cause the varnish layer to crack and flake, often

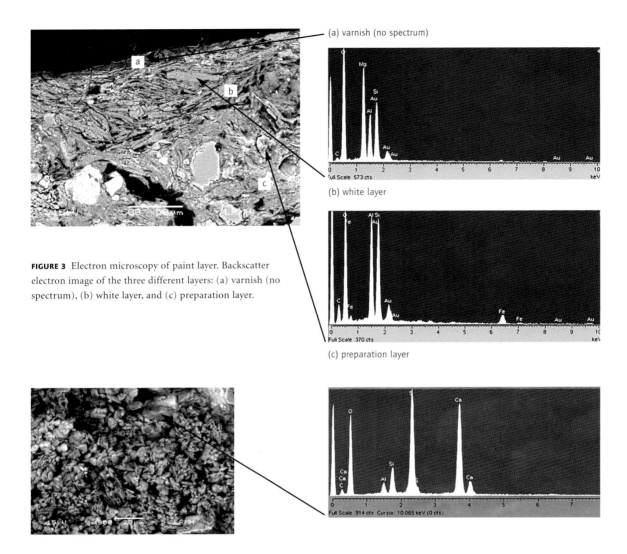

(a) varnish (no spectrum)

(b) white layer

(c) preparation layer

FIGURE 3 Electron microscopy of paint layer. Backscatter electron image of the three different layers: (a) varnish (no spectrum), (b) white layer, and (c) preparation layer.

FIGURE 4 SEM backscatter electron image showing gypsum crystals that have accumulated in the adobe pores. Spectrum shows peaks of calcium and sulfur, indicating the presence of calcium sulfate.

taking with it some of the paint layer (Fig. 5). This type of damage may be normal, since it is common practice to reapply the varnish to the decorated surfaces every one to two years. Fluctuations in the temperature and humidity inside the cathedral can be partially controlled by adjusting the shutters on the east and the west walls according to the sun exposure, which will reduce the incident ultraviolet light on the decorated surfaces.

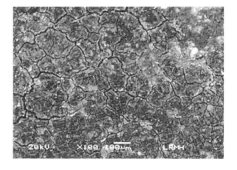

FIGURE 5 SEM backscatter electron image showing microcracking of varnish.

Conclusion

Original materials cannot always be positively identified; however, when raw materials or knowledge of the application technique disappear, scientific investigations can help shed light on the paint technology and materials used, as well as on alteration products and patterns. Such analysis also helps conservators design treatment materials and techniques that are compatible with the original painting and appropriate for use.

Scientific analysis is fundamental to understanding painting materials and techniques, and should be carried out routinely and systematically in the field when undertaking in situ conservation of decorated surfaces on earth. Additional research on decorated surfaces is needed, specifically on application techniques, on understanding how the composition or texture affects cohesion of the materials, and on identification of the primary causes of weathering of earthen decorated surfaces.

Acknowledgments

The author would like to thank the director of the Laboratoire de Recherche des Monuments Historiques (LRMH), Isabelle Pallot-Frossard, who gave a young researcher the opportunity to conduct studies in her laboratory. Many thanks to Philippe Bromblet, at the time researcher for the Stone section of the LRMH, and Paulette Hugon, engineer for the Wall Painting section. I am also grateful to CRATerre Director Patrice Doat and Thierry Joffroy, as well as Sébastien Moriset and Gisèle Taxil, for their great field support. I address my greatest thanks to the Sirigu women who called me by their daughter's name.

Notes

1   For further information on the painting materials, see Navrongo, Ghana, Conservation of "Our Lady of Seven Sorrows" Cathedral, Final Report, 1996–2004. Bolgatanga Diocese, Ghana Museums and Monuments Boards, CRATerre-EAG, and the Getty Grant Program (now the Getty Foundation).

References

Pibot, Jacques. 2000. *Les Peintures murales des femmes kasséna du Burkina Faso*. Paris: Harmattan.

Rainer, L. H. 1992. Decorated surfaces on earthen architecture: A methodological approach toward their conservation. Case study: Kassena wall paintings. Master's thesis, Antioch University.

Closing Dedication

Michael Kabotie/Lomawywesa

I' kwa tsi mu, my friends—
For the last four days we have sat in a gathering
Of faces from many ways of life
Sharing friendship and learning
Among the ancestral homes of the First Ones who utilized
These same qualities of sharing and learning to build these
Wondrous communities here at Mesa Verde.

We have shared much knowledge and learned much from
Each other about our diverse cultural traditions and values
Understanding the challenges that lie ahead in our paths
                              and
Now the time has come that we journey back to our homes
And places of work
With renewed appreciation for traditional ways and truths
To protect, preserve, and enhance those values that are still alive.

So in the spirit of the trickster I wish each and every one
Of you a safe journey to your homes and workplaces
With the prayer and wisdom of the Sacred Clown:

                    With one fart may life be a relief
                              and
                    With one smile may life be joyful.

Kwakhai.
Thank you.

Summary Discussion

Colloquium Organizing Committee: Angelyn Bass Rivera, Claudia Cancino, Rebecca J. Carr, Kecia Fong, Mary Hardy, and Leslie Rainer

The colloquium on the conservation of decorated surfaces made of earth and embellishing earthen architecture brought together a diverse group of professionals from different continents to present their recent research and conservation projects and to discuss issues for future research and collaboration. The participants shared knowledge and experience in the technical aspects of earth as a building material and a deep concern about the disappearance of the traditions and technology of decorating with earth and the loss of fragile architectural decoration.

The colloquium was structured into sessions on the conservation of decorated surfaces in the context of archaeological sites, museums, historic buildings, and living traditions. Within each theme, presentations focused on both traditional and new approaches to documentation and conservation treatment, as well as on the fundamental issues of decorative style and meaning, historical change, and cultural identity and values. This organization of the sessions was a functional way to stimulate dialogue on specific conservation issues. However, it became evident from the discussions that numerous points were common to all the themes and that many concerns, needs, and ideas about how to advance the field transcended the themes.

On the final day of the event, moderators of each session summarized and highlighted key issues that had emerged from the presentation, followed by a groupwide discussion. This summary evolved from those discussions and additional contributions from colloquium participants. The following sums up ten key discussion points and the identified needs for future research.

I. Research and field testing of noninvasive or less-invasive investigation and in situ conservation treatments for decorated surfaces on archaeological sites is needed to preserve their physical integrity and archaeological significance. The scientific and cultural information these surfaces contain is essential for reliable future study. Preventive treatments that address the causes of damage or decay of the decorated surfaces and the architectural systems they embellish are preferred over remedial or direct intervention for preserving material integrity. New technologies such as virtual reconstruction of sites offer options for interpretation and research. This can be a means of shifting the risks of tourism-related damage away from the sites themselves.

II. An understanding of the relationship between the condition of the decorated architectural surface and causes of decay is fundamental to the design of a conservation plan. It is essential to conduct a survey and document the findings in order to understand this causal relationship and to prioritize conservation needs, including treatment, monitoring, and maintenance. Due to the complexity of decorated surfaces on earth, conservation must integrate laboratory research and analysis with treatment in an iterative process.

III. Detaching and removing wall paintings and other decorated surfaces from their original context, while a common treatment in the past, is now considered a treatment option only of last resort (e.g., if the site is threatened with complete destruction). The conservation profession needs to explore alternatives to detachment—such as reburial or presentation—that allow the decorated surface to remain in situ and preserve its significance. Conservation solutions must also appropriately respond to other issues such as maintenance and tourism. If it is necessary to detach a decorated architectural finish, guidelines are needed to help site managers determine the appropriateness of this action. The guidelines should not only steer the decision-making process but also provide direction and standards for documentation, analysis (of context, cultural significance, environmental conditions, and materials), methods of removal, and preservation. The environment of the treated and remounted fragment in storage or on exhibit may be radically different from its original setting, and such environmental change can be detrimental to preservation. Unless an institution has provisions in place for appropriate conservation, installation, and interpretation, wall paintings and other decorated surfaces may best be protected in situ.

IV.   Conservation is often faced with the challenge of preserving the past while also allowing for change. This is particularly true in historic buildings, when adaptive use is the most viable option for long-term preservation of a structure and its architectural decoration. Adaptive use does not preclude sound conservation practice. Determination of appropriate reuse of buildings and conservation of surface decoration must take into account the lifestyle, values, and traditions of the people who created, use, and care for the buildings in question.

V.   The source of living traditions is the surviving community. If conservation of decorated surfaces is to be a respected and relevant practice in the context of living traditions, the community must be integrated into the conservation process—and should benefit from it. The most successful conservation strategies include community participation in all phases of the project, from planning to implementation, maintenance, and management.

VI.   Decorated architectural surfaces are the material expression of the culture in which they are created. To humanize the material heritage, the individuals as well as the communities who create decorated architectural surfaces on earth must be recognized. Documentation is vital for the conservation not only of the materials used

in surface finishes but also as a way to acknowledge and record the work of artists and their living traditions. This is especially critical in the case of dying traditions, where documentation may be their only form of preservation. Documentation also becomes crucial in the rare case of tradition revival, where these records can provide vital yet forgotten information.

VII.   Conservators involved in the conservation and transmission of living traditions should study and learn from the masters and practitioners of the craft to gain knowledge about the materials and techniques they use. This empirical knowledge should be supported by scientific research into the physico-chemical characteristics and working properties of the materials. The acceptance or rejection of any new materials requires not only in situ testing and evaluation of the results prior to widespread use but also consultation with and the concurrence of the local community.

VIII.   Better understanding of the properties of materials used in building and decorating with earth is needed, as is further research and dissemination of information on the following:
- preparation of traditional decorative materials and application techniques (ground and paint layers, varnishes or coatings, organic binders and additives);
- deterioration mechanisms of decorated earthen architectural surfaces caused by salts, and appropriate treatment of such damage;
- testing protocols for the easy identification of plaster and paint materials, especially for use in the field;
- adhesion tests specifically designed for earthen plasters, for use in both the laboratory and the field to determine the adhesion properties between the decorative finish layer and the substrate, which can be of similar or dissimilar materials; and
- composition, preparation, and use of earth-based grouts.

IX.   Formal criteria and a sound methodology to qualitatively and quantitatively evaluate the effectiveness of past treatments applied to decorated earthen architectural surfaces are needed, particularly when modern conservation materials have been used (e.g., resins, ethyl silicates, cements). Evaluation requires a thorough knowledge of past treatments and a reexamination of present conditions. Monitoring and recording of the type and location of changes in condition over time is a critical tool for evaluation. Information regarding site context, original and treatment materials, results of monitoring, and evaluation of treatment success or failure should be disseminated to the wider conservation and heritage management community.

X.   The conservation field would benefit from the coordination of collaborative research and dissemination of information on the topic of earthen decorated surfaces. The establishment of a central reference collection could facilitate this, and should include a material reference library as well as an archive of photographic and written documentation.

Conclusion

Angelyn Bass Rivera

This colloquium and volume focusing on the conservation of decorated surfaces gives us a glimpse of the diversity of decorated earthen architecture from around the world, as well as the complex cultural traditions associated with creating and conserving them. From wall paintings on archaeological sites in China, the Americas, and Egypt to detached decorative fragments in museums, and from the ornamental architecture of the Middle East to the painted, relief adornment on shrines and churches in West Africa, these papers clearly demonstrate how the human desire to embellish or elaborate their dwellings is evident throughout history and how earth is commonly used as the decorative medium. Through these examples, we also begin to see and understand how decorated surfaces speak to us across the barriers of time and language about our individual and collective humanity. As the art historian James Trilling has pointed out, "To grasp a culture's ornament . . . is to grasp its heritage, its uniqueness, and its joy."*

It became clear from the colloquium presentations and papers that future conservation of this decorative art and tradition is a matter of both materials and social science. To con-serve decorated surfaces and the buildings they embellish, as well as the cultures they represent, we must not only have a commanding understanding of the physical properties of the earthen materials—including the environmental processes affecting them and the technologies used to create and treat them—but we must also understand the past and present cultural, political, and economic climate and the unique qualities of the cultures to which they belong.

In the face of globalization and increasing worldwide population growth, and the resulting demolition of buildings and loss of cultural traditions as sustainable practice, conservation of earthen buildings and their decorated surfaces is imperative—as is conserving the knowledge of how to create and maintain them and transmitting this art to future generations. Through this meeting of experts from different countries and disciplines, a dialogue and exchange of information in this area of heritage conservation has begun and will result in new collaborative research projects for our future.

* James Trilling, *Ornament: A Modern Perspective* (Seattle: University of Washington Press, 2003), 3.

Bibliography

This bibliography provides an overview of the literature on the conservation of decorated surfaces made of earth and embellishing earthen architecture. Due to the great diversity of materials and techniques of such decorated architectural surfaces, and the different contexts in which these surfaces can be found, the literature on the topic is widely varied. It ranges from scholarly papers in professional journals in the fields of conservation, anthropology, architecture, and archaeology, to photographic essays describing living traditions and documenting the processes of decorating earthen surfaces.

This bibliography was compiled from searches in the following areas:

- proceedings of international conferences and symposia on earthen architecture and wall paintings
- university theses and dissertations available in one or more libraries
- previous earthen architecture bibliographies
- relevant references from this volume's papers
- contributions from colleagues in the field

The references are current up to 2004.

This is the first published bibliography specific to the topic of decorated surfaces on or made of earth. We intend it to be far reaching and comprehensive, and as a result, it includes a broad selection of papers, articles, and theses. It is hoped that more references will be added to further this area of study.

Acknowledgment and gratitude are extended to Claudia Cancino, Amel Chabbi, and Valerie Greathouse for their hard work on the compilation of this bibliography.

Adams, Sarah Margaret. 2002. Hand to hand: *Uli* body and wall painting and artistic identity in Southeastern Nigeria. PhD diss., Yale University.

Adande, Joseph C. E. 1999. Les bas-reliefs du Palais de Glélé: Un art au-delà de l'image et de l'histoire. In *Passé, présent et futur des palais et site royaux d'Abomey: 22–26 septembre 1997: Actes de la conférence,* ed. Getty Conservation Institute, ICCROM, and Ministère de la culture et de la communication du Bénin, 17–25. Los Angeles: Getty Conservation Institute.

Agarawala, R. A. 1977. *Marwar Murals.* Delhi: Agam Prakashan (distributed by D. K. Publishers' Distributors, New Delhi).

Agnew, Neville, ed. 1997. *Conservation of Ancient Sites on the Silk Road: Proceedings of an International Conference on the Conservation of Grotto Sites.* Los Angeles: Getty Conservation Institute.

———. 2003. Sins of omission: Diagnosis, risk assessment and decision: Lessons from three sites. In *Conserving the Painted Past: Developing Approaches to Wall Painting Conservation: Post-Prints of a Conference Organised by English Heritage, London, 2–4 December, 1999,* ed. Robert Gowing and Adrian Heritage, 75–84. London: James & James.

Agrawal, O. P. 1986. Conservation problems of Ajanta wall paintings. In *Case Studies in the Conservation of Stone and Wall Paintings: Preprints of the Contributions to the Bologna Congress, 21–26 September 1986,* ed. N. S. Brommelle and Perry Smith, 86–89. London: International Institute for Conservation of Historic and Artistic Works.

Agrawal, O. P., and Kamal K. Jain. 1984. Problems of conservation of wall paintings in India. In *International Symposium on the Conservation and Restoration of Cultural Property, November 17–21, 1983, Tokyo, Japan: Conservation and Restoration of Mural Paintings (I),* ed. Organizing Committee of the International Symposium on the Conservation and Restoration of Cultural Property, 31–40. Tokyo: Tokyo National Research Institute of Cultural Properties.

Akiyama, Terukazu. 1985. Japanese wall painting: An art historical overview. In *International Symposium on the Conservation and Restoration of Cultural Property, November 18–21, [1984], Tokyo, Japan: Conservation and Restoration of Mural Paintings (II),* ed. Organizing Committee of the International Symposium on the Conservation and Restoration of Cultural Property, 21–36. Tokyo: Tokyo National Research Institute of Cultural Properties.

Al-Anbar, Ali Saleh. 1999. *A Study of the interiors and their decoration in the traditional mud-brick architecture of the Najd region of Saudi Arabia and the factors that have influenced the development of interior decoration and spatial organization.*

PhD thesis, Heriot Watt University, School of Design and Applied Arts, Edinburgh College of Art.

Alçada, M., ICCROM, and CRATerre-EAG, eds. 1993. *Terra 93: 7a Conferência Internacional sobre o Estudo e Conservação da Arquitectura de Terra: Silves, Portugal, 24 a 29 de Outubro, 1993 = 7th International Conference on the Study and Conservation of Earthen Architecture: Silves, Portugal 24–29 October, 1993 = 7ème conférence internationale pour l'étude et la conservation de l'architecture de terre: Silves, Portugal, 24 au 29 Octobre, 1993.* Lisbon: Direcção Geral dos Edifícios e Monumentos Nacionais (DGEMN).

Alva, Alejandro, Hugo Houben, ICCROM, and CRATerre-EAG, eds. 1988. *5th International Meeting of Experts on the Conservation of Earthen Architecture: Rome, Italy, 22–23 October 1987 = 5e réunion internationale d'experts sur la conservation de l'architecture de terre: Rome, 22–23, X, 1987.* Rome: ICCROM; Villefontaine, France: CRATerre.

Alva Balderrama, Alejandro, and Giacomo Chiari. 1995. Protection and conservation of excavated structures of mudbrick. In *Conservation on Archaeological Excavations, with Particular Reference to the Mediterranean Area,* 2nd ed., ed. N. P. Stanley Price, 101–12. Rome: ICCROM.

Arkum, Burcum Hanzade. 2003. Neolithic plasters of the Near East: Catal Hoyuk building 5, a case study. Master's thesis, University of Pennsylvania.

Arnon, Nancy, and Sam Baca. 1990. Churches, symbols of community: The preservation of New Mexico's adobe churches. In *6th International Conference on the Conservation of Earthen Architecture: Adobe 90 Preprints: Las Cruces, New Mexico, U.S.A., October 14–19, 1990,* ed. Kirsten Grimstad, 143–48. Marina del Rey, CA: Getty Conservation Institute.

Aryan, K. C. 1977. *Punjab Murals.* New Delhi: Rekha Prakashan.

Ashurst, John. 2002. *Mortars, Plasters and Renders in Conservation.* 2nd ed. London: Ecclesiastical Architects' and Surveyors' Association.

Bandaranayake, Senake. 1997. The Dambulla Rock Temple Complex, Sri Lanka: Ten years of management, research, and conservation. In *Conservation of Ancient Sites on the Silk Road: Proceedings of an International Conference on the Conservation of Grotto Sites,* ed. Neville Agnew, 46–55. Los Angeles: Getty Conservation Institute.

Barger, M. Susan. 1995. Materials characterization of natural adobe plasters: New approaches for preservation strategies based on traditional practice. In *Materials Issues in Art and Archaeology IV: Symposium Held May 16–21, 1994, Cancun, Mexico,* ed. Pamela B. Vandiver, James R. Druzik, José Luis

Galván Madrid, Ian C. Freestone, and George Segan Wheeler, 389–94. Materials Research Society Symposia Proceedings, vol. 352. Pittsburgh: Materials Research Society.

Barrio Martin, Joaquin. 1993. Architecture de terre du village préromain de Cuellar: Prélèvement et conservation (Segovia, Espagne). In *Terra 93: 7a Conferência Internacional sobre o Estudo e Conservação da Arquitectura de Terra: Silves, Portugal, 24 a 29 de Outubro, 1993 = 7th International Conference on the Study and Conservation of Earthen Architecture: Silves, Portugal 24–29 October, 1993 = 7ème conférence internationale pour l'étude et la conservation de l'architecture de terre: Silves, Portugal, 24 au 29 Octobre, 1993,* ed. M. Alçada, ICCROM, and CRATerre-EAG, 310–16. Lisbon: Direcção Geral dos Edifícios e Monumentos Nacionais (DGEMN).

Bass, Angelyn. 1998. Design and evaluation of hydraulic lime grouts for in situ reattachment of lime plaster to earthen walls. Master's thesis, University of Pennsylvania.

Beas, Maria Isabel G. 1991. Traditional architectural renders on earthen surfaces. Master's thesis, University of Pennsylvania.

Beas, Maria Isabel, Patricia Navarro Grau, and Cesar Maguina. 2000. La arquitectura religiosa del Valle de Oyón, Perú. In *Terra 2000: 8th International Conference on the Study and Conservation of Earthen Architecture, Torquay, Devon, UK, May 2000: Preprints,* ed. English Heritage, ICOMOS-UK, and University of Plymouth Centre for Earthen Architecture, 4–8. London: James & James.

Beas Guerrero de Luna, Maria Isabel. 1993. Consolidation of traditional plasters: A laboratory research. In *Terra 93: 7a Conferência Internacional sobre o Estudo e Conservação da Arquitectura de Terra: Silves, Portugal, 24 a 29 de Outubro, 1993 = 7th International Conference on the Study and Conservation of Earthen Architecture: Silves, Portugal 24–29 October, 1993 = 7ème conférence internationale pour l'étude et la conservation de l'architecture de terre: Silves, Portugal, 24 au 29 Octobre, 1993,* ed. M. Alçada, ICCROM, and CRATerre-EAG, 410–16. Lisbon: Direcção Geral dos Edifícios e Monumentos Nacionais (DGEMN).

Berman, Esmé. 1983. Ndebele painting. In *Art and Artists of South Africa: An Illustrated Biographical Dictionary and Historical Survey of Painters, Sculptors & Graphic Artists Since 1875,* ed. Esmé Berman, 305–6. Cape Town: Balkema.

Biancifiori, Maria Antonietta. 1994. *Biancifiori: Works of Architectural Restoration in Oman.* Rome: De Luca.

Blair, Katherine D. 1983. *Four Villages: Architecture in Nepal: Studies in Village Life.* Los Angeles: Craft and Folk Art Museum (distributed by University of Chicago Press).

Blier, Suzanne Preston. 1999. L'histoire en relief: Las bas-reliefs des palais royaux du Danxomè, création et conservation d'une tradition. In *Passé, présent et futur des palais et site royaux d'Abomey: 22–26 septembre 1997: Actes de la conférence,* ed. Getty Conservation Institute, ICCROM, and Ministère de la culture et de la communication du Bénin, 26–38. Los Angeles: Getty Conservation Institute.

———. 2003–4. Butabu: West Africa's extraordinary earthen legacy. *World Monuments Icon* (Winter): 34–39.

Bogin, Stephanie. 2004. A technical study of the early Buddhist wall paintings at Nako, Himachal Pradesh, India. Master's thesis, University of London, Courtauld Institute of Art, Conservation of Wall Painting Department.

Bohnert, Allen S. 1990. The preservation of prehistoric mud plaster at Mesa Verde National Park. In *6th International Conference on the Conservation of Earthen Architecture: Adobe 90 Preprints: Las Cruces, New Mexico, U.S.A., October 14–19, 1990,* ed. Kirsten Grimstad, 261–66. Marina del Rey, CA: Getty Conservation Institute.

Bomin, Su, and Li Ru. 1996. The influence of three kinds of consolidants to the color of wall paintings. *Dunhuang Research* 48:171–79.

Bonavia, Duccio. 1985. *Mural Painting in Ancient Peru.* Translated by Patricia J. Lyon. Bloomington: Indiana University Press.

Borelli, Caterina, Diane Torr, and Ian Murray. 2000. *The Architecture of Mud.* VHS. Watertown, MA: Documentary Educational Resources.

Bourgeois, Jean-Louis, Carollee Pelos, and Basil Davidson. 1989. *Spectacular Vernacular: The Adobe Tradition.* New York: Aperture Foundation.

Bouwens, Dirk. 1993. English mud-brick and mud building. In *Terra 93: 7a Conferência Internacional sobre o Estudo e Conservação da Arquitectura de Terra: Silves, Portugal, 24 a 29 de Outubro, 1993 = 7th International Conference on the Study and Conservation of Earthen Architecture: Silves, Portugal 24–29 October, 1993 = 7ème conférence internationale pour l'étude et la conservation de l'architecture de terre: Silves, Portugal, 24 au 29 Octobre, 1993,* ed. M. Alçada, ICCROM, and CRATerre-EAG, 58–63. Lisbon: Direcção Geral dos Edifícios e Monumentos Nacionais (DGEMN).

Bowen, Cole. 1957. *15 Essays in Half-Tone.* Pretoria: Van Schaik.

Brody, J. J. 1991. *Anasazi and Pueblo Painting*. Albuquerque: University of New Mexico Press.

Brommelle, N. S., and Perry Smith, eds. 1986. *Case Studies in the Conservation of Stone and Wall Paintings: Preprints of the Contributions to the Bologna Congress, 21–26 September 1986*. London: International Institute for Conservation of Historic and Artistic Works.

Brown, Roy B., Beatriz Sandoval, and Haydee Orea M. 1990. The protection and conservation of the adobe structures at Paquimé, Casas Grandes, Chihuahua, Mexico. In *6th International Conference on the Conservation of Earthen Architecture: Adobe 90 Preprints: Las Cruces, New Mexico, U.S.A., October 14–19, 1990*, ed. Kirsten Grimstad, 204–8. Marina del Rey, CA: Getty Conservation Institute.

Burch, Rachel. 1997. The reburial of wall paintings: A critical assessment of the technique of reburial for the conservation in situ of excavated painted plasters. Post-diploma diss., University of London, Courtauld Institute of Art, Conservation of Wall Painting Department.

Burkina Faso Ministère de l'enseignement de base et de l'alphabétisation de masse, Bureau du Projet Education III, Patrice Doat, and CRATerre. 1991. *Étude sur les savoirs constructifs au Burkina Faso*. Villefontaine, France: Centre international de la construction en terre; Burkina Faso: Le Ministère.

Butler, William. B. 1973. The Avila Adobe: The determination of architectural change. *Historical Archaeology* 7:30–45.

C. T. Loo, Inc. 1949. *Chinese Frescos of the Northern Sung*. New York: C. T. Loo.

Cancino Borge, Claudia N. 2001. Assessment of grouting methods for cracks and large scale detachment repair at Casa Grande: Casa Grande Ruins National Monument. Master's thesis, University of Pennsylvania.

Caron, Peter, and Michael F. Lynch. 1988. Making mud plaster. *APT Bulletin* 20 (4): 7–9.

Carr, Rebecca J. 2002. Evaluation of adhesive binders for the preservation of in-situ aboriginal surface finishes at Mesa Verde National Park. Master's thesis, University of Pennsylvania.

Casoli, Antonella, Giacomo Chiari, Richard Burger, Lucy Salazar-Burger, Margherita Vizzari, and Gerardo Palla. 2000. Identification of the binder in the paintings of the ancient Manchay culture (Peru). In *Terra 2000: 8th International Conference on the Study and Conservation of Earthen Architecture, Torquay, Devon, UK, May 2000: Preprints*, ed. English Heritage, ICOMOS-UK, and University of Plymouth Centre for Earthen Architecture, 120–25. London: James & James.

Castellanos, Carolina, and Ana Maria Hoyle. 2000. Conservation and management planning for earthen architecture Chan Chan, Peru. In *Terra 2000: 8th International Conference on the Study and Conservation of Earthen Architecture, Torquay, Devon, UK, May 2000: Preprints*, ed. English Heritage, ICOMOS-UK, and University of Plymouth Centre for Earthen Architecture, 13–18. London: James & James.

Cather, Sharon. 2003. Assessing causes and mechanisms of detrimental change to wall paintings. In *Conserving the Painted Past: Developing Approaches to Wall Painting Conservation: Post-Prints of a Conference Organised by English Heritage, London, 2–4 December, 1999*, ed. Robert Gowing and Adrian Heritage, 64–74. London: James & James.

Celedón, Pedro Pablo, Pía Domingues, Mahasti Ziai Afshar, Getty Conservation Institute, and ActionCineVideo Productions. 1997. *History Told on Walls*. VHS Getty Conservation Video. Los Angeles: Getty Conservation Institute.

Cellauro, Louis, and Gilbert Richaud. 1984. Le système du pisé décoré et sa diffusion sous la Révolution et l'Empire. In *Facciate dipinte: conservazione e restauro: Atti del convegno di studi Genoa, 15–17 aprile 1982*, ed. Giovanna Rotondi Terminiello and Farida Simonetti, 23–26. Genoa: Sagep.

Centre de recherche de l'École d'Architecture de Grenoble. CRATerre-EAG. http://terre.grenoble.archi.fr/.

Chayet, Anne, Corneille Jest, and John Sanday. 1990. Earth used for building in the Himalayas, the Karakoram, and Central Asia—Recent research and future trends. In *6th International Conference on the Conservation of Earthen Architecture: Adobe 90 Preprints: Las Cruces, New Mexico, U.S.A., October 14–19, 1990*, ed. Kirsten Grimstad, 29–34. Los Angeles: Getty Conservation Institute.

Chiari, Giacomo. 1976. Adobe in Peru: Treatment of a painted frieze (abstract). In *Deuxième colloque international pour la conservation des monuments en brique crue = Second International Conference on the Conservation of Mud-brick Monuments, Yazd [Iran], 6–11 March 1976*, ed. ICOMOS, 33–34. Paris: ICOMOS.

————. 1980. Treatment of adobe friezes in Peru. In *Üçüncü Uluslararasi Kerpiç Koruma Sempozyumu: 29 Eylül–4 Ekim, 1980, Ankara = Third International Symposium on Mudbrick (Adobe) Preservation: 29 September–4 October, 1980, Ankara*, ed. International Council of Museums, Türkiye Milli Komitesi, and International Council of Monuments and Sites, Türkiye Milli Komitesi, 39–45. Ankara: ICOM-Turkey; ICOMOS-Turkey.

———. 1988. Consolidation of adobe with ethyl silicate: Control of long term effects using SEM. In *5th International Meeting of Experts on the Conservation of Earthen Architecture: Rome, Italy, 22–23 October 1987 = 5e réunion internationale d'experts sur la conservation de l'architecture de terre: Rome, 22–23, X, 1987*, ed. Alejandro Alva, Hugo Houben, ICCROM, and CRATerre-EAG, 25–32. Rome: ICCROM; Villefontaine, France: CRATerre.

———. 1990. Chemical surface treatments and capping techniques of earthen structures: A long-term evaluation. In *6th International Conference on the Conservation of Earthen Architecture: Adobe 90 Preprints: Las Cruces, New Mexico, U.S.A., October 14–19, 1990*, ed. Kirsten Grimstad, 267–73. Marina del Rey, CA: Getty Conservation Institute.

———. 1993. Conservazione in situ di fregi dipinti su mattone crudo. In *Archeologia: recupero e conservazione*, ed. Luisa Masetti Bitelli, Istituto per i beni artistici, culturali e naturali della Regione Emilia-Romagna, and Restauro '91, Ferrara, 169–83. Arte e restauro. Florence: Nardini.

Chiari, Giacomo, Antonio Invernizzi, and Giuseppina Bertolotto. 1993. Investigation and restoration of clay fragmentary statues from Old Nisa, Turkmenistan. In *Terra 93: 7a Conferência Internacional sobre o Estudo e Conservação da Arquitectura de Terra: Silves, Portugal, 24 a 29 de Outubro, 1993 = 7th International Conference on the Study and Conservation of Earthen Architecture: Silves, Portugal 24–29 October, 1993 = 7ème conférence internationale pour l'étude et la conservation de l'architecture de terre: Silves, Portugal, 24 au 29 Octobre, 1993*, ed. M. Alçada, ICCROM, and CRATerre-EAG, 228–30. Lisbon: Direcção Geral dos Edifícios e Monumentos Nacionais (DGEMN).

Chiari, Giacomo, and Roger Ravinez. 1976. Huaca Garagay (Peru). In *Deuxième colloque international pour la conservation des monuments en brique crue = Second International Conference on the Conservation of Mud-Brick Monuments, Yazd [Iran], 6–11 March 1976*, ed. ICOMOS, 31–32. Paris: ICOMOS.

Chiari, Giacomo, Marisa Rigoni, and Thierry Joffroy. 1993. Ethyl silicate treatments and humidity. In *Terra 93: 7a Conferência Internacional sobre o Estudo e Conservação da Arquitectura de Terra: Silves, Portugal, 24 a 29 de Outubro, 1993 = 7th International Conference on the Study and Conservation of Earthen Architecture: Silves, Portugal 24–29 October, 1993 = 7ème conférence internationale pour l'étude et la conservation de l'architecture de terre: Silves, Portugal, 24 au 29 Octobre, 1993*, ed. M. Alçada, ICCROM, and CRATerre-EAG, 422–25. Lisbon: Direcção Geral dos Edifícios e Monumentos Nacionais (DGEMN).

Clark, Liesl, Liev Schreiber, WGBH Television, (Boston, MA), WGBH Video, and Channel Four (Great Britain). 2003. *Lost Treasures of Tibet*. VHS NOVA. South Burlington, VT: WGBH Video.

Cobau, Andreina Costanzi. 1986. Excavated wall plasters: Conservation problems. In *Preventive Measures During Excavation and Site Protection: Conference Ghent, 6–8 November 1985 = Mesures Préventives En Cours De Fouilles Et Protection Du Site: Gand, 6–8 Novembre 1985*, ed. ICCROM and Rijksuniversiteit te Gent, 103–10. Rome: ICCROM.

Cointeraux, François. 1803. *L'Art de peindre à fresque sur le pisé avec la découverte de l'auteur pour rendre durable cette peinture: Ensemble les enduits, les tapisseries et l'épreuve du canon dans le pisé*. Saint-Mandé: Ecole d'architecture rurale.

Compton, Edwin Binda. 1993. Ancestral techniques and materials used in the architecture and mural paintings of the pre-plateau sierra of the Chilean Andes. In *Terra 93: 7a Conferência Internacional sobre o Estudo e Conservação da Arquitectura de Terra: Silves, Portugal, 24 a 29 de Outubro, 1993 = 7th International Conference on the Study and Conservation of Earthen Architecture: Silves, Portugal 24–29 October, 1993 = 7ème conférence internationale pour l'étude et la conservation de l'architecture de terre: Silves, Portugal, 24 au 29 Octobre, 1993*, ed. M. Alçada, ICCROM, and CRATerre-EAG, 37–42. Lisbon: Direcção Geral dos Edifícios e Monumentos Nacionais (DGEMN).

Conlon, James, Pamela Jerome, and Selma Al-Radi. 2003. Documentation of the Tarimi Palaces 2002–2003: Qasr al-'Ishshah. *Yemen Update: Bulletin of the American Institute for Yemeni Studies* 45:9–22.

Courtney-Clarke, Margaret. 1986. *Ndebele: The Art of an African Tribe*. New York: Rizzoli.

———. 1990. *African Canvas: The Art of West African Women*. New York: Rizzoli.

Crocker, E. 1993. The purpose and mechanics of lime renders. In *Terra 93: 7a Conferência Internacional sobre o Estudo e Conservação da Arquitectura de Terra: Silves, Portugal, 24 a 29 de Outubro, 1993 = 7th International Conference on the Study and Conservation of Earthen Architecture: Silves, Portugal 24–29 October, 1993 = 7ème conférence internationale pour l'étude et la conservation de l'architecture de terre: Silves, Portugal, 24 au 29 Octobre, 1993*, ed. M. Alçada, ICCROM, and CRATerre-EAG, 433–38. Lisbon: Direcção Geral dos Edifícios e Monumentos Nacionais (DGEMN).

Crosby, Anthony. 1980. Conservation of painted lime plaster on mud brick walls at Tumacacori National Monument, U.S.A. In *Üçüncü Uluslararasi Kerpiç Koruma Sempozyumu: 29 Eylül–4 Ekim, 1980, Ankara = Third International*

Symposium on Mudbrick (Adobe) Preservation: 29 September–4 October, 1980, Ankara, ed. International Council of Museums, Türkiye Milli Komitesi, and International Council of Monuments and Sites, Türkiye Milli Komitesi, 59–78. Ankara: ICOM-Turkey; ICOMOS-Turkey.

De Silva, R. H. 1971. The evolution of the technique of Sinahalese wall painting and comparison with Indian painting methods. *Ancient Ceylon* 1:90–104.

De Vos, Ashley. 1985. A survey of the painted mud Viharas of Sri Lanka. In *Adobe: International Symposium and Training Workshop on the Conservation of Adobe: Final Report and Major Papers: Lima, Cuzco (Peru) 10–22 September 1983,* ed. ICCROM, Regional Project on Cultural Heritage and Development UNDP/UNESCO, and National Institute of Culture (Peru), 91–95. Lima: Regional Project on Cultural Heritage and Development UNDP/UNESCO; Rome: ICCROM.

Demas, Martha, and Neville Agnew, ed. 2002. *Principles for the Conservation of Heritage Sites in China.* Los Angeles: Getty Conservation Institute. (Available for download at http://www.getty.edu/conservation/publications/ pdf_publications/china_prin_2english.pdf.)

Denyer, Susan. 1978. *African Traditional Architecture: An Historical and Geographical Perspective.* London: Heinemann Educational Books.

Dethier, Jean. 1981. *Des architectures de terre, ou, l'avenir d'une tradition millénaire.* Paris: Centre Georges Pompidou, Centre de création industrielle.

Dinsmore, J., and H. Howard. 1988. The treatment of an Eighteenth Dynasty wall painting fragment at the British Museum. In *Conservation of Ancient Egyptian Materials*: Preprints of the conference organized by the United Kingdom Institute for Conservation, Archaeology Section, held at Bristol, December 15–18, 1988), ed. S. Watkins and C. Brown, 61–68. London: United Kingdom Institute for Conservation.

Dix, Linnaea A. 1996. Characterization and analysis of prehistoric earthen plasters, mortars, and paints from Mug House, Mesa Verde National Park, Colorado. Master's thesis, University of Pennsylvania.

Dmochowski, Z. R. 1990. *An Introduction to Nigerian Traditional Architecture: Vol. 1, Northern Nigeria, Vol. 2, South-West and Central Nigeria, Vol. 3, South-Eastern Nigeria: The Igbo-Speaking Areas.* London: Ethnographica.

Dolske, Donald A., and William T. Petuskey. 1987. Monitoring air pollution impacts on Anasazi ruins at Mesa Verde National Park, Colorado, USA. In *8th General Assembly and International Symposium "Old Cultures in New Worlds": Washington, District of Columbia, United States of America, October 10–15, 1987: Symposium Papers,* ed. ICOMOS, 285–92. Washington, DC: ICOMOS United States Committee.

Dowdy, Katherine, and Michael Romero Taylor. 1993. Investigations into the benefits of site burial in the preservation of prehistoric plasters in archaeological ruins. In *Terra 93: 7a Conferência Internacional sobre o Estudo e Conservação da Arquitectura de Terra: Silves, Portugal, 24 a 29 de Outubro, 1993 = 7th International Conference on the Study and Conservation of Earthen Architecture: Silves, Portugal 24–29 October, 1993 = 7ème conférence internationale pour l'étude et la conservation de l'architecture de terre: Silves, Portugal, 24 au 29 Octobre, 1993,* ed. M. Alçada, ICCROM, and CRATerre-EAG, 480–87. Lisbon: Direcção Geral dos Edifícios e Monumentos Nacionais (DGEMN).

Elleh, Nnamdi. 1997. *African Architecture: Evolution and Transformation.* New York: McGraw-Hill.

Elliot, Aubrey. 1993. *The Ndebele: Art and Culture.* 2nd ed. Cape Town: Struik.

English Heritage, ICOMOS-UK, and University of Plymouth Centre for Earthen Architecture, eds. 2000. *Terra 2000: 8th International Conference on the Study and Conservation of Earthen Architecture, Torquay, Devon, UK, May 2000: Preprints.* London: James & James.

Fewkes, Jesse Walter. 1911. *Antiquities of the Mesa Verde National Park: Cliff Palace.* Bureau of American Ethnology Bulletin, 51. Washington, DC: Smithsonian Institution.

Fiero, K., F. Matero, and A. Bass Rivera. 2000. Preservation of prehistoric earthen architectural finishes in Mesa Verde National Park, Colorado. In *Terra 2000: 8th International Conference on the Study and Conservation of Earthen Architecture, Torquay, Devon, UK, May 2000: Preprints,* ed. English Heritage, ICOMOS-UK, and University of Plymouth Centre for Earthen Architecture, 31–38. London: James & James.

Fodde, E. 2000. Decorative interior features of twentieth-century *ladiri* buildings of Campidano and their traditional repair methods. In *Terra 2000: 8th International Conference on the Study and Conservation of Earthen Architecture, Torquay, Devon, UK, May 2000: Preprints,* ed. English Heritage, ICOMOS-UK, and University of Plymouth Centre for Earthen Architecture, 125–31. London: James & James.

Fong, Kecia Lee. 1999. Design and evaluation of acrylic-based grouts for earthen plasters. Master's thesis, University of Pennsylvania.

Forrest, Kathleen Anne. 2001. An architectural analysis and earthen finish: characterization of cavate M-100, Frijoles Canyon, Bandelier National Monument, Los Alamos, NM. Master's thesis, University of Pennsylvania.

French, Pamela. 1987. The problems of in situ conservation of mudbrick and mud plaster. In *In Situ Archaeological Conservation: Proceedings of Meetings, April 6–13, 1986, Mexico,* ed. Henry W. M. Hodges and Miguel Angel Corzo, 78–83. Marina del Rey, CA: Getty Conservation Institute; Mexico City: Instituto Nacional de Antropología e Historia de Mexico.

Gamarra, Ricardo Morales. 1985. Conservation of structures and decorative elements in Chan Chan. In *Adobe: International Symposium and Training Workshop on the Conservation of Adobe: Final Report and Major Papers: Lima, Cuzco (Peru) 10–22 September 1983,* ed. ICCROM, Regional Project on Cultural Heritage and Development UNDP/UNESCO, and National Institute of Culture (Peru), 83–89. Lima: Regional Project on Cultural Heritage and Development UNDP/UNESCO; Rome: ICCROM.

Gerassimova, N. G., and E. P. Mel'nikova. 1978. The effect of the treatment with polybutyl methacrylate solutions on physical and mechanical properties of Loess plaster. In *ICOM Committee for Conservation 5th Triennial Meeting: Zagreb, 1–8 October 1978: Preprints,* ed. ICOM Committee for Conservation, 78/15/13/1–78/15/13/11. Paris: International Council of Museums.

Gettens, Rutherford J. 1938. The materials in the wall paintings from Kizil in Chinese Turkestan. *Technical Studies in the Field of the Fine Arts* 6 (4): 281–94.

———. 1938. The materials in the wall paintings of Bamiyan, Afghanistan. *Technical Studies in the Field of the Fine Arts* 6 (3): 186–93.

———. 1938. Pigments in a wall painting from Central China. *Technical Studies in the Field of the Fine Arts* 7 (2): 99–105.

Getty Conservation Institute. Project Bibliographies: Terra. http://gcibibs.getty.edu/asp/.

Getty Conservation Institute, ICCROM, and Ministère de la culture et de la communication du Bénin, eds. 1999. *Passé, présent et futur des palais et site royaux d'Abomey: 22–26 septembre 1997: Actes de la conférence.* Los Angeles: Getty Conservation Institute.

Ghana Museums and Monuments Board, and CRATerre-EAG. 2004. *Larabanga.* Grenoble, France: CRATerre edition.

Ghana Museums and Monuments Board, and World Heritage Centre. 1999. *Asante Traditional Buildings = Bâtiments Traditionnels Asante.* 1st ed. Ghana: Ghana Museums and Monuments Board.

Goldberger, Mina Eliana. 1992. A conservation study of an Anasazi earthen mural at Aztec Ruins National Monument. Master's thesis, University of Pennsylvania.

Gordon, Eric. 1997. Conservation treatment of two Ming Dynasty temple wall paintings. In *Conservation of Ancient Sites on the Silk Road: Proceedings of an International Conference on the Conservation of Grotto Sites,* ed. Neville Agnew, 112–19. Los Angeles: Getty Conservation Institute.

Griffin, Isobel. 1999. Earthen grouts in wall painting conservation: An investigation of their working properties and performance characteristics. Master's thesis, Conservation of Wall Paintings Department, Courtauld Institute of Art, University of London.

Grimstad, Kirsten, ed. 1990. *6th International Conference on the Conservation of Earthen Architecture: Adobe 90 Preprints: Las Cruces, New Mexico, U.S.A., October 14–19, 1990.* Los Angeles: Getty Conservation Institute.

Hanna, S. B., and J. K. Dinsmore. 1991. Conservation of Central Asian wall painting fragments from the Stein Collection in the British Museum. In *The Conservation of Wall Paintings: Proceedings of a Symposium Organized by the Courtauld Institute of Art and the Getty Conservation Institute, London, July 13–16 1987,* ed. Sharon Cather, 77–86. Marina del Rey, CA: Getty Conservation Institute.

Hanna, Seamus, Nicholas Lee, and Geoffrey Foster. 1988. Three bodhisattvas: The conservation of a fifteenth century Chinese wall painting in the British Museum collection. In *Conservation Today: Papers Presented at the UKIC 30th Anniversary Conference, 1988,* ed. Victoria Todd, 130–34. London: United Kingdom Institute of Conservation.

Hansen, Eric F., Sue Walston, and Mitchell Hearns Bishop, ed. 1993. *Matte Paint: Its History and Technology, Analysis, Properties and Conservation Treatment, with Special Emphasis on Ethnographic Objects.* (A bibliographic supplement to Art and Archaeology Technical Abstracts, Vol. 30). Marina del Rey, CA: Getty Conservation Institute in association with the International Institute for Conservation of Historic and Artistic Works (IIC), London.

Hartmann, Andreas. 1996. Investigations on injection grouts to readhere lime mortars to adobe grounds. In *Proceedings of the 8th International Congress on Deterioration and Conservation of Stone: Berlin, 30. Sept.–4. Oct. 1996,* ed. Josef Riederer, 1535–46. Berlin: Möller Druck und Verlag.

Hartzler, Bob. 1997. Acrylic-modified earthen mortar. *CRM* 20 (10): 50–52.

Hibben, Frank C. 1975. *Kiva Art of the Anasazi at Pottery Mound.* Las Vegas, NV: KC Publications.

Houben, Hugo, and Hubert Guillaud. 1994. *Earth Construction: A Comprehensive Guide.* London: Intermediate Technology Publications.

Houben, Hugo, Hubert Guillaud, and CRATerre. 1989. *Traité de construction en terre.* L'Encyclopédie de la construction en terre, vol. 1. Marseille: Parenthèses.

Hoyle, Ana Maria. 1990. Chan Chan: aportes para la conservacion de la arquitectura de tierra. In *6th International Conference on the Conservation of Earthen Architecture: Adobe 90 Preprints: Las Cruces, New Mexico, U.S.A., October 14–19, 1990,* ed. Kirsten Grimstad, 225–29. Marina del Rey, CA: Getty Conservation Institute.

Hu Jigao. 1989. Dunhuang Mogaoku bihua xiufu jiagu gongzuo do jiantao yu zhanwang = Retrospective of and prospects for the restoration and consolidation of the mural paintings of Mogao Grottoes in Dunhuang. *Wen wu bao hu yu kao gu ke xue = Sciences of Conservation & Archaeology* 1 (2): 10–18.

Huang Kezhong, Jiang Huaiying, Cai Run, and Feng Lijuan. 1990. The weathering characteristics of the rocks of the Kezier Grottoes and research into their conservation. In *6th International Conference on the Conservation of Earthen Architecture: Adobe 90 Preprints: Las Cruces, New Mexico, U.S.A., October 14–19, 1990,* ed. Kirsten Grimstad, 283–88. Marina del Rey, CA: Getty Conservation Institute.

ICCROM, Regional Project on Cultural Heritage and Development UNDP/UNESCO, and National Institute of Culture (Peru), eds. 1985. *Adobe: International Symposium and Training Workshop on the Conservation of Adobe: Final Report and Major Papers: Lima, Cuzco (Peru) 10–22 September 1983.* Lima: Regional Project on Cultural Heritage and Development UNDP/UNESCO; Rome: ICCROM.

ICOMOS, ed. 1976. *Deuxième colloque international pour la conservation des monuments en brique crue = Second International Conference on the Conservation of Mud-Brick Monuments: Yazd [Iran], 6–11 March 1976.* Paris: ICOMOS-Iran.

ICOMOS, and ICOMOS, Iran, eds. 1976. *Premier colloque international sur la conservation des monuments en brique crue: Yazd, Iran, 25–30. XI. 1972 = First International Conference on the Conservation of Mud-Brick Monuments: Yazd, Iran, 25–30. XI. 1972.* Tehran: Ministry of Culture and Arts.

Iftekhar, Ahmed. 1993. Earthen architecture in the wet climate of Bangladesh and future direction for its conservation and upgrading. In *Terra 93: 7a Conferência Internacional sobre o Estudo e Conservação da Arquitectura de Terra: Silves, Portugal, 24 a 29 de Outubro, 1993 = 7th International Conference on the Study and Conservation of Earthen Architecture: Silves, Portugal 24–29 October, 1993 = 7ème conférence internationale pour l'étude et la conservation de l'architecture de terre: Silves, Portugal, 24 au 29 Octobre, 1993,* ed. M. Alçada, ICCROM, and CRATerre-EAG, 52–57. Lisbon: Direcção Geral dos Edifícios e Monumentos Nacionais (DGEMN).

International Council of Museums, Türkiye Milli Komitesi, and International Council of Monuments and Sites, Türkiye Milli Komitesi, eds. 1980. *Üçüncü Uluslararasi Kerpiç Koruma Sempozyumu: 29 Eylül–4 Ekim, 1980, Ankara = Third International Symposium on Mudbrick (Adobe) Preservation: 29 September–4 October, 1980, Ankara.* Ankara: ICOM-Turkey; ICOMOS-Turkey.

J. Paul Getty Museum, and Getty Conservation Institute. 1992. *In the Tomb of Nefertari: Conservation of the Wall Paintings.* Malibu, CA: J. Paul Getty Museum; Marina del Rey, CA: Getty Conservation Institute.

Jain, Kulbhushan, and Minakshi Jain. 2000. *Architecture of the Indian Desert.* Ahmedabad, India: AADI Centre.

Jerome, Pamela. 2000. The use of lime plasters for waterproofing and decoration of mudbrick buildings in Yemen. In *Terra 2000: 8th International Conference on the Study and Conservation of Earthen Architecture, Torquay, Devon, UK, May 2000: Preprints,* ed. English Heritage, ICOMOS-UK, and University of Plymouth Centre for Earthen Architecture, 144–49. London: James & James.

Jerome, Pamela, Giacomo Chiari, and Caterina Borelli. 1999. The architecture of mud: Construction and repair technology in the Hadhramaut region of Yemen. *APT Bulletin: The Journal of Preservation Technology* 30 (2–3): 39–48.

Jerome, Pamela, Selma Al-Radi, James Conlon, and Gina Crevello. 2003. Preservation of the mudbrick palaces of Tarim, Yemen. In *Terra 2003: Preprints of Papers, 9th International Conference on the Study and Conservation of Earthen Architecture, Yazd, Iran, 29 November–2 December, 2003,* ed. Sazman-i Miras-i Farhangi-i Kishvar (Iran), 319–28. Tehran: Iranian Cultural Heritage Organization.

Jing, Anning. 1991. The Yan Buddhist Mural of the Paradise of Bhaisajyaguru. *Metropolitan Museum Journal* 26:147–66.

Joffroy, Thierry. 1999. Actions des cinq dernières années: Volet "architecture" du projet PREMA-Bénin II. In *Passé, présent et futur des palais et site royaux d'Abomey: 22–26 septembre 1997: Actes de la conférence,* ed. Getty Conservation Institute, ICCROM, and Ministère de la culture et de la communication du Bénin, 55–66. Los Angeles: Getty Conservation Institute.

Joffroy, Thierry, and Sébastien Moriset. 1996. *Palais royaux d'Abomey 1. Circonstances et processus de dégradation [Projet PREMA-Bénin]*. Rome: ICCROM; Grenoble: CRATerre-EAG; Paris: UNESCO.

———. 1996. *Palais Royaux d'Abomey 2. Guide d'entretien [Projet PREMA-Bénin II]*. Rome: ICCROM; Grenoble: CRATerre-EAG; Paris: UNESCO.

Kirkpatrick, David Teal. 1990. Prehistoric Mogollon and Anasazi earthen architecture of the southwestern United States. In *6th International Conference on the Conservation of Earthen Architecture: Adobe 90 Preprints: Las Cruces, New Mexico, U.S.A., October 14–19, 1990*, ed. Kirsten Grimstad, 86–91. Marina del Rey, CA: Getty Conservation Institute.

Kopelson, Evan. 1996. Analysis and consolidation of architectural plasters from Çatalhöyük, Turkey. Master's thesis, University of Pennsylvania.

Kuchitsu, Nobuaki, Duan Xiuye, Chie Sano, Guo Hong, and Li Jun. 1997. Color change of pigments in the Mogao Grottoes of Dunhuang. In *Conservation of Ancient Sites on the Silk Road: Proceedings of an International Conference on the Conservation of Grotto Sites*, ed. Neville Agnew, 329–33. Los Angeles: Getty Conservation Institute.

Lal, B. B. 1970. Preservation of Buddhist monuments and paintings at Bami-yan-Afghanistan. *Kabul Times* 9 (166): 3–4.

Lewcock, Ronald B. 1986. *Wadi Hadramawt and the Walled City of Shibam*. Paris: UNESCO.

Li, Kuang-Han. 2004. Conservation of vernacular Ladakhi architecture: The Munshi House in old town Leh, Ladakh. Master's thesis, University of Pennsylvania.

Li Shi, Tetuo Sinkai, Masamitsu Inaba, and Ryutiro Sugisita. 1994. Analysis of binding media used in the wall paintings of Dunhuang Mogao-ku grottos. *Kobunkazai no kagaku = Scientific Papers on Japanese Antiques and Art Crafts* 39:19–27.

Li Yunhe, Li Shi, Li Tiechao, and Xiang Xiaomei. 1993. Researches in the application of polyvinyl alcohol and polyvinyl acetate on the restoration of mural paintings. In *Dunhuang yan jiu wen ji. Shi ku bao hu pian*, ed. Dunhuang yan jiu yuan (China), Vol. 2, 166–77, 311. Lanzhou: Gansu min zu chu ban she.

Li Zuixiong, and Nishiura Tadateru. 1993. A study in the choice of a suitable strengthening substance for the Dunhuang wall paintings. In *Dunhuang yan jiu wen ji. Shi ku bao hu pian*, ed. Dunhuang yan jiu yuan (China), Vol. 2, 191–94, 313–14. Lanzhou: Gansu min zu chu ban she.

Liddell, Marlane A., and Margaret Courtney-Clarke. 1990. Fine artists who paint their lives on a canvas of mud. *Smithsonian* 21 (2): 128–35.

Lister, Florence Cline. 2000. *Behind Painted Walls: Incidents in Southwestern Archaeology*. Albuquerque: University of New Mexico Press.

Luk, Cynthia, Ingrid Neuman, James Martin, Cynthia Kuniej Berry, and Judy Greenfield. 1997. The treatment of two Chinese wall painting fragments. In *Conservation of Ancient Sites on the Silk Road: Proceedings of an International Conference on the Conservation of Grotto Sites*, ed. Neville Agnew, 95–104. Los Angeles: Getty Conservation Institute.

MacHenry, P. G. Jr. 1976. Mud-brick construction in the Southwestern United States past and present. In *Premier colloque international sur la conservation des monuments en brique crue: Yazd, Iran, 25–30. XI. 1972 = First International Conference on the Conservation of Mud-Brick Monuments: Yazd, Iran, 25–30. XI. 1972*, ed. ICOMOS and ICOMOS, Iran, 24–28. Tehran: Ministry of Culture and Arts.

Maekawa, Shin, Yongjun Zhang, Wang Baoyi, Fu Wenli, and Xue Ping. 1997. Environmental monitoring at the Mogao Grottoes. In *Conservation of Ancient Sites on the Silk Road: Proceedings of an International Conference on the Conservation of Grotto Sites*, ed. Neville Agnew, 301–13. Los Angeles: Getty Conservation Institute.

Malenka, Sally, and Beth A. Price. 1997. A Chinese wall painting and a palace hall ceiling: Materials, technique, and conservation. In *Conservation of Ancient Sites on the Silk Road: Proceedings of an International Conference on the Conservation of Grotto Sites*, ed. Neville Agnew, 127–38. Los Angeles: Getty Conservation Institute.

Malisius, Ulrich. 1993. Ghadames: A historic town in the northern Sahara. In *Terra 93: 7a Conferência Internacional sobre o Estudo e Conservação da Arquitectura de Terra: Silves, Portugal, 24 a 29 de Outubro, 1993 = 7th International Conference on the Study and Conservation of Earthen Architecture: Silves, Portugal 24–29 October, 1993 = 7ème conférence internationale pour l'étude et la conservation de l'architecture de terre: Silves, Portugal, 24 au 29 Octobre, 1993*, ed. M. Alçada, ICCROM, and CRATerre-EAG, 64–67. Lisbon: Direcção Geral dos Edifícios e Monumentos Nacionais (DGEMN).

Markovic, Sasha. 1993. Impermanence/permanence: Mural decoration in northern Ghana. In *Terra 93: 7a Conferência Internacional sobre o Estudo e Conservação da Arquitectura de Terra: Silves, Portugal, 24 a 29 de Outubro, 1993 = 7th International Conference on the Study and Conservation of Earthen Architecture: Silves, Portugal 24–29 October, 1993 =*

7ème conférence internationale pour l'étude et la conservation de l'architecture de terre: Silves, Portugal, 24 au 29 Octobre, 1993, ed. M. Alçada, ICCROM, and CRATerre-EAG, 68–72. Lisbon: Direcção Geral dos Edifícios e Monumentos Nacionais (DGEMN).

Marshak, Boris. 1990. Panjikent: A pre-Islamic town in Central Asia. In *6th International Conference on the Conservation of Earthen Architecture: Adobe 90 Preprints: Las Cruces, New Mexico, U.S.A., October 14–19, 1990,* ed. Kirsten Grimstad, 230–32. Marina del Rey, CA: Getty Conservation Institute.

Matero, Frank G. 1995. A programme for the conservation of architectural plasters in earthen ruins in the American Southwest: Fort Union National Monument, New Mexico, USA. *CRM* 1 (1): 5–24.

———. 1997. Managing change: Conservation of surface finishes at Mesa Verde's cliff dwellings. *CRM* 20 (10): 39–42.

———. 1999. The conservation of plasters in earthen archeological sites. *CRM* 22 (6): 59–62.

———. 1999. Lessons from the Great House: Condition and treatment history as prologue to site conservation and management at Casa Grande Ruins National Monument. *Conservation and Management of Archaeological Sites* 3 (4): 203–24.

———. 2000. The conservation of an excavated past. In *Towards Reflexive Method in Archaeology: The Example at Çatalhöyük,* ed. Ian Hodder, 71–88. BIAA monograph, no. 28. Cambridge and Oxford: McDonald Institute for Archaeological Research, University of Cambridge (distributed by Oxbow Books).

———. 2003. Managing change: The role of documentation and condition survey at Mesa Verde National Park. *Journal of the American Institute for Conservation* 42 (1): 39–58.

Matero, Frank G., and Angelyn Bass. 1994. Orphans of the storm: The preservation of architectural plasters in earthen ruins. *CRM* 17 (4): 21–26.

———. 1995. Design and evaluation of hydraulic lime grouts for the reattachment of lime plasters on earthen walls. *Conservation and Management of Archaeological Sites* 1 (2): 97–108.

Matero, Frank, Elisa del Bono, Kecia L. Fong, Rick Johansen, and John Barrow. 2000. Condition and treatment history as prologue to site conservation at Casa Grande Ruins National Monument. In *Terra 2000: 8th International Conference on the Study and Conservation of Earthen Architecture, Torquay, Devon, UK, May 2000: Preprints,* ed. English Heritage, ICOMOS-UK, and University of Plymouth Centre for Earthen Architecture, 52–64. London: James & James.

Matero, Frank G., and Claudia Cancino. 2000. The conservation of earthen archaeological heritage: An assessment of recent trends. In *Terra 2000 Postprints: 8th International Conference on the Study and Conservation of Earthen Architecture, Torquay, Devon, UK, May 2000,* ed. English Heritage, ICOMOS-UK, and University of Plymouth Centre for Earthen Architecture, 11–21. London: James & James.

Matthews, T. H. 1971. Tribal painting in South Africa with particular reference to Xhosa painting (vols. 1–2). PhD diss., University of South Africa.

Mauger, Thierry. 2002. *Arabie, jardin des peintres: Architecture et art mural du Asîr.* Paris: A. Biro.

McDonald, John K. 1996. *House of Eternity: The Tomb of Nefertari.* Los Angeles: Getty Conservation Institute; J. Paul Getty Museum.

McHenry, Paul G. Jr. 1990. Acoma: A case study in preservation philosophy and implementation. In *6th International Conference on the Conservation of Earthen Architecture: Adobe 90 Preprints: Las Cruces, New Mexico, U.S.A., October 14–19, 1990,* ed. Kirsten Grimstad, 159–65. Marina del Rey, CA: Getty Conservation Institute.

Meiring, A. L. 1955. The Amandebele of Pretoria. *South African Architectural Record* 40:26–35.

Mellaart, James. 1962. Excavations at Çatal Hüyük: First preliminary report, 1961. *Anatolian Studies* 12:41–65.

Meyer, Kurt W., and Pamela Deuel. 1999. Who are the Tharu? National minority and identity as manifested in housing forms and practices. In *Nepal: Tharu and Tarai Neighbours,* ed. Herald O. Skar, 121–59. Kathmandu: EMR.

———. 2003. The granary of the Tharu of Nepal. In *The Art of Rice: Spirit and Sustenance in Asia,* ed. Roy W. Hamilton, 143–51. Los Angeles: UCLA Fowler Museum of Cultural History.

Michon, Jean-Louis. 1990. Mud castles (kasbas) of south Morocco— Will they survive? In *6th International Conference on the Conservation of Earthen Architecture: Adobe 90 Preprints: Las Cruces, New Mexico, U.S.A., October 14–19, 1990,* ed. Kirsten Grimstad, 99–104. Marina del Rey, CA: Getty Conservation Institute.

Miller, Eric G., Nicholas J. Lee, and Diane R. Ellam. 1987. Remounting and conservation of archaeological wall paintings at the British Museum. In *Recent Advances in the Conservation and Analysis of Artifacts: Jubilee Conservation Conference, London 6–10 July, 1987,* ed. James Black, 289–95. London: Summer Schools Press.

Miura, Sadatoshi, Tadateru Nishiura, Zhang Yongjun, Wang Baoyi, and Li Shi. 1997. Microclimate of Cave Temples 53 and 194,

Mogao Grottoes. In *Conservation of Ancient Sites on the Silk Road: Proceedings of an International Conference on the Conservation of Grotto Sites,* ed. Neville Agnew, 294–300. Los Angeles: Getty Conservation Institute.

Montgomery, Ross Gordon, Watson Smith, John Otis Brew, and J. Franklin Ewing. 1949. *Franciscan Awatovi: The Excavation and Conjectural Reconstruction of a 17th-Century Spanish Mission Establishment at a Hopi Indian Town in Northeastern Arizona.* Papers of the Peabody Museum of American Archaeology and Ethnology, Harvard University, Reports of the Awatovi Expedition. Peabody Museum, Harvard University, Report No. 3, vol. 36. Cambridge: The Museum.

Mora, Paolo, Laura Mora, and Paul Philippot. 1984. *Conservation of Wall Paintings.* London: Butterworths.

Moss, Elizabeth. 1998. Protection and environmental control of the plastered mudbrick walls at Çatalhöyük. Master's thesis, University of Pennsylvania.

Mturi, Amini. 1984. The conservation of the African architectural heritage: Part I. *Monumentum* 27 (3): 181–96.

———. 1984. The conservation of the African architectural heritage: Part II. *Monumentum* 27 (4): 275–84.

Nandadeva, Bilinda D. 1990. Traditions and techniques of earthen architecture of Sri Lanka. In *6th International Conference on the Conservation of Earthen Architecture: Adobe 90 Preprints: Las Cruces, New Mexico, U.S.A., October 14–19, 1990,* ed. Kirsten Grimstad, 105–10. Marina del Rey, CA: Getty Conservation Institute.

———. 1997. Materials and techniques of Kandyan and southern schools of mural painting of Sri Lanka mid-eighteenth to late-nineteenth centuries. PhD diss., University of Delaware.

Nath, Birendra. 1983. *Nalanda Murals.* New Delhi: Cosmo Publications.

National Park Service. Mesa Verde National Park. http://www.nps.gov/meve/home.htm.

Navrongo-Bolgatanga Diocese, Ghana Museums and Monuments Board, Getty Grant Programme, French Embassy in Ghana, and CRATerre-EAG. 2004. *Navrongo Cathedral: The Merge of Two Cultures.* Villefontaine, France: CRATerre Editions.

Nordby, Larry V. 2001. *Prelude to Tapestries in Stone: Understanding Cliff Palace Architecture.* Archeological Research Series: Architectural Studies No. 4. Mesa Verde, CO: Division of Research and Resource Management, Mesa Verde National Park.

Oates, David. 1990. Innovations in mud-brick: Decorative and structural techniques in ancient Mesopotamia. *World Archaeology* 21 (3): 388–406.

Odul, Pascal, ed. 1993. *Bibliographie sur la préservation, la restauration et la réhabilitation des architectures de terre = Bibliography on the Preservation, Restoration and Rehabilitation of Earthen Architecture.* Rome: CRATerre-EAG; ICCROM.

Oliver, A. B., and R. L. Hartzler. 2000. Understanding the deterioration of adobe walls: Fort Union National Monument, New Mexico, U.S.A. In *Terra 2000: 8th International Conference on the Study and Conservation of Earthen Architecture, Torquay, Devon, UK, May 2000: Preprints,* ed. English Heritage, ICOMOS-UK, and University of Plymouth Centre for Earthen Architecture, 78–85. London: James & James.

Olivier, Myriam, Ali Mesbah, and Willy Adam. 1990. Restauration des murailles de Sana'a, Yémen du Nord: Amélioration du Zabour, méthode traditionelle de construction en terre. In *6th International Conference on the Conservation of Earthen Architecture: Adobe 90 Preprints: Las Cruces, New Mexico, U.S.A., October 14–19, 1990,* ed. Kirsten Grimstad, 233–39. Marina del Rey, CA: Getty Conservation Institute.

Paramasivan, S. 1939. Technique of the painting process in the rock-cut temples of Badami. *Proceedings of the Indian Academy of Sciences, Section A* 10:145–49.

———. 1939. Wall paintings in the Bagh Caves: Investigation into their methods. *Proceedings of the Indian Academy of Sciences, Section A* 10:85–95.

Pibot, Jacques. 2001. *Les peintures murales des femmes kasséna du Burkina Faso.* Paris: Harmattan.

Pillsbury, Joanne. 1992. Technical evidence for temporal placement: Sculpted adobe friezes of Chan Chan, Peru. In *Materials Issues in Art and Archaeology III: Symposium Held April 27–May 1 1992, San Francisco, California, U.S.A.,* ed. Pamela B. Vandiver, James R. Druzik, George Segan Wheeler, and I. C. Freestone, 989–95. Pittsburgh: Materials Research Society.

Piqué, Francesca, and Leslie H. Rainer. 1999. Actions des cinq dernières années: La conservation des bas-reliefs de l'ajalala du roi Glélé au Musée historique, palais royaux d'Abomey. In *Passé, présent et futur des palais et site royaux d'Abomey: 22–26 septembre 1997: Actes de la conférence,* ed. Getty Conservation Institute, ICCROM, and Ministère de la culture et de la communication du Bénin, 67–81. Los Angeles: Getty Conservation Institute.

———. 1999. The conservation of polychrome earthen bas-reliefs from the Royal Palaces of Abomey in the West African

Republic of Benin. In *12th Triennial Meeting, Lyon, 29 August–3 September 1999: Preprints (ICOM Committee for Conservation),* ed. Janet Bridgland, 443–48. London: James & James.

———. 1999. *Palace Sculptures of Abomey: History Told on Walls.* Los Angeles: Getty Conservation Institute; J. Paul Getty Museum.

Playdon, Dennis G., and Brian D. Vallo. 2000. Restoring Acoma: The Pueblo revitalization projects. *CRM* 23 (9): 20–24.

Preusser, Frank. 1991. Scientific and technical examination of the tomb of Queen Nefertari at Thebes. In *The Conservation of Wall Paintings: Proceedings of a Symposium Organized by the Courtauld Institute of Art and the Getty Conservation Institute, London, July 13–16 1987,* ed. Sharon Cather, 1–12. Marina del Rey, CA: Getty Conservation Institute.

Prussin, Labelle. 1969. *Architecture in Northern Ghana: A Study of Forms and Functions.* Berkeley: University of California Press.

Qi Yingtao. 1984. Studies on conservation of the grotto temples and the mural paintings of ancient graves in China. In *International Symposium on the Conservation and Restoration of Cultural Property, November 17–21, 1983, Tokyo, Japan: Conservation and Restoration of Mural Paintings (I),* ed. Organizing Committee of the International Symposium on the Conservation and Restoration of Cultural Property, 19–29. Tokyo: Tokyo National Research Institute of Cultural Properties.

Rainer, Leslie H. 1992. Decorated surfaces on earthen architecture: A methodological approach toward their conservation. Case study: Kassena wall paintings. Master's thesis, Antioch University.

———. 1992. The writing on the wall. *Places* 8 (1): 42–45.

———. 1993. The tradition of Kassena wall painting: Burkina Faso. In *Terra 93: 7a Conferência Internacional sobre o Estudo e Conservação da Arquitectura de Terra: Silves, Portugal, 24 a 29 de Outubro, 1993 = 7th International Conference on the Study and Conservation of Earthen Architecture: Silves, Portugal 24–29 October, 1993 = 7ème conférence internationale pour l'étude et la conservation de l'architecture de terre: Silves, Portugal, 24 au 29 Octobre, 1993,* ed. M. Alçada, ICCROM, and CRATerre-EAG, 439–44. Lisbon: Direcção Geral dos Edifícios e Monumentos Nacionais (DGEMN).

Rich, Peter. 1995. Pride of Ndebele. *Architectural Review* 197 (1177): 73–77.

Richert, Roland Von S., and R. Gordon Vivian, ed. 1974. *Ruins Stabilization in the Southwestern United States.* Publications in Archeology (United States, National Park Service), vol. 10. Washington DC: National Park Service; U.S. Government Printing Office.

Rodrigues, P. F. 2000. Renderings for earth construction. In *Terra 2000: 8th International Conference on the Study and Conservation of Earthen Architecture, Torquay, Devon, UK, May 2000: Preprints,* ed. English Heritage, ICOMOS-UK, and University of Plymouth Centre for Earthen Architecture, 444. London: James & James.

Rohn, Arthur H. 1971. *Mug House, Mesa Verde National Park, Colorado.* Archeological Research Series, no. 7-D 7/4. Washington, DC: National Park Service.

Roth, James. 1952. The separation of two layers of ancient Chinese wall-painting. *Artibus Asiae* 15:145–50.

Rua, Carlos, and Anton Rajer. 1990. Restoration of the sixteenth century church at Curahuara de Carangas, Bolivia: A case study. In *6th International Conference on the Conservation of Earthen Architecture: Adobe 90 Preprints: Las Cruces, New Mexico, U.S.A., October 14–19, 1990,* ed. Kirsten Grimstad, 171–75. Marina del Rey, CA: Getty Conservation Institute.

Rua, Carlos, Anton Rajer, and Nelson Mostacedo. 1993. A case study of conservation/restoration of the seventeenth century adobe church at Carabuco, Bolivia. In *Terra 93: 7a Conferência Internacional sobre o Estudo e Conservação da Arquitectura de Terra: Silves, Portugal, 24 a 29 de Outubro, 1993 = 7th International Conference on the Study and Conservation of Earthen Architecture: Silves, Portugal 24–29 October, 1993 = 7ème conférence internationale pour l'étude et la conservation de l'architecture de terre: Silves, Portugal, 24 au 29 Octobre, 1993,* ed. M. Alçada, ICCROM, and CRATerre-EAG, 205–9. Lisbon: Direcção Geral dos Edifícios e Monumentos Nacionais (DGEMN).

Samánez Argumedo, Roberto. 1986. Mural painting on adobe walls during Peruvian colonial times—Its restoration and conservation. In *Case Studies in the Conservation of Stone and Wall Paintings: Preprints of the Contributions to the Bologna Congress, 21–26 September 1986,* ed. N. S. Brommelle and Perry Smith, 75–79. London: International Institute for Conservation of Historic and Artistic Works.

———. 1990. Criterios y técnicas de restauracion aplicadas en los monumentos de adobe en el Peru. In *6th International Conference on the Conservation of Earthen Architecture: Adobe 90 Preprints: Las Cruces, New Mexico, U.S.A., October 14–19, 1990,* ed. Kirsten Grimstad, 342–47. Marina del Rey, CA: Getty Conservation Institute.

Sazman-i Miras-i Farhangi-i Kishvar (Iran), ed. 2003. *Terra 2003: Preprints of Papers, 9th International Conference on the Study and Conservation of Earthen Architecture, Yazd, Iran, 29*

November–2 December, 2003. Tehran: Iranian Cultural Heritage Organization.

Schaewen, Deidi von, Laurence Dougier, Frédéric Couderc, and Angelika Taschen. 2003. *Inside Africa.* Cologne: Taschen.

Schilling, Michael R., Li Jun, Li Tie Chao, Guo Hong, Li Zuixiong, and Duan Xu Xe. 1997. Color measurement at the Mogao Grottoes. In *Conservation of Ancient Sites on the Silk Road: Proceedings of an International Conference on the Conservation of Grotto Sites,* ed. Neville Agnew, 341–47. Los Angeles: Getty Conservation Institute.

Schmid, Werner, ed. 2000. *GraDoc: Graphic Documentation Systems in Mural Painting Conservation: Research Seminar, Rome 16–20 November 1999.* Rome: ICCROM.

Schneider, Elizabeth Ann. 1985. Ndebele mural art. *African Arts* 18 (3): 60–67.

———. 1986. Paint, pride and politics: Aesthetic and meaning in Transvaal Ndebele wall art. PhD diss., University of the Witwatersrand.

Schorer, Fabian. 1997. *Zur Konservierung der Deckenmalerei im Oratorium des Schlosses zu Brühl: Prüfung und Umsetzung zweier Sicherungsmethoden am Putzsystem.* Kölner Beiträge zur Restaurierung und Konservierung von Kunst-und Kulturgut, Bd. 6. Munich: A. Siegl.

Schwartzbaum, Paul M., Wannipa Na Songkhla, and Ippolito Massari. 1986. The conservation of mural paintings in Thailand. In *Case Studies in the Conservation of Stone and Wall Paintings: Preprints of the Contributions to the Bologna Congress, 21–26 September 1986,* ed. N. S. Brommelle and Perry Smith, 90–95. London: International Institute for Conservation of Historic and Artistic Works.

Schwartzbaum, Paul M., Constance S. Silver, and Christopher Wheatley. 1980. The conservation of a Chalcolithic mural painting on mud brick from the site of Teleilat Ghassul, Jordan. In *Üçüncü Uluslararasi Kerpiç Koruma Sempozyumu: 29 Eylül–4 Ekim, 1980, Ankara = Third International Symposium on Mudbrick (Adobe) Preservation: 29 September–4 October, 1980, Ankara,* ed. International Council of Museums, Türkiye Milli Komitesi, and International Council of Monuments and Sites, Türkiye Milli Komitesi, 177–200. Ankara: ICOM-Turkey; ICOMOS-Turkey.

Seignobos, Christian, and Fabien Jamin. 2004. *La Case Obus: histoire et reconstitution.* Marseille: Editions Parenthèses–Patrimoine sans frontiers.

Sengupta, Rakhaldas. 1985. Conservation and restoration of mural paintings in India. In *International Symposium on the Conservation and Restoration of Cultural Property, November*

18–21, [1984], Tokyo, Japan: Conservation and Restoration of Mural Paintings (II), ed. Organizing Committee of the International Symposium on the Conservation and Restoration of Cultural Property, 37–54. Tokyo: Tokyo National Research Institute of Cultural Properties.

Seymour, Z. Lewin, and Paul M. Schwartzbaum. 1985. Investigation of the long-term effectiveness of an ethyl silicate-based consolidant on mudbrick. In *Adobe: International Symposium and Training Workshop on the Conservation of Adobe: Final Report and Major Papers: Lima, Cuzco (Peru) 10–22 September 1983,* ed. ICCROM, Regional Project on Cultural Heritage and Development UNDP/UNESCO, and National Institute of Culture (Peru), 77–81. Lima: Regional Project on Cultural Heritage and Development UNDP/UNESCO; Rome: ICCROM.

Shekede, Lisa. 1997. English domestic wall paintings on earthen supports: Materials and deterioration. Master's thesis, Conservation of Wall Paintings Department, Courtauld Institute of Art, London.

———. 2000. Wall paintings on earthen supports: Evaluating analytical methods for conservation. In *Terra 2000: 8th International Conference on the Study and Conservation of Earthen Architecture, Torquay, Devon, UK, May 2000: Preprints,* ed. English Heritage, ICOMOS-UK, and University of Plymouth Centre for Earthen Architecture, 169–75. London: James & James.

Shipman, J. G. T. 1984. The Hadhramaut. *Asian Affairs* 15:154–62.

Sickman, Laurence. An early Chinese wall-painting newly discovered. *Artibus Asiae* 15:137–44.

Sikka, Sandeep. 2003. Conservation of historic earth structures in the western Himalayas. In *Terra 2003: Preprints of Papers, 9th International Conference on the Study and Conservation of Earthen Architecture, Yazd, Iran, 29 November–2 December, 2003,* ed. Sazman-i Miras-i Farhangi-i Kishvar (Iran), 531–38. Tehran: Iranian Cultural Heritage Organization.

Silver, Constance S. 1987. Architectural finishes of the prehistoric Southwest: A study of the cultural resource and prospects for its conservation. Master's thesis, Columbia University.

———. 1990. Analyses and conservation of Pueblo architectural finishes in the American Southwest. In *6th International Conference on the Conservation of Earthen Architecture: Adobe 90 Preprints: Las Cruces, New Mexico, U.S.A., October 14–19, 1990,* ed. Kirsten Grimstad, 176–81. Marina del Rey, CA: Getty Conservation Institute.

———. 1997. The conservation of tempera mural paintings and architectural finishes. In *Conservation of Ancient Sites on the Silk Road: Proceedings of an International Conference on the*

Conservation of Grotto Sites, ed. Neville Agnew, 139–46. Los Angeles: Getty Conservation Institute.

Silver, Constance S., Joel Snodgrass, and Richard Wolbers. 1993. A program for the conservation of prehistoric mural paintings on mud renderings in the American Southwest. In *Terra 93: 7a Conferência Internacional sobre o Estudo e Conservação da Arquitectura de Terra: Silves, Portugal, 24 a 29 de Outubro, 1993 = 7th International Conference on the Study and Conservation of Earthen Architecture: Silves, Portugal 24–29 October, 1993 = 7ème conférence internationale pour l'étude et la conservation de l'architecture de terre: Silves, Portugal, 24 au 29 Octobre, 1993,* ed. M. Alçada, ICCROM, and CRATerre-EAG, 215–21. Lisbon: Direcção Geral dos Edifícios e Monumentos Nacionais (DGEMN).

Singh, R. P., and R. K. Sharma. 1993. Conservation problems of murals in Du-khang Gumpha, Tabo Monastery, Spiti, Himachal Pradesh. *Conservation of Cultural Property in India* 26:75–87.

Slater, Mary E. 1999. Characterization of earthen architectural surface finishes from Kiva Q, Cliff Palace, Mesa Verde National Park, Colorado. Master's thesis, University of Pennsylvania.

Smith, Watson. 1990. *When Is a Kiva? And Other Questions About Southwestern Archaeology.* Tucson: University of Arizona Press.

Smith, Watson, and Louie Ewing. 1952. *Kiva Mural Decorations at Awatovi and Kawaika-a, with a Survey of Other Wall Paintings in the Pueblo Southwest.* Papers of the Peabody Museum of American Archaeology and Ethnology, Harvard University, vol. 37. Cambridge: The Museum.

Steen, Charlie R., and Rutherford J. Gettens. 1962. Tumacacori interior decorations. *Arizoniana* 3 (3): 7–21.

Suzuki, Kakichi. 1985. Administrative measures for the conservation of mural paintings on Japanese architecture. In *International Symposium on the Conservation and Restoration of Cultural Property, November 18–21, [1984], Tokyo, Japan: Conservation and Restoration of Mural Paintings (II),* ed. Organizing Committee of the International Symposium on the Conservation and Restoration of Cultural Property, 55–63. Tokyo: Tokyo National Research Institute of Cultural Properties.

Szabó, Zoltán. 1978. The conservation of adobe walls decorated with mural paintings and reliefs in Peru. In *ICOM Committee for Conservation 5th Triennial Meeting: Zagreb, 1–8 October 1978: Preprints,* ed. ICOM Committee for Conservation, 78/15/7/1–78/15/7/7. Paris: International Council of Museums.

Torraca, Giorgio. 1971. An international project for the study of mud-brick preservation. In *Preprints of the Contributions to the New York Conference on Conservation of Stone and Wooden Objects: 7–13 June 1970,* ed. International Institute for Conservation of Historic and Artistic Works, 47–57. London: International Institute for Conservation of Historic and Artistic Works.

———. 1984. Environmental protection of mural paintings in caves. In *International Symposium on the Conservation and Restoration of Cultural Property, November 17–21, 1983, Tokyo, Japan: Conservation and Restoration of Mural Paintings (I),* ed. Organizing Committee of the International Symposium on the Conservation and Restoration of Cultural Property, 1–18. Tokyo: Tokyo National Research Institute of Cultural Properties.

Turton, Catherine E. 1998. Plan for the stabilization and removal of wall paintings at Çatalhöyük. Master's thesis, University of Pennsylvania.

United Nations Centre for Human Settlements. 1986. *Manual on Surface Protection.* Earth Construction Technology series. Nairobi: United Nations Centre for Human Settlements (Habitat).

van Vuuren, C. J. 1986. Muurversiering by die Ndebele = Mural art of the Ndebele. *Suid-Afrikaanse tydskrif vir etnologie = South African Journal of Ethnology* 9 (3): 101–11.

———. 1988. The KwaNdebele monuments committee: Ethnological contributions. *SAMAB* 8 (1): 89.

Wacziarg, Francis, and Aman Nath. 1982. *Rajasthan: The Painted Walls of Shekhavati.* London: Croom Helm.

Wainwright, Ian N. M., Elizabeth A. Moffatt, P. Jane Sirois, and Gregory S. Young. 1997. Analysis of wall painting fragments from the Mogao and the Bingling Temple grottoes. In *Conservation of Ancient Sites on the Silk Road: Proceedings of an International Conference on the Conservation of Grotto Sites,* ed. Neville Agnew, 334–40. Los Angeles: Getty Conservation Institute.

Warren, John. 1999. *Conservation of Earth Structures.* Oxford: Butterworth-Heinemann.

Waterlot, Em. G. 1926. *Les bas-reliefs des bâtiments royaux d'Abomey (Dahomey).* Université de Paris, Travaux et mémoires de l'Institut d'Ethnologie, vol. 1. Paris: Institut d'Ethnologie.

Whitfield, Roderick, Susan Whitfield, and Neville Agnew. 2000. *Cave Temples of Mogao: Art and History on the Silk Road.* Los Angeles: Getty Conservation Institute and J. Paul Getty Museum.

Xu Yuming. 1985. Exploration in conservation and restoration of mural paintings in ancient temples and Taoist temples in China. In *International Symposium on the Conservation and Restoration of Cultural Property: November 18–21, [1984], Tokyo, Japan: Conservation and Restoration of Mural Paintings (II)*, ed. Organizing Committee of the International Symposium on the Conservation and Restoration of Cultural Property, 215–21. Tokyo: Tokyo National Research Institute of Cultural Properties.

———. 1991. The conservation and restoration of the wall painting in Jokhang Temple in Lhasa City, Tibet. *Wen wu bao hu yu kao gu ke xue = Sciences of Conservation & Archaeology* 3 (1): 11–13.

List of Colloquium Participants

Titles and affiliations of participants are given as of the time of the colloquium.

First Name	Last Name	Title	Affiliation	Country
George	Abungu	Heritage Management and Planning Consultant; Chair, Kenya Cultural Center	Independent consultant	Kenya
Karel	Bakker	Professor of Architecture	Department of Architecture, University of Pretoria	Republic of South Africa
Jake	Barrow	Senior Exhibit Specialist	National Park Service, Intermountain Region	USA
Angelyn	Bass Rivera	Architectural Conservator	National Park Service, Bandelier National Monument	USA
Maribel B.	Beas	Architectural Conservator	Historic Building Architects	USA
Ann	Bourgès	Research Lab Associate	Getty Conservation Institute	USA
Jerry J.	Brody	Professor Emeritus of Art and Art History	University of New Mexico	USA
Gary	Brown	Archaeologist	National Park Service, Aztec National Monument	USA
Rachel	Burch	Wall Paintings Conservator	Independent conservator	USA
Claudia	Cancino	Associate Project Specialist	Getty Conservation Institute	USA
Rebecca	Carr	Exhibit Specialist, Architectural Conservator	National Park Service, Archeological Site Conservation Program, Mesa Verde National Park	USA
David	Carson	Assistant Scientist	Getty Conservation Institute	USA
Giacomo	Chiari	Chief Scientist	Getty Conservation Institute	USA
Anthony	Crosby	Chair US/ICOMOS, Earthen Architecture Committee	Independent consultant	USA
Veronica	Cuthair	Director	Ute Mt. Tribal Park	USA
Kathleen	Fiero	Archaeologist	National Park Service, Mesa Verde National Park (retired)	USA
Preston	Fisher	Structural Engineer	National Park Service, Mesa Verde National Park	USA
Kecia	Fong	Project Specialist	Getty Conservation Institute	USA
Kathleen	Garland	Head, Objects Conservation	Nelson-Atkins Museum of Art	USA
Dulce Maria	Grimaldi Sierra	Assistant Director, Department of Archaeological Conservation	Coordinaciòn Nacional de Conservaciòn del Patrimonia Cultural, Instituto Nacional de Antropología e Historia	Mexico
Divay	Gupta	Program Director	Indian National Trust for Cultural Heritage	India
Mary	Hardy	Senior Project Specialist	Getty Conservation Institute	USA
Delbridge	Honanie	Artist	Hopi Tribe	USA

First Name	Last Name	Title	Affiliation	Country
Hugo	Houben	Research Engineer	CRATerre-EAG	France
Pamela	Jerome	Director of Preservation	Wank Adams Slavin Associates	USA
Michael	Kabotie	Artist	Hopi Tribe	USA
Laura	Kochanski	Resources Manager	National Park Service, Pu'uhonua o Honaunau National Historical Park	USA
François	LeBlanc	Head, Field Projects	Getty Conservation Institute	USA
Frank	Matero	Professor of Architecture and Chair of the Graduate Program in Historic Preservation, School of Design	University of Pennsylvania	USA
Eric	Miller	Conservator	British Museum, Department of Conservation, Documentation and Science	United Kingdom
Sébastien	Moriset	Architect	CRATerre-EAG	France
Karla	Muñoz-Alcocer	Program Specialist, Conservator	Smithsonian Center for Materials Research and Education	USA
Claire	Munzenrider	Director of Conservation	Museums of New Mexico	USA
Larry	Nordby	Field Director, Archeological Site Conservation Program	National Park Service, Mesa Verde National Park (retired)	USA
Alastair	Northedge	Professor of Islamic Art and Archaeology	Université de Paris I	France
Ishanlosen	Odiaua	Lecturer in Architecture	Architecture Program, Abubakar Tafawa Balewa University	Nigeria
Anne	Oliver	Principal	Oliver Conservation Group	USA
Francesca	Piqué	Wall Paintings Conservator	Private conservator	Italy
Leslie	Rainer	Senior Project Specialist	Getty Conservation Institute	USA
Stephen	Rickerby	Wall Paintings Conservator	Private conservator	United Kingdom
Joe	Rogers	Conservation Associate	Nelson-Atkins Museum of Art	USA
Lisa	Shekede	Wall Paintings Conservator	Private conservator	United Kingdom
David	Singleton	Conservator	Bristol Museums and Art Gallery	United Kingdom
Mary	Slater	Architectural Conservator	National Park Service, Bandelier National Monument	USA
James	Stratis	Preservation Projects Manager	Colorado Historical Society	USA
Gisèle	Taxil	Architect, Earthen Architecture Specialist	Independent consultant	France
Susan	Thomas	Supervisory Museum Curator	Bureau of Land Management, Canyons of the Ancients National Monument/Anasazi Heritage Center	USA
Linda	Towle	Chief, Research and Resource Management	National Park Service, Mesa Verde National Park	USA
Lydia	Vagts	Paintings Conservator	Private practice	USA
Henri	Van Damme	Professor of Physical Chemistry	Ecole Supérieure de Physique et de Chimie Industrielles	France
Clemencia	Vernaza	Wall Paintings Conservator	Private conservator	Switzerland
Jagath	Weerasinghe	Senior Lecturer in Art History, Archaeology, and Conservation	University of Kelaniya, Post Graduate Institute of Archaeology	Sri Lanka
Larry	Wiese	Superintendent	National Park Service, Mesa Verde National Park	USA
Lori	Wong	Associate Project Specialist	Getty Conservation Institute	USA
Jun	Zheng	Wall Paintings Conservator	Courtauld Institute of Art, Conservation of Wall Painting Department	United Kingdom

Contributors

George H. Okello Abungu is a Cambridge-trained archaeologist, chairman of the Kenya Cultural Center, and CEO of Okello Abungu Heritage Consultants. Formerly director-general of the National Museums of Kenya, he is also chairman of Africa 2009, ISCOTIA, and the Programme for Museum Development in Africa, among other organizations. In 2005, he was a guest scholar at the Getty Conservation Institute, researching strategies for sustainable management and utilization of intangible heritage in Africa. Apart from his work on the conservation of African heritage, G. Abungu has also widely published in the disciplines of archaeology, heritage management, museology, and the subject of culture and development.

Karel Anthonie Bakker was born in Vryburg, Republic of South Africa, and obtained a PhD with a focus on archaic Hellenic architectural history from the University of Pretoria. His main fields of study and research are pedagogy, classical architecture, African built environments, heritage impact assessment, and urbanism. He serves on the executive committee of ICOMOS South Africa and the ICOMOS CIF. He is a member of the Education Committee of the South African Council of the Architectural Professions, and of Cultmatrix cc conservation management practice. In addition, he is an associate professor in the department of architecture at the University of Pretoria, and has published widely on heritage impact assessment and urban conservation issues.

Angelyn Bass Rivera is a conservator with the National Park Service, specializing in the conservation of architectural finishes and management of archaeological sites. She currently directs the Vanishing Treasures Program at Bandelier National Monument in New Mexico, which integrates archaeological site conservation with Native American consultation and training in heritage management. She received an MS in historic preservation from the University of Pennsylvania in 1998. A. Bass Rivera has been involved in conservation projects in the United States, Africa, and Central America. She was one of the members of the organizing committee of the colloquium, and was one of the principal conservators of the Awatovi and Kawaika-a murals at the Museum of Northern Arizona.

Ann Bourgès holds three master's degrees in physics, applied to archaeology, archeometry, and conservation of earthen architecture. She has successfully joined her laboratory research at LRMH and CRATerre, where she analyzed materials and traditional building techniques, to fieldwork at Huaca de la Luna in Peru, and Our Lady of Seven Sorrows Cathedral in Ghana. Formerly a research lab associate with the Building Materials Section at the Getty Conservation Institute and associated with Project Terra, she is now a research scientist for the Centre National de la Recherche Scientifique (CNRS) at the Institut des Sciences Apliquées (INSA) lab's metallurgy physics and material physics group in Lyon, France.

Claudia Cancino, a native of Lima, Peru, was trained as an architect at the Architecture and Urban Planning School, Universidad Ricardo Palma, in Lima, followed by additional training in architectural conservation at ICCROM (1995) and in business administration in Lima (1998). From 1996 to 1999, she was a member of the architecture faculty at the Universidad Peruana de Ciencias Aplicadas in Lima. C. Cancino earned an MS in historic preservation and an advanced certificate in conservation in 2001 and 2002, respectively, from the University of Pennsylvania. She has worked as a conservator on archaeological sites with earthen plasters in the southwestern United States, and is currently an associate project specialist at the Getty Conservation Institute, where she mainly works on the Earthen Architecture Initiative. She was a member of the organizing committee for the colloquium.

Rebecca Carr, currently on staff at Casa Grande Ruins National Monument in Arizona, holds a BA from the University of Delaware with dual majors in anthropology and photography. She also holds an undergraduate certificate in museum curation and has recently completed coursework to obtain an MS in historic preservation with an advanced certificate in architectural conservation from the University of Pennsylvania. From 2001 to 2005 she was the architectural conservator at Mesa Verde National Park. She has worked as archaeologist and assistant lab supervisor for an international engineering firm and has served as executive director for the Telluride Historical Museum during the initial phases of that museum's award-winning building renovation project. R. Carr's other experience includes work for the National Endowment for the Humanities, the Anasazi Heritage Center, the Mancos Historical Society, and the Wadsworth Atheneum.

Giacomo Chiari, chief scientist at the Getty Conservation Institute, was born in Carmagnola, Italy. As professor of applied mineralogy at the University of Turin, he carried out research on an array of significant works of art and architecture, including the *Last Judgment* by Michelangelo, the earthen architecture of the Hadhramaut region of Yemen, and the polychrome earthen architectural reliefs of Huaca Garagay in Peru. His research in conservation science includes the chemical and mineralogical characterization of earthen building materials and methods for their treatment, and the elucidation of the structure of Maya Blue. He has developed a method for dating mural paintings based on magnetic preferential orientation of hematite.

Anthony Crosby is an architectural conservator in private practice, formerly with the National Park Service, working in the protection of cultural properties in the United States and internationally. His projects include surveys, reports, workshops, assessments, construction documents and construction supervision of structures in the American Southwest, Central America, and Egypt, and oversight of mural painting conservation projects at Arizona's Tumacacori National Historical Park; San Antonio Missions, in Texas; and the Lincoln Memorial, Washington, DC. A. Crosby has written on preservation in national and international publications and professional jour-

nals. He teaches at local, regional, national, and international meetings and courses, including the architectural conservation course at ICCROM in Rome (1993–95) and courses on the protection of archaeological sites and historic structures constructed of earth in Grenoble and Peru (1989–99). Currently, he is chair of the US/ICOMOS Specialized Committee on Earthen Architecture and a member of the ICOMOS International Scientific Committee on Earthen Architecture.

Kecia Fong is a project specialist for Built Heritage Education and Training at the Getty Conservation Institute. She is an architectural and archaeological site conservator. She received her MS in historic preservation with an Advanced Certificate in Conservation from the University of Pennsylvania. K. Fong helped develop pilot conservation treatments for the decorated surface finishes of Mesa Verde National Park, and has worked for the National Park Service on the condition assessment and conservation treatment of ancient Puebloan sites throughout the American Southwest. She is currently involved in the development of didactic materials for the conservation of earthen architecture, the development of a training workshop for the conservation and management of archaeological sites, and an assessment of education and training needs in built heritage conservation for the Asia-Pacific region.

Kathleen M. Garland received her BA in art history from Brown University, and her MA in art conservation from the State University of New York, Cooperstown. She completed her internship in the Sculpture Conservation Department at the Victoria and Albert Museum. From 1986 to 1989 she held the position of senior sculpture conservator for the National Trust for Great Britain, and in 1989 she established the Objects Conservation Lab at the Nelson-Atkins Museum of Art, where she is presently working on the Chinese sculpture collection. In 2001 she was the first Luce Fellow in Chinese Paintings Conservation at the Freer and Sackler Galleries, Smithsonian Institution.

Mary Hardy is a senior project specialist in Field Projects at the Getty Conservation Institute, where she manages Project TERRA, a collaborative initiative of the GCI, CRATerre, and ICCROM for the study and conservation of earthen architecture. She is a conservation architect and conservator with master's degrees in architecture from the University of California, Berkeley, and in historic preservation from Columbia University. She has also completed postgraduate training at the International Laboratory of Architecture and Urban Design in Siena, Italy. M. Hardy was a consulting conservator to the University of Pennsylvania's Conservation of Architectural Surfaces Program for Archaeological Resources at Mesa Verde (1999, 2000), and was a member of the organizing committee of the colloquium.

Delbridge Honanie/Coochsiwukioma (Falling White Snow), is a Hopi painter, sculptor, kachina carver, and teacher. He was born into the Bear Clan on January 7, 1946, in Winslow, Arizona. Receiving his early education on the Hopi Reservation, he attended Phoenix Indian High School. After graduating from the Institute of American Indian Arts in Santa Fe, New Mexico, he returned to Phoenix in 1970 as an arts and craft instructor at his alma mater. As a member of Artist Hopid (see Michael Kabotie, below), he began carving sculptures from cottonwood root. Carving traditional dolls for yearly ceremonies fueled his innovation, yet still showing the old way. This work is now considered the contemporary style. He is one of the most respected and collected carvers of the Southwest. Coochsiwukioma is an award-winning artist whose paintings and sculptures are in public and private collections throughout the United States and abroad.

Pamela Jerome is a registered architect and architectural conservator. She is director of preservation and a senior associate with Wank Adams Slavin Associates LLP, a New York–based architecture and engineering firm. She is also an adjunct associate professor at Columbia University's Graduate School of Architecture, Planning and Preservation, where she has taught since 1995. She sits on the board of trustees of US/ICOMOS. P. Jerome has worked on cultural property preservation in North and South America, the Mediterranean and Black Sea regions, and the Middle East. Her expertise is in masonry conservation and waterproofing, with a particular emphasis on earthen architecture and archaeological site preservation.

Michael Kabotie/Lomawywesa (Walking in Harmony), was born September 3, 1942, into the Water/Snow Clan, village of Shungopavi, on the Hopi Reservation in northeastern Arizona. Introduced to silver overlay in 1958, he was influenced by his cousins and his father, Fred Kabotie. He became a recognized painter after a one-man exhibit in 1966 at the Heard Museum in Phoenix, and in 1973 was a founding member of Artist Hopid, a group of five painters, carvers, and song-poets now referred to as the modernist Indian arts movement. Lomawywesa's inspirations are rooted in the Awatovi kiva murals and Sikyatki pottery designs. With assistance from Hopi painter and carver Delbridge Honanie, Lomawywesa created *Journey of the Human Spirit,* a 48-foot contemporary kiva mural at the Museum of Northern Arizona, in Flagstaff. His most recent mural, *Sacred Eruption,* is at the Sunset Crater

Volcano National Monument visitor center in Arizona. In 2003, he was recognized with an Arizona Living Treasure Award. He lectures globally, and his works are found in collections and museums worldwide.

Eric Miller left South Africa and a career in insurance brokerage at age 30 and retrained as a graphic designer at the Wimbledon School of Art. He later followed this with postgraduate training in conserving sculpture and church monuments at Croydon Art School. He joined the Stone Section (later the Stone, Wall Paintings, and Mosaics Section) of the Department of Conservation of the British Museum in 1979. Since 1999 he has made yearly visits to Egypt to work on wall paintings.

Sébastien Moriset, an architect specializing in earthen architecture, has worked since 1993 at CRATerre-EAG, the International Centre for Earth Construction at the School of Architecture, University of Grenoble. In addition to extensive fieldwork experience, he has developed conservation programs, management plans, and World Heritage nominations for a range of sites in Africa and Central Asia. He is currently serving as a resource person in training activities and a technical coordinator in the field projects of the Africa 2009 program (CRATerre-EAG, ICCROM, UNESCO-WHC). Apart from the Asante shrines in Ghana, he has conducted conservation activities and trained conservation teams on various sites, including Larabanga mosque and Navrongo cathedral in Ghana, the Abomey palaces in Benin, James Island Fort in Gambia, Timbuktu mosques in Mali, Kasubi tombs in Uganda, Tchogha-Zanbil ziggurat in Iran, and Ancient Merv in Turkmenistan.

Larry Nordby is currently the field director of the Archeological Site Conservation Program at Mesa Verde National Park. Before coming to Mesa Verde, from 1984 to 1995 he served as the National Park Service's Southwest regional archaeologist and chief of the Branch of Cultural Research and Chaco Center. He worked with the University of Colorado field school and contract archaeology program between 1965 and 1975, when he started working with the National Park Service. His research interests include behavior and proxemics, underwater archaeology, and creating modular interdisciplinary databases that link conservation and anthropological objectives.

Alastair Northedge is an historical archaeologist and professor of Islamic art and archaeology at Université de Paris 1. He has worked in Syria, Jordan, Saudi Arabia, Kazakhstan, and Turkmenistan, and conducted projects at Amman, Jordan, and in Samarra and Ana, Iraq. He is author of *Studies on*

Roman and Islamic Amman and joint author of *Excavations at Ana* with Andrina Bamber and Michael Roaf.

Ishanlosen Odiaua is an architect and teacher in the architecture program of Abubakar Tafawa Balewa University, Bauchi, Nigeria. She has a postgraduate degree in earth construction from the School of Architecture, University of Grenoble. She has been an assistant to the coordination team of Africa 2009 training activities in Bafoussam, Cameroon, and Mombasa, Kenya. She has also coordinated and executed an inventory exercise of immovable cultural heritage in Bauchi State of Nigeria. I. Odiaua is also involved in various activities in the field of earth construction and heritage conservation in her home country of Nigeria.

Leslie Rainer, a senior project specialist in Field Projects at the GCI, received an independent MA in the conservation of wall paintings and decorated architectural surfaces in 1991 from Antioch University, and certificates in mural paintings conservation (ICCROM), and the preservation of earthen architecture (ICCROM-CRATerre-EAG). She has worked as an independent conservator with museums, regional conservation centers, and international organizations on projects in the Americas, Europe, China, and West Africa, many of these working with decorated surfaces on earthen supports. She was one of the members of the organizing committee of the colloquium, and is a former chair of the US/ICOMOS Specialized Committee on Earthen Architecture. She was the lead conservator on the Hopi Mural Fragment Project at the Peabody Museum (Harvard University) and the Museum of Northern Arizona. L. Rainer has published several articles on the conservation of decorated earthen architectural surfaces.

Stephen Rickerby received his MA in art history before undertaking the Courtauld Institute of Art/Getty Conservation Institute (GCI) postgraduate diploma in the conservation of wall paintings (1985–89). He has since worked as a wall painting conservator in private practice and as a consulting conservator on a number of GCI projects, including the tomb of Nefertari in Egypt; the Royal Palaces of Abomey in Benin, West Africa; and the Cave 85 Project at Mogao, China. He has been involved in conservation teaching in China, and cosupervises the Courtauld Institute's fieldwork sites in Cyprus and Malta. He is also on the Board of Examiners and the Board of Studies for the master's degree course at the Courtauld Institute's Conservation of Wall Painting Department.

Joe C. Rogers has been a staff member of the Nelson-Atkins Museum of Art since 1983. He worked as conservation assistant in the Paintings Conservation Department from 1983 to 1990, and is currently the objects conservation associate. His responsibilities include the care of furniture in the Museum's permanent collection and the sculpture in the Kansas City Sculpture Park.

Pamela Rose has worked on archaeological sites in Egypt and Sudan for many years. She is currently director of the excavations at Qasr Ibrim on behalf of the Egypt Exploration Society.

Lisa Shekede obtained a postgraduate diploma in the conservation of wall paintings at the Courtauld Institute of Art, Conservation of Wall Painting Department (1991–94), followed by a master's degree in 1997. Her particular area of expertise is the technology and conservation of wall paintings on earthen supports. Besides working in private practice in the United Kingdom and Malta, she currently cosupervises the fieldwork programs of the Courtauld Institute master's degree students and is also a Getty Conservation Institute consultant on the Cave 85 project at the Mogao Grottoes, Dunhuang, China.

David Singleton trained initially as a musical instrument maker. He spent periods working in a circus, the antique furniture trade, and on the inland waterways before entering the three-year sculpture conservation diploma course at the City and Guilds of London Art School in 1985. He then worked on architectural conservation projects and joined the British Museum in the Stone, Wall Paintings, and Mosaics Conservation Section in 1991. In 1995 he moved to the Organic Materials Conservation Section, where he specialized in decorated surfaces in the Egyptian and ethnographic collections. In 2000 he moved to Bristol Museums and Art Gallery, where he works in preventive conservation.

Gisèle Taxil, architect and artist, earned a specialized degree in earthen architecture at CRATerre-EAG in Grenoble. Winning two scholarships, she studied earthen architecture in France, Egypt, and the United States, where she worked in the architectural field for three years. She is currently working on the preservation of architectural heritage built and decorated with gypsum in the southern Alps, and works as an independent specialist for CRATerre-EAG. During the past few years she has focused on the restoration of Our Lady of Seven Sorrows Cathedral in Ghana. As an artist, she does architectural photography and decoration works with earth and gypsum plasters.

Susan Thomas received a BA in anthropology from the University of Oklahoma and served as field archaeologist, laboratory director, collections manager, and curator at several institutions in the South and Midwest United States before becoming curator of the Anasazi Heritage Center (AHC) in 1988. At AHC, she is responsible for the protection and management of all collections and for supervising museum specialists within the curation program and interns and contractors working on collection data entry. In addition, she has conducted several facility assessments of nonfederal museums for compliance with federal curation regulations. S. Thomas is the NAGPRA (Native American Graves Protection and Repatriation Act) coordinator for the Bureau of Land Management, Colorado, and is the primary contact with the tribes and other federal agencies in resolving NAGPRA issues as they relate to the collections at the AHC.

Lydia Vagts is a paintings conservator in private practice in the Boston area. She works for both museums and private collectors, and currently has projects at the Museum of Fine Arts, Boston, and the Worcester Art Museum. She is also the conservator of the mural paintings in the public art collection of the City of Cambridge, Massachusetts. Lydia has worked on a variety of wall painting projects in the United States, Italy, and France, and in 1999 carried out the conservation of the murals of John Singer Sargent at the Museum of Fine Arts, Boston. L. Vagts was one of the principal conservators of the Awatovi and Kawaika-a murals at the Peabody Museum, Harvard University.

Chris J. van Vuuren was born in Pretoria, Republic of South Africa, and holds a diploma in museum science and a PhD in anthropology from the University of Pretoria. He designed the Ndebele Open Air Museum in Middelburg, of which he was the first curator. The research for the project described in his paper was the topic of a master's dissertation, "The Settlement Pattern of the South Ndebele" (1984). He has published several articles on Ndebele history, architecture, and beadwork and ritual.

Jun Zheng has been working as a conservator for painted surfaces on architecture and polychrome sculptures since 1986, when he joined the China National Institute of Cultural Property. He has carried out extensive conservation projects and taught in various training courses both inside and outside of China, and has served on the boards of the Expert Committee of Science and Technology in Conservation and the Consultation Board for Architectural Conservation of the State Administration of Cultural Heritage of China. He received his BS in chemistry from Beijing University in 1986; a postgraduate diploma from the Conservation of Wall Painting Department of the Courtauld Institute of Art, University of London, in 1994; and is currently undertaking PhD research at the Courtauld Institute on conservation planning for heritage sites.